The Rigveda

Guides to Sacred Texts

THE DAODE JING
Livia Kohn

THE YIJING
Joseph Adler

THE RIGVEDA
Stephanie Jamison and Joel Brereton

The Rigveda

A Guide

JOEL P. BRERETON
STEPHANIE W. JAMISON

OXFORD
UNIVERSITY PRESS

OXFORD
UNIVERSITY PRESS

Oxford University Press is a department of the University of Oxford. It furthers the University's objective of excellence in research, scholarship, and education by publishing worldwide. Oxford is a registered trade mark of Oxford University Press in the UK and certain other countries.

Published in the United States of America by Oxford University Press
198 Madison Avenue, New York, NY 10016, United States of America.

Library of Congress Cataloging-in-Publication Data
Names: Brereton, Joel P., 1948– author. | Jamison, Stephanie W., author.
Title: The Rigveda : a guide / Joel P. Brereton and Stephanie W. Jamison.
Description: New York : Oxford University Press, 2020. |
Series: Guides to sacred texts | Includes bibliographical references and index. |
Identifiers: LCCN 2019035401 (print) | LCCN 2019035402 (ebook) |
ISBN 9780190633363 (hardback) | ISBN 9780190633370 (paperback) |
ISBN 9780190633394 (epub) | ISBN 9780190633387 (updf) | ISBN 9780190633400 (online)
Subjects: LCSH: Vedas. Ṛgveda—Criticism, interpretation, etc. |
Vedic literature—History and criticism.
Classification: LCC BL1112.56 .B74 2020 (print) | LCC BL1112.56 (ebook) |
DDC 294.5/9212046—dc23
LC record available at https://lccn.loc.gov/2019035401
LC ebook record available at https://lccn.loc.gov/2019035402

Hardback printed by Bridgeport National Bindery, Inc., United States of America

Contents

Guides to Sacred Texts

What is a sacred text? The Oxford English Dictionary offers a definition of "sacred" as "Set apart for or dedicated to some religious purpose, and hence entitled to veneration or religious respect." The definition is necessarily vague. What does it mean to be "set apart?" What constitutes a "religious purpose?" How formal is "veneration?" Does minimal "religious respect" qualify? The sphere of meanings surrounding the word "sacred" will depend on the religion involved. For that reason "sacred texts" in this series is a term conceived broadly. All of the texts covered by this series have held special regard—they have been "set apart"—in a religion either ancient or modern. Such texts are generally accorded more serious attention than other religious documents. In some cases the texts may be believed to be the words of a deity. In other cases the texts may be part of an atheistic religion. This breadth of application indicates the rationale behind Guides to Sacred Texts.

This series offers brief, accessible introductions to sacred texts, written by experts upon them. While allowing for the individuality of each text, the series follows a basic format of introducing the text in terms of its dates of composition, traditions of authorship and assessment of those traditions, the extent of the text, and the issues raised by the text. For scripture that continues to be utilized, those issues will likely continue to generate controversy and discussion among adherents to the text. For texts from religions no longer practiced, the issues may well continue to address concerns of the present day, despite the antiquity of the scripture. These volumes are useful for introducing sacred writings from around the world to readers wanting to learn what these sacred texts are.

Note on the Title

Although throughout this book we use the scholarly transliteration of the name of the text, the Ṛgveda, we have chosen the rendering Rigveda in the title of the book to avoid the problems that might arise from having a diacritic in the first letter.

1

Introduction

The R̥gveda is a monumental text with signal significance for both world religion and world literature; yet it is comparatively little known outside a small band of specialists, even among those who study the religious traditions of India. The oldest Sanskrit text, composed probably in the latter half of the second millennium BCE, it stands, at least nominally, as the foundational text of what will later be called Hinduism, and one of its verses, the so-called Gāyatrī mantra, is part, at least nominally, of the daily practice of those initiated into Vedic learning.

The text consists of over a thousand hymns dedicated to various divinities, composed in highly sophisticated and often enigmatic poetry. Its range is very large—encompassing profound and uncompromising meditations on cosmic enigmas, joyful and exuberant tributes to the wonders of the world, ardent praise of the gods and their works, moving and sometimes painful expressions of personal devotion, and penetrating reflections on the ability of mortals to make contact with and affect the divine and cosmic realms through sacrifice and praise. Thus, much of what will distinguish later Indian religious literature is already present in the R̥gveda. Yet, though its name is widely known, the celebration of the R̥gveda is muted at best, even within its own tradition, and, save for a few famous hymns, its contents go largely unnoticed outside of that tradition.

This guide to the R̥gveda proposes to help remedy this situation. It will provide an overview of the text, its structure, and the process of its composition and collection; treat its purpose—to serve as

The Rigveda. Joel P. Brereton and Stephanie W. Jamison, Oxford University Press (2020). © Oxford University Press.
DOI: 10.1093/oso/9780190633363.001.0001

the recited verbal portion of an extremely elaborate ritual system—and how this purpose is reflected in the contents and structure of the text; give some indication of the flavor of the text by quoting and discussing particular portions of it; situate it in the religious practices of its time (insofar as they are known or inferred); and treat its use and reception both in the periods immediately following the time of its composition and in the post-Vedic period, which saw profound changes in religious practices and beliefs, up to the modern era. It will also introduce readers to the literary qualities of the text and to the poets' belief in the role of their poetry in making sense of, and indeed creating, cosmic order and function—examining the exuberance with which the poets press the boundaries of language to create their own reflection of the complex and ultimately impenetrable mysteries of the cosmos and the verbal devices they developed to mirror these cosmic intricacies.

What is the R̥gveda: A brief overview

The R̥gveda is one of the four Vedas, which together constitute the oldest texts in Sanskrit and the earliest evidence for what will become Hinduism. Collectively they belong to the class of texts known as *śruti*, literally "hearing," a concept roughly equivalent to "revelation"; that is, the texts were later considered to have been *heard*, rather than composed, by humans, although the internal evidence of the Vedas shows no such concept. The four Vedas are the R̥gveda, the Atharvaveda, the Yajurveda, and the Sāmaveda. On grounds of both language and content, the R̥gveda is the oldest of the four and foundational for the others. The second oldest is the Atharvaveda, a text that in some ways continues the compositional style of the R̥gveda (and contains many repetitions from the R̥gveda), but whose contents consist in large part, of personal spells and healing charms. Despite its age and affinity with R̥gvedic poetic practice, it stands somewhat apart from the religious system of the Vedic period. In contrast, the other two Vedas, the Yajurveda and the Sāmaveda, form a ritually associated trio with the R̥gveda, with each providing the ritual script for a different part of the spoken liturgy and for a different priest active in the joint ritual system of the middle Vedic period. The R̥gveda was the source for the recitations of the Hotar priest (and assistants); the Yajurveda contained the formulae linked to ritual actions, which were principally carried out by the Adhvaryu priest (and assistants); and the Sāmaveda comprised the chants performed by the Udgātar priest (and assistants). We will have occasion to refer to all three other Vedas particularly in chapter 10.

The R̥gveda consists of 1028 hymns, called *sūkta*s "well-spoken (speech)," most of which are devoted to praising the gods associated with the elaborate sacrificial rituals also depicted in the hymns. The hymns consist of verses, ranging from 1 to 58, composed in strictly regulated meters. There are approximately 10,000 verses. In fact the text takes its name from these verses: the Sanskrit word for "verse" is *r̥c*; when compounded with the word for knowledge, it yields *r̥g-veda*, literally "knowledge/wisdom (consisting of) verses." The separate hymns are ascribed to a surprising number of individual poets—over 200 are named in the later indices to the text—and most of these poets belong to delineated bardic families. Hymns attributed to members of one family are generally transmitted together in books, or *maṇḍala*s, literally "circles," and these family *maṇḍala*s form the heart of the text. Composition of the hymns was entirely oral, as was the transmission of the text for much of its history: as far as we can tell, it was first written down no earlier than the second half of the first millennium CE, approximately two millennia after its likely period of composition, and its transmission probably remained primarily oral for centuries after that.

The language of the hymns is Vedic (or Vedic Sanskrit), an archaic form of the language that developed into the Sanskrit of the epics and the classical period. The place of composition was largely in the greater Punjab region, including areas of present-day

Pakistan and northwestern India, as the Indo-Aryans made their way into the subcontinent sometime in the early to mid-second millennium BCE. The language of these peoples belongs to the Indo-European family and is most closely related to Old Iranian; the Indo-Aryan languages (of which Sanskrit is the oldest form attested) and Iranian languages together form the Indo-Iranian sub-branch of Indo-European. The early Indo-Aryans and the early Iranians share many social, cultural, religious, and literary features, and these shared features are very prominent in the R̥gveda.

A significant moment

The R̥gveda thus inhabits a significant moment in the history of greater India. Janus-faced, it looks both backward and forward. As just mentioned, it displays a shared Indo-Iranian culture, with agreements between the R̥gveda and the Old Iranian texts, especially those composed in the Old Iranian language Avestan, astonishing both in their number and in their granular detail. The separation of the Indo-Aryan and Iranian languages and of their speakers must have been fairly recent to account for the pervasive structural similarities in both language and culture. To go back even further, the language of the R̥gveda is not only Indo-European in grammar and lexicon but also in literary sensibility. The R̥gveda represents the last full flowering in the Indian subcontinent of the Indo-European genre of praise poetry. The same spirit reverberates in the R̥gvedic bard's encomia of his gods as in the archaic Greek poet Pindar's of the victors in the Greek athletic games.

But the text looks forward as well. Although Vedic religion is very different in many regards from what is known as Classical Hinduism, the seeds are there. Gods like Viṣṇu and Śiva (under the name Rudra), who will become so dominant later, are already present in the R̥gveda, though in roles both lesser than and different from those they will later play, and the principal R̥gvedic gods like

Indra remain in later Hinduism, though in diminished capacity. Although the great Vedic sacrifices generally give way to other forms of worship, they remain narrative touchstones in the epics and later. Terms such as *brahman* and *dharma(n)* that will resonate in later Hinduism are also already present in the Ṛgveda, though with different senses. And, perhaps most important, the signal literary achievement of Classical India, the elaborate poetic genre known as *kāvya*, has its roots in the equally intricate poetry of the Ṛgveda.

The text is thus poised between the cultural tradition from which it—and its composers—came and the new culture that the melding of the Indo-Aryans and the traditions they encountered in the subcontinent would create in the ensuing centuries, as the Indo-Aryans moved farther south and east. Yet in acknowledging the importance of the traditional milieu from which the Ṛgveda emerged and the very different culture to which it is prelude, we should not underestimate its present. The Ṛgveda is not an uneasy amalgam of evocation of the past and anticipatory hints of the future, notable only for the light it sheds in both directions. It has a consistency and originality of vision that are entirely its own, reflecting a world in which the poets and ritualists who dominate the text count themselves as partners with the gods they celebrate in the imaging of the cosmos and their control of its forces. Despite their respect for tradition, there is little or no elegiac nostalgia for a glorious past; the poets and their patrons use their past as a foundation for what they envision as a glorious future. The people of the Ṛgveda seem to have a sense of their own power—whether exerted by arms, or by words, or by correctly performed rituals—and a sense that the *now* they inhabit is one of great promise, though also of commensurable risk.

But the Ṛgveda is our only contemporary witness of this moment. There are no other texts of the same period and no archaeological remains that manifest Vedic culture of this period. The later Vedic texts do help fill out the picture, but they already reflect a sociocultural, political, and religious (and indeed geographical) landscape significantly changed from that of the Ṛgveda. And all Vedic texts leave out an enormous amount. As texts focused on a high-culture ritual system limited to the elite, they provide information about everyday secular life and ordinary people only by chance. In evaluating what the Ṛgveda can tell us about this moment and this place and these people, we must always keep in mind how limited the snapshot provided really is.

World literature and religion

But the Ṛgveda is not only significant for its position in Indian religious and literary history at a particularly defining moment. It also deserves to be treated as a monument in world literature and world religion, a voice—or indeed many voices—from deep antiquity testifying to the sophistication and complexity of the culture of which it was a product. It is among the oldest preserved texts from antiquity (though predated by Egyptian, Sumerian, and Akkadian texts from the Near East, literary traditions entirely independent of it), but the Ṛgveda shows no signs of the hesitant or false experimental ventures of a nascent literary enterprise, nor of even the appealing straightforward simplicity of what used to be celebrated as "primitive" art. These are not the unmediated artless outpourings of unshaped praise arising in a naïve heart struck with awe. Instead Ṛgvedic poetry belongs to a fully mature literary tradition, with an awareness of the multiple ways in which words can relate to each other, formally and functionally, a wealth of intricate poetic devices at hand, and the daring to push the boundaries of intelligibility within the limits of the traditional poetic culture. As noted earlier, it is clear that this poetic tradition had a long development behind it, reaching back into Indo-European prehistory, and although we have no preserved texts from the intervening period, stock phrases (formulae) and standard techniques are shared across the archaic literary cultures of the older attested Indo-European languages. It is also clear that in the time of the R̥gveda there was a vibrant poetic scene, with multiple poets competing with each other for patronage as well as for artistic excellence, all very conscious both of the tradition they belong to and the new, personal stamp each hopes to put on this tradition. Although some earlier Western scholars of the R̥gveda sought (and found, at least by their own lights) the rough and primitive simplicity they expected to characterize poetry of this antiquity, coming at the dawn of recorded Indian history, this attitude—forged in great part by their experience with the poetry of their own Victorian and Edwardian age—is long out of date, and indeed the bold complexity of much of twentieth-century poetry awakened later Vedic scholars to the same boundary-pushing literary qualities and attitudes in the R̥gvedic corpus.

The same level of mature development is true also of the R̥gvedic religious system. Vedic "high" ritual (technically known, starting in the middle Vedic period, as *śrauta* ritual) is one of the most complex ritual systems the world has ever known, with multiday extravaganzas involving a small army of priestly participants and ceremonies in which every gesture and every word of each participant was fixed. Thousands of pages of the later ritual manuals are devoted to getting all this right, and although the R̥gvedic ritual system differs in some ways from classical *śrauta* ritual, it demonstrably presupposes the same basic set of rituals with the same basic sets of participants and patterned actions. Again, this is not the spontaneous free-form worship of deified cosmic forces occasioned by awe, fear, or humble gratitude, but a highly developed system of rites, built of smaller units arranged in clearly articulated structures, all loaded with symbolic significance—which is expertly decoded by the theological authors of the somewhat later exegetical prose texts known as the *brāhmaṇa*s.

The sophistication and complexity that meet us in every detail of the verbal and ritual materials available from this period are all the more astounding when compared with the complete lack of correspondingly sophisticated material remains. The composers of the Rgveda, the practitioners of śrauta ritual, did not leave behind great intricately organized cities with monumental buildings and well-designed urbanscapes. In fact there are no archaeological remains reliably associated with the early Vedic people, and what we can glean from the texts about the material aspects of their lives sketches a way of life involving mobile or semi-mobile pastoralism and goods appropriate to such mobility: wheeled vehicles, simple dwellings, no fixed temples or places of assembly. This is contrary to the assumptions most of us have about antiquity, where our informal measures of cultural development are derived from archaeology. But it befits an ever-mobile lifestyle to focus on a genre of art that can be carried in the head (oral poetry) and on a religion that can be practiced anywhere where a piece of ground can be properly prepared.

2

Historical Context

Migration

Were the peoples who produced the Ṛgveda, the peoples who called themselves "Āryas," indigenous to South Asia or did they migrate there? The most widely accepted scholarly view is that the Indo-Aryan peoples came into South Asia during the second millennium BCE and gradually extended cultural dominance in the subcontinent during the first millennium BCE. Some earlier scholars had envisioned this migration as an invasion and conquest, but this rather simplistic interpretation has given way to one of a more gradual movement into South Asia, perhaps in different waves, of Indo-Aryan speakers. To be sure, there were battles between these peoples and other peoples already settled in India, but there were also battles among different Ārya tribes. However, a number of scholars have strongly opposed the idea not only of an Ārya invasion but also of an Ārya migration into India. They have argued that there is little material evidence to support the theory that the Indo-Aryans migrated into South Asia and that the Ṛgveda shows no clear memory of migration or locations outside of South Asia. But linguistic and textual evidence has made it certain, or at least as nearly certain as knowledge of the very distant past can be, that the Indo-Aryans did migrate into South Asia. As remarked earlier, they were an Indo-European people, and they were especially closely related to early Iranian peoples. Theories that have tried to explain these connections by means of migration out of South Asia rather than into it create unlikely historical reconstructions (as, for

The Rigveda. Joel P. Brereton and Stephanie W. Jamison, Oxford University Press (2020). © Oxford University Press.
DOI: 10.1093/oso/9780190633363.001.0001

example, Hock 1999a has demonstrated). Moreover, careful study of central Asian archaeology and linguistic exchange between central Asian cultures, including the predecessor cultures of the Indo-Aryan peoples, has allowed scholars to reconstruct a plausible map and general timeline for the Indo-Aryan migration.

Around the end of the third millennium BCE, ancestors of the Indo-Aryan and Iranian speaking peoples lived on the Russian steppes, south of the Russian/Siberian taiga, the "snow forests" of the high latitudes, which stretched from the Ural Mountains eastward toward the Yenisei River, and north of the Caspian and Black Seas. These Indo-Iranians were semi-nomadic pastoralists, whose livelihood depended primarily on their herds. At least part of the year they needed to relocate to find pasturage for their herds, and this brought them into competition with one another and with other peoples of the steppes. Therefore, they were a mobile people and a people able to fight to secure or to defend the pasturelands they required. They used ox-drawn carts and horse-drawn, two-wheeled chariots, which contributed to their mobility and to their success in battle.

During the first half of the second millennium, Indo-Iranian peoples had continued to move south, and during that period they apparently came into contact with peoples associated with the Bactria-Margiana Archaeological Complex (BMAC). In its mature phase, from approximately the middle of the third through the first quarter of the second millennium BCE, the area it encompassed included regions of northern Afghanistan (ancient Bactria), southern Turkmenistan (overlapping with ancient Margiana), and southern Uzbekistan (see Parpola 2015: 69–83; Witzel 2003). The exact nature of the contact between the peoples who established this culture and the migrating Indo-Iranians is not clear, but one possibility is that the leaders of the Indo-Iranian peoples became rulers within the BMAC either during its mature or during its later phase. Whatever the nature of the contact between the Indo-Iranian peoples and those of the BMAC was, it may have been a crucial one for the development of Indo-Aryan and early Iranian religion and culture. In particular, it may have been at this period and in this place that the Indo-Iranians developed rituals that were based on older ritual forms centered on a drink of life or of immortality, but whose principal offering became the juice of the *soma* plant (or in Iranian, *haoma* plant). In the later Indo-Aryan tradition, the various *soma* rituals became the most prestigious non-royal rites and the dominant rituals for which the liturgical poetry of the R̥gveda was largely composed. While the development of the *soma* rites may have been a significant religious innovation in the early second millennium, cultural continuities among the Indo-Iranian peoples during this period were also remarkable. The Indo-Iranians retained their language and their traditions of poetic composition, even while the poetry was adapted for use within newer ritual forms.

The Indo-Aryan and Iranian peoples eventually lost contact with one another as the Indo-Aryans moved farther south into South Asia and the Iranian peoples west into the Iranian plateau. Even before they fully separated, cultural and linguistic differences had already developed between the ancestors of the Indo-Aryans and early Iranians. Beginning around 1500 BCE, a segment of the Indo-Aryans established rule in the Mitanni kingdom of northwestern Mesopotamia. The population of the kingdom were Hurrian speakers, but their rulers had Indo-Aryan names and invoked Indo-Aryan deities, which were distinct from Iranian names and gods. Presumably the segment of Indo-Aryans who established this rule had moved west before other segments migrated to the south and east into South Asia.

Indo-Iranian background

As already noted, the Indo-Aryan languages are most closely related to the Iranian languages. In particular, Vedic Sanskrit and the Old Iranian languages are so similar in grammar and lexicon that their separation cannot be temporally very deep. Two Old Iranian languages are attested, Old Persian, the language of the monumental inscriptions of the Achaemenid Empire, and Avestan. The former is not attested until the reign of Darius I (sixth century BCE), and the contents of the inscriptions are shaped by the imperial program. By contrast, Avestan is dated considerably earlier, at least in its older form, and the preoccupations of its texts are very similar to those of the Ṛgveda—praise poetry based on traditional models and an elaborate ritualism. There are two forms of Avestan, generally called Old (or Gāthic) Avestan and Young(er) Avestan. The former is primarily attested in the hymns, called Gāthās, attributed to the religious figure Zarathustra, the eponymous (though possibly legendary) founder of the religion Zoroastrianism (via the Greek form of his name, Zoroaster). With due allowance for some differences in their religious focus, these hymns are startlingly like those of the Ṛgveda. The phraseology is often superimposable or rings changes on the same underlying formulae; the same type of poetic risk-taking, of exploiting the extreme possibilities of the verbal tools at hand, is found in both. Moreover, the apparently "personal" voice of the poet that pervades the Gāthās is found in the hymns of certain Ṛgvedic bards, particularly Vasiṣṭha. Although ritual is muted in the Gāthās, it is clear that a ritual system similar to that of the Ṛgveda is presupposed. This becomes even clearer in the texts of the Younger Avesta, which testify to a cult centered on the offering of a ritual drink called *haoma*, which, as we saw earlier, is etymologically identical to Vedic *soma*, the focus of the most solemn Vedic rituals. There are pervasive similarities between the haoma and soma rituals, with identical names for the chief priest (*zaotar* = *hotar*) and for various actions and paraphernalia in the ritual. The Younger Avesta also preserves myths and the names of mythical figures that find their exact counterparts in the Ṛgveda. The Avesta and the Ṛgveda thus mirror each other in remarkable ways, and evidence from each has been (and continues to be) invaluable for interpreting difficult problems in the other.

3

Dating and Authorship

Dating

As should be clear from the previous chapter, it can be difficult to disentangle the preserved R̥gveda from the penumbra of poetic tradition from which it emerged. Since poets built their new structures using older verbal materials, a particular crystallization of traditional elements could be hundreds of years old or, as it were, (re-)made yesterday. Young poets would redeploy and repurpose formulations used by their fathers or grandfathers—or generations even further back. Nonetheless, despite the continuities with the Indo-Iranian and Indo-European poetic tradition, the R̥gveda is of course a distinct and bounded text in a distinct language and reflects not merely its ancient sources but also the contemporary historical context it inhabits. Before exploring that more fully, we should attempt to provide a rough dating of the text. As we will see, it is nearly impossible to assign an absolute date to the text, even within several centuries. It is also difficult to determine how long a time span was required for the composition of the whole text, no matter what absolute date we might assign. But we can start with the time of the presumed advent of the Indo-Aryans into the geographical area reflected in the R̥gveda.

The hymns of the R̥gveda were likely composed during the period in which the Indo-Aryans migrated from the area of present-day Afghanistan into the greater Punjab. The dating of the R̥gveda has been and is likely to remain a matter of contention and

The Rigveda. Joel P. Brereton and Stephanie W. Jamison, Oxford University Press (2020). © Oxford University Press.
DOI: 10.1093/oso/9780190633363.001.0001

reconsideration because as yet little has been uncovered in the material record or in the hymns themselves that allows us to establish a date with precision. Since the R̥gveda does not mention iron but does speak of other kinds of metal, it is likely a Bronze Age text. If we could determine the period in which iron began to be manufactured, therefore, we would have a date by which the hymns would have been composed. However, while the dates at which iron appears in the archaeological record in South Asia differ in different parts of the subcontinent, generally the manufacture of iron appears around 1200–1000 BCE. The R̥gvedic hymns, therefore, would have to have been composed no later than this period. Iron is attested in the Atharvaveda, which is the Vedic collection closest in age to the R̥gveda. While the R̥gveda is older than the Atharvaveda and while there may have been a gap between the close of the R̥gveda and the emergence of the Atharvaveda and the other early Vedic collections, there is no basis for assuming a great passage of time between the R̥gveda and the Atharvaveda. Although its language is younger than that of the R̥gveda, the Atharvaveda's traditions of hymnic composition continued those of the R̥gveda, and hymns like those of the Atharvaveda already appear in the late R̥gveda. Therefore the date of the latest portions of the R̥gveda is not likely to be very much earlier than the end of the Bronze Age.

It is also likely that the period of the composition of R̥gvedic hymns did not extend more than several centuries before this period. The poets to whom the R̥gvedic indices attribute the hymns and the kings mentioned within the hymns themselves comprise perhaps half a dozen generations. Rounding these numbers, we can then place the period of the composition of the R̥gvedic hymns sometime within the broad period 1500–1000 BCE. At best these dates encompass only the extant hymns of the R̥gveda. But as we have remarked before, the poetic conventions on which the R̥gveda was built are very much older, extending back to the Indo-Iranian period with even deeper roots into the Indo-European period. The R̥gveda is the surface of a very long tradition.

Oral tradition and composition

As has been emphasized earlier, the R̥gveda was composed entirely orally and is the product of a long oral tradition of praise poetry that goes back to the unity of Proto-Indo-European before the various branches split off. This can be demonstrated by adducing poetic formulae in the separate poetic traditions that are superimposable and can be reconstructed to a single Proto-Indo-European phrase. The most famous of these phrases is Greek κλέος ἄφθιτον: Vedic *śrávaḥ . . . ákṣitam*, sound-for-sound equivalent and both meaning "imperishable fame," first identified by Adalbert Kuhn in 1853. Numbers of others have been added to the dossier in the ensuing years.

The theory and practice of oral composition have been much studied and discussed in the last near century, associated in the first instance with Milman Parry and further developed by his student Albert Lord. (For brief but incisive discussion of formulas and oral composition, see Watkins 1995: 12–19.) The form in which this theory is best known was developed on and exclusively treats epic (especially Homer) and the type of narrative songs that develop into epic (especially the Yugoslavian bardic tradition studied, while it was still alive, by Parry and Lord). In this form the poet deploys fairly substantial blocks (often full verse lines or half lines) of identical or nearly identical formulaic material but in a sprawling and loose-jointed structure, which can vary from telling to telling—so-called "(re)composition in performance." At some point in an epic tradition the text may get fixed, but this fixation postdates the period of oral composition. This model applies (at least in our opinion, which is perhaps not shared by most specialists of the Indian epic) to the genesis and development of the Mahābhārata (but less so, if at all, to the Rāmāyaṇa). Indeed, there was no fixation of the text of the Mahābhārata in the sense of the Homeric epics, as even a glance at its critical edition, with its multitude of significant and lengthy variants, shows clearly.

However, this model is emphatically *not* applicable to the R̥gveda, and the ways in which the R̥gveda does not conform to what was, for a while, the only model for oral composition recognized in modern scholarship are probably responsible for how long it has taken to bring the R̥gveda under that conceptual umbrella. On the one hand, R̥gvedic formulaic language is generally not manifested as large blocks of identical text. Instead, strict formulae (that is, identically repeated phrases) tend to be brief—considerably shorter than a verse line. In addition, many formulae do not involve exact repetition but exist as "deep structure," with multiple variations on the deep structure showing up on the surface. Repeated full verse lines are fairly rare in the R̥gveda (though see Bloomfield 1916 for those that exist), but patterned alternates of underlying formulae are pervasive in the text. The prime example of a short, strictly repeated formula is the encapsulation of the great Indra myth, in which he kills the archenemy, the snake Vr̥tra. This deed is succinctly summarized by the phonologically driven two-word formula *áhann áhim* "he/you smote the serpent," which occurs numerous times in the text. But such exactly repeated phrases are relatively rare, and even this particular formula is regularly subject to variation—by, inter alia, morphological manipulation (e.g., V.31.7 *áhiṃ yád ghnán* "when, smiting the serpent . . ." with a participle [*ghnán*] substituting for the finite verb [*áhan*]), elaboration of one or the other of the terms (e.g., I.32.3 *áhann enam prathamajā́m áhīnām* "he smote him, the first born of the serpents"), or lexical substitution (e.g., IV.17.3 *vádhīd vr̥trám* "he smote Vr̥tra," where a form of the root √*vadh*, which is suppletive to √*han*, supplies the verb, and the name of the enemy, beginning with *v*-, replaces *ahim* "serpent" but reestablishes the alliterative pattern of the original formula).

Moreover, though in the standard model of oral composition, the poem itself is ever-changing and is the joint (or rather successive) product of a series of anonymous bards, with fixation of the text—if it comes at all—coming much later, a R̥gvedic hymn was fixed at the time of composition and thereafter transmitted without alteration. And it was "owned" by the poet who composed it. Poets often refer to themselves by name within their compositions, proudly asserting that the hymn is their product. Though they make use of formulaic language, they aim to put their personal stamp on that language, often by the types of variation just described, and to make each composition distinctively their own. They painstakingly acquire the tools and skills that belong to the oral tradition but also explicitly aim to put those tools and skills to new uses. There is always tension between the weight of the tradition and the pressure for novelty. As one poet puts it (R̥V III.31.10), "I make new (the song) born of old," acknowledging both the legacy of his poetic forebears and his own contribution in creating something original.

Poets and poetic lineages

What then do we know about the composers of these hymns? First, as already pointed out, it is clear that the text as we have it was the product of several generations of poets, at least, and that these poets often belonged to named lineages. There are several types of evidence that support this view.

We possess a later index to the R̥gveda, the Sarvānukramaṇī (hereafter Anukramaṇī), dating from the end of the Vedic period, perhaps to the mid-4th century BCE, but probably drawing on older materials. It lists each hymn, the deity to which it is dedicated, and its meter—*and* attributes each hymn to a particular poet, identified both by his name and by his patronymic. In a number of cases, the (given) name of a poet is found as a patronymic to another poet, indicating that this second poet is a son or descendant of the first. For example, the given name of the poet Vasiṣṭha Maitrāvaruṇi recurs as the patronymic to a series of poets including Vasukra Vāsiṣṭha, Indrapramati Vāsiṣṭha, etc.; a segment of one hymn (VII.33.10–14), which treats the birth of

Vasiṣṭha, is also ascribed to Vasiṣṭhaputrāḥ "the sons of Vasiṣṭha." These poetic lineages can stretch for several generations; e.g., the given name of Dīrghatamas Aucathya (himself perhaps the son of Ucathya Āṅgirasa), responsible for a remarkable set of hymns in Maṇḍala I, recurs as the patronymic of another memorable poet of Maṇḍala I, Kakṣīvant Dairghatamasa, who in turn supplies the patronymic for several other poets, Śabara Kākṣīvata, Sukīrti Kākṣīvata, and (supposedly a female poet) Ghoṣā Kākṣīvatī. Although the Anukramaṇī is considerably later than the Ṛgveda and not all of its attributions can be relied on, its data seem surprisingly accurate for the most part and conform to Ṛgveda-internal clues. Poets also refer to their own fathers and forefathers in their own compositions.

The second major type of evidence is linguistic. Although the core sections of the Ṛgveda are remarkably consistent linguistically, there are parts of the text, primarily concentrated in Maṇḍala X, that show linguistically younger forms, indicating a period of linguistic development spanned by the contents of the text. Although the issue of Ṛgvedic language, archaic and archaizing, is a complex one, the younger features of the so-called "popular" hymns are a good indication that the period of composition extended through some significant amount of time. The naming practices discussed in the previous paragraph often dovetail nicely with the linguistic indications. For example, the Kakṣīvant descendants referred to above are all poets of the Xth Maṇḍala.

The organization of the Ṛgveda also reflects—and therefore implicitly provides evidence for—the grouping of poets into generational lineages. As we will see, of the ten maṇḍalas making up the Ṛgveda, Maṇḍalas II through VII are referred to as the "Family Books," with each one ascribed to various poets belonging to a particular family, as witnessed both by the ascriptions of the hymns in the Anukramaṇī and by the hymn-internal statements of the poets themselves. For example, Maṇḍala V is the Atri Maṇḍala. Some 14 of the 87 hymns in this book are attributed by the Anukramaṇī to the eponymous founder of the lineage, Atri Bhauma; most of the other hymns are assigned to his descendants, designated by the patronymic Ātreya. An astonishing 36 different Ātreyas are identified as poets belonging to this line. Hymn-internal evidence supports this later picture. For example, V.22, a hymn to Agni, is assigned by the Anukramaṇī to Viśvasāman Ātreya. In the hymn itself, the poet addresses himself by name (as R̥gveda poets often do), urging himself to "chant like Atri (or the Atris)" (*atrivát árcā*), that is, like his father or forefather(s). In the last verse of this little hymn (vs. 4) he asserts that the Atris (plural) (*átrayaḥ*) strengthen and beautify Agni with praise songs and hymns. The poet thus situates himself within his family and poetic lineage.

The non-Family Books also generally consist of hymns grouped by poet or poetic lineage, though in units smaller than a maṇḍala. Maṇḍala VIII consists largely of hymns attributed to two families, the Kāṇvas and the Āṅgirasas. Most of Maṇḍala I is similarly organized by poet, and some of the most distinctive poetic voices are found there—Kakṣīvant and Dīrghatamas were already mentioned earlier. The first part of Maṇḍala X also contains small groups of hymns arranged by poet, though the second half contains only single hymns by individual poets. Maṇḍala IX is the exception to this pervasive organizational pattern. It is thematically focused, containing only hymns to the deified ritual drink Soma Pavamāna ("Self-purifying Soma") to be performed at the most elaborate of the non-royal Vedic rituals, the Soma Sacrifice. The Anukramaṇī of course assigns poets to all of the hymns therein; significantly, many of these are either poets found elsewhere in the R̥gveda in their appropriate family section or have patronymics that link them to poets elsewhere in the text. For example, Kakṣīvant is assigned one hymn in IX (IX.74) in addition to his run of hymns in I (I.116–25); most of the descendants of Vasiṣṭha mentioned earlier, identified by the patronymic Vāsiṣṭha, contributed sections to a single hymn in IX (IX.97), whose first three verses are assigned to their eponymous ancestor Vasiṣṭha himself.

4

Structure of the Text

Collection and ordering of the hymns

As should be clear from the previous chapter, the R̥gveda is a very complex text with numerous moving parts: over a 1,000 hymns consisting of approximately 10,000 verses, over 200 named poets, 10 large books with a variety of organizing principles. It is also astoundingly systematic in its organization, a quality not always encountered in textual materials from antiquity. Further detail on the organization will be given in the discussion of the transmission of the text, pp. 23–25; for now what is important is that the systematic organization strongly suggests that a centralized authority or agency oversaw the gathering and structuring of these disparate materials and, further, that this activity postdated the time of active composition.

As we will see in chapter 5, judging from the internal evidence of the R̥gveda, the sociopolitical situation during the period of composition consisted of a loose network of family- and clan-based circles that could form larger alliances when confronted with certain challenges (such as warfare with outside groups) but that generally operated at a certain level of autonomy and indeed competition among themselves. These groups were led by "kings" (whatever that term meant at the time), and these kings and the poets who celebrated them existed in a patron-client relationship, with each group having its own family of poets. The larger network in which they claimed membership was what they themselves called the Ārya, but the operative day-to-day social unit was the family/clan (*víś*).

The Rigveda. Joel P. Brereton and Stephanie W. Jamison, Oxford University Press (2020).
DOI: 10.1093/oso/9780190633363.001.0001

The Family Books of the Ṛgveda (II–VII), as well as the smaller family collections in Maṇḍalas I, VIII, and X, must have grown out of the individual compilations of hymns produced by the bardic families, each associated with such a social group, compilations perhaps preserved as training tools for each new generation of poets, or as evidence of a lineage's poetic expertise, or just out of ancestral pride and, of course, preserved only orally. These collections were no doubt made and maintained during the compositional period itself, though probably only loosely organized. Some editing and culling may have been performed in the process: it is remarkable how little bad, banal, or tiredly repetitive poetry there is in the Ṛgveda, though surely every bardic family was cursed with dull-witted and uninspired members and the first efforts of even good poets-to-be must have had their flaws. Of course this editing may have been done in the second stage of the process, when the family collections were consolidated (or at both stages), but given how many hymns must have been composed over the decades or lifetimes of every family, we must assume that most of it was lost—or judged unworthy of preserving.

At some point the balanced equilibrium of power existing among the various clan groups must have become disturbed, with the emergence of a group or groups that established hegemony over the other groups in the loose confederacy—quite possibly the Bharatas, as Michael Witzel has suggested in a number of publications (e.g., 1995a).

Thereafter, again in Witzel's formulation, there arose a consolidated state (whatever "state" meant in this period) presided over by a group called the Kurus (see Witzel 1995b). It seems that one of the aims of this new political power was to produce a unified religious culture out of the patchwork of clan-based practices—leading to the uniform śrauta ritual system of the middle Vedic period. It was most likely in this era and for these reasons that the individual family hymn collections were brought together and systematically organized into the super-collection we now term the R̥gveda. This compilation coincided with the end of free composition of R̥gvedic-style hymns. The new religious landscape emphasized an ecumenical ritual, with the appropriation, repurposing, and redeployment of ritual materials, both verbal and physical, culled from the various smaller groups and integrated into a single system. The freewheeling poet, following his poetic whim and answerable only to his clan-patron, gave way to the priestly reciter, mouthing the words of previous poets, a cog in the ritual machine.

Thus the production of the great collection that we know as the R̥gveda was an entirely separate process from the composition of the individual hymns and happened at a later time. It was motivated not by literary or religious factors, but sociopolitical ones—which saw a uniform ritual system built from materials originally belonging to a range of different social groups as one way to impose political hegemony. There are several telling if indirect indications of the purpose behind the creation of the collected R̥gveda. For one thing, the final hymn in the text, X.191, is dedicated to "unity" (*saṃjñāna*) and models the production of a common ritual and a common purpose. Earlier in the R̥gveda in the Soma maṇḍala, there is a hymn that shows how the forging of a common ritual could be done: IX.67 consists of three-verse units each attributed to a different poet, and these poets are representatives of the most prominent bardic families, whose hymns are otherwise collected in their individual Family Books. The hymn seems a conscious attempt to create a shared ritual from the competing family traditions. The final two verses of the hymn (IX.67.31–32), which appear to be a later addition, promise great success to whoever studies "the sap assembled by the seers," namely the verses collected in this very hymn.

For further on the collection and redaction of the text, see chapter 10.

The transmission of the text and the state of the transmitted text

The unusual circumstances obtaining both in the composition of the individual hymns (that is, immediate fixation upon composition) and in the compilation of the text (that is, systematic collection and arrangement in service of a sociopolitical agenda) are probably some of the underlying causes of the unusual state of the text as we have it. The Ṛgveda is essentially unique among texts preserved from antiquity in being entirely complete, without lacuna, without variants, and, as far as we can tell, almost entirely without corruptions. The apparatus criticus collecting the manuscript variants for every word that is a standard bottom-of-the-page feature of editions of Classical texts, the suspension dots in and around an edited text that represent gaps in manuscripts, and the sad jagged boundaries of transcribed cuneiform texts representing the broken edges of the tablets are all absent from editions of the Ṛgveda, whose text is presented unadorned. The text we work with is that of the Śākala school, established by Śākalya, a teacher of the late Vedic period. Though other schools and recensions are mentioned in the tradition, they appear to have differed minimally from each other, generally only in the ordering of a few hymns and the inclusion or not of a few late verses or hymns. (See further on this in chapter 7.) There are various reasons for the remarkable integrity of the text.

We are already fortunate in the fact that the transmission of the text was entirely oral for several millennia, for manuscripts are prone to decay and destruction in the climate of the subcontinent. Even after writing had penetrated deeply into Indian culture, the sacred texts, especially the Ṛgveda, were forbidden to be written. It is not clear when the text was first written down—the best guesses are in the second half of the first millennium CE—but even afterward oral transmission remained the more robust means, even into modern times, and this oral transmission was more reliable than any manuscript tradition. But the faithful transmission of the text also arose from other factors.

The immediate fixation of the individual hymns and the closing of the text in the very act of compiling it resulted in a single text that was, in principle, not to be altered—unlike the looser attitude toward variation and expansion of, say, the great Sanskrit epic, the Mahābhārata, with its separate recensions and plethora of manuscripts often differing significantly from each other. What subsequently guaranteed the faithful and invariant transmission of this single, frozen text from deepest antiquity to modern times was the attitude toward the text that arose in the post-compositional period. The R̥gveda itself manifests an extraordinary respect for the power of properly spoken speech, and as the language of the R̥gveda became increasingly archaic and separated from ordinary speech (as it surely was in part already at the time of composition)—and as the text came to be considered to belong to the newly identified category of *śruti*, or divinely inspired texts produced without human agency—it became imperative on religious grounds to preserve the exact verbal form of the text, with the preservation of the meaning of the text far less important (though see chapter 10).

Thus, on the one hand, the sacrality of the text was considered to inhere in absolute fidelity to its original wording, and, on the other, it was not subject to the corruptions that creep into transmission by manuscript copying or by attempts to modernize the language or make better sense of the contents. To ensure that corruptions did not alter the verbal form during oral transmission, elaborate methods of oral recitation were devised to provide cross-checks. In addition to the Saṃhitāpāṭha, the "continuous recitation" of the text, with sandhi (phonological adjustments across word boundaries) applied, a number of methods were based on the word-by-word analysis of the text. The result of this concentration on the exact verbal form of the text, with a major de-emphasis on the meaning of the text in the lineages of the reciters (thus discouraging attempts to change it to make more sense as the language itself changed), was the fortunate recipe for delivering an almost perfectly preserved time capsule over the millennia. On metrical grounds we can identify some places in the text where clusters of consonants (generally a consonant followed by *y* or *v*) need to be distracted to produce another syllable (that is, read as consonant plus *iy* or *uv*), and other metrical disturbances suggest minor phonological adjustments to the text, but these restorations are highly restricted. There is good reason to believe that the text we have is essentially the same text the composers and compilers dealt with.

The dawning realization in Western scholarship about the fidelity of the transmission ultimately produced a deep-seated and principled reluctance to emend it. In the early days of R̥gvedic scholarship in the West, emendations were routinely and frequently proposed, and given the frequent obscurity of the text, these adjustments often yielded an easy (or easier) sense. But sometime around the turn of the twentieth century, this attitude changed, and Vedicists today almost never accept or propose emendations to the text. The few that are proposed and accepted must involve minimal change of the transmitted text and some explanation for why the change would have happened. There are few if any texts from antiquity where such a sternly practiced "hands-off" attitude prevails.

Structure of the text

Whenever the compilation was made and whoever made it, it was done with a brisk efficiency that one hopes prevailed in other parts of the administration. As was sketched briefly in the first section of this chapter, the R̥gveda consists of over a 1,000 hymns divided into 10 maṇḍalas of unequal length. The core of the text is the group of Family Books, Maṇḍalas II–VII, each of which contains hymns ascribed to a single bardic family. These six books are arranged in order of size, with II (ascribed to the Gr̥tsamada family) containing the fewest hymns (43) and VII (the Vasiṣṭha maṇḍala) the most

(104). Within each maṇḍala the hymns are arranged first by the deity addressed, with Agni, the fire god, first, followed by Indra, the great warrior god, and then collections of hymns to other deities, generally arranged by the decreasing number of hymns to each deity within the maṇḍala. Within the various deity collections, further organizational principles apply: the hymns are arranged by length—longest first—and if two hymns contain an equal number of verses, they are arranged by meter, with longer meters preceding shorter ones.

Not all the arrangements in these books conform to the principles just laid out. Hymns of the "wrong" length are sometimes found within an otherwise well-ordered sequence, and in several cases the length of a particular maṇḍala breaks the pattern: Maṇḍala III contains 62 hymns, while IV has only 58; V has 87 but VI 75. Rather than viewing these breaches as the sign of incomplete or imperfect application of their own principles by the original compilers, modern Vedic scholarship has recognized these anomalies as evidence for later manipulation of the text, by appending newer hymns to older sections or by combining several hymns into one or splitting one into several. Examining these breaks in the pattern has given us numerous insights into the layers of compilation in our received text.

Enclosing the Family Books, the other maṇḍalas are structured somewhat differently. Maṇḍala VIII primarily contains hymns from two bardic families, the Kāṇvas (in 1–48 and 60–66) and the Āṅgirasas (in 67–103), though hymns attributed to poets from other families sometimes intrude, often because they exhibit features associated with the same liturgical purpose as the Kāṇva/Āṅgirasa hymns. Within these larger collections, the hymns attributed to particular poets are grouped together in small collections. The rigid arrangement by deity of the Family Books is not followed in this maṇḍala, though within the smaller groupings hymns to the same deity cluster together, with Indra often leading off. What really characterizes this maṇḍala is its frequent strophic structure. Many hymns have their verses grouped together in two- or three-verse units, known as *pragāthas* and *tṛcas* respectively. These strophic structures are especially associated with the sung portions of the ritual, which in the classical form of śrauta ritual were performed by the Udgātar priest of the Sāmaveda and his associated priests. Indeed, many of the hymns in VIII were incorporated into the Sāmaveda. Maṇḍala VIII thus appears to be in great part a specialized liturgical collection within the liturgical text that is the Ṛgveda. The strophic principle allowed quite large hymns to be assembled, and the dominant impression of the maṇḍala is of long, loosely structured—one might say rambling—hymns, whose intermediate units, the strophes, often show unity on this smaller scale.

Nestled in the middle of this maṇḍala is a set of 11 apocryphal or "half-apocryphal" hymns known as the Vālakhilya hymns (VIII.49–59). Although these are clearly supplements to the Ṛgveda, they were transmitted with accents, included with the rest of the Śākala text, and treated by the Padapāṭha (word-by-word text) and by the Anukramaṇī index, so they are more closely associated with the Ṛgveda than the other apocrypha. The first eight hymns in this collection proceed in pairs, dedicated to the same divinity and containing the same number of verses, and especially the first two pairs appear to be variants of each other, utilizing the same words and themes, deployed slightly differently. They have the air of set school exercises and, though the level of skill displayed in the poetry is lower than much of the Ṛgveda, they may give us valuable insights into the process of creating a Ṛgvedic hymn.

Maṇḍala I also consists of smaller groups of hymns attributed to particular poets, but falls into two sections: I.1–50 and I.51–191. The first group consists of six groups belonging to individual poets, with the hymns often in the short gāyatrī meter and arranged in pragāthas, like the hymns in VIII. Also, like VIII, several of the poets belong to the Kāṇva family. It is almost certainly later than the rest of I, and, with some notable exceptions like the great Indra hymn I.32, the quality of the hymns is comparatively low, with banal phraseology and simple sentiments. The second, and considerably longer, part of I is quite different. It is divided into nine groups of hymns, each attributed to a particular poet and arranged according to the same principles as the Family Books. The poetry is some of the most glorious—intricate, bold, deeply original—in the R̥gveda, and the poets' names are a roll call of some of the most distinctive poetic voices in the text, among them the well-known Kakṣīvant, Dīrghatamas, Agastya, but also lesser known but no less distinguished ones such as Nodhas and Paruchepa.

Maṇḍala IX is the most unusual, in that it contains only hymns dedicated to Soma Pavamāna (Self-purifying Soma), that is, the deified ritual drink, and it only concerns a small episode in the preparation of that drink, when the pressed soma liquid is poured over a sheep's wool filter to remove its impurities and is collected in vessels and mixed with other ritual substances. The collection may have been created for the Potar, the "purifier" priest, in charge of this rite. Although these few ritual actions are imbued with cosmic significance and decorated with every verbal trick the R̥gvedic poet had at hand, the subject matter is both extremely limited and, at least superficially, not very promising as a topic for poetry. It is an astounding feat that 114 hymns devoted only to this ritual moment, all different, and including the longest hymn in the R̥gveda (IX.97), could be assembled and preserved, and no doubt an even larger number of such hymns were not deemed worthy of preservation. The hymns were in part extracted from family collections elsewhere in the R̥gveda. The Anukramaṇī ascribes a number of hymns in IX to poets it also names elsewhere in the R̥gveda, especially in I, V, and VIII, and it is noteworthy that, though there are a few hymns dedicated to Soma in various other roles and guises elsewhere in the R̥gveda, there are none outside of IX to Soma Pavamāna. Some of the poets in IX listed by the Anukramaṇī appear to be descendants of poets elsewhere in the R̥gveda, as shown by their patronymics, and so there is also a newer layer within IX. The hymns in IX are arranged by meter and within the metrical groups by decreasing number of verses.

Maṇḍala X is the latest addition to the text and contains a wider variety of subject matter than any of the other maṇḍalas—including hymns devoted to life-cycle rites such as marriage and funeral, meta-reflections on the sacrifice, speculative reconstructions of the origin of the cosmos, hymns dedicated to deities and forces peripheral to the Soma Sacrifice, spells for personal and trivial matters, and so on. In many of its parts its language belongs to a younger and more vernacular stratum than the rest of the R̥gveda, with many "popular" linguistic features reflecting a lower register; these younger portions are linguistically comparable to the second-oldest Vedic text, the Atharvaveda, and many such hymns also have Atharvan subject matter. Indeed, a number of them are found both in the R̥gveda and in the Atharvaveda.

However, Maṇḍala X is not as distinct from the rest of the R̥gveda as it is sometimes depicted. As in the rest of the text, the first half (approximately) is organized into collections attributed to individual poets; as the maṇḍala continues, there are fewer and fewer hymns per poet, until by X.85 there is only one hymn apiece. It is primarily the latter half of X that exhibits the popular characteristics just outlined. The earlier parts of X are not markedly or consistently younger in appearance than other parts of the core R̥gveda, and some of the most highly wrought and sophisticated hymns of the R̥gveda are found in this portion. It is often loosely stated that Maṇḍalas I and X form the younger R̥gveda, and many linguistic judgments have been rendered on the basis of this crude classification. It is one that must be applied with care: especially the second part of I but also the first part of X can be linguistically indistinguishable from the core R̥gveda, and even in the other parts of I and X, supposedly younger forms and concepts should be evaluated carefully.

It should be clear from the foregoing that the whole structure of the R̥gveda follows a consciously devised plan, rather than being a haphazardly gathered grab bag. One further piece of evidence shows just how deliberate the plan was: the two outer maṇḍalas, I and X, the latest to be assembled, contain an identical number of hymns—191—though the internal structures of I and X are quite different and the hymns therein must have been brought together under quite different circumstances. But someone must have felt the need to make the two outer books symmetrical and therefore to fiddle with the contents in order to make the numbers come out right.

5

Social and Political Context

Way of life

During the composition period of the R̥gveda, the Indo-Aryans carried on the way of life that had long defined the Indo-Iranians. They continued to be pastoralists, who raised cattle, goats, sheep for wool, horses for the two-wheeled chariots that made them formidable in battle, and other livestock. They continued a long-established tradition of periods of settlement alternating with periods of movement. This pattern appears in the R̥gveda itself, which distinguishes the period of *kṣéma* "settlement" from the period of *yóga*, literally the "hitching up" of vehicles for mobility. In the period of settlement, the Indo-Aryans tended their herds and flocks, which provided their principal economic support, and they also practiced some agriculture. They grew grains, *dhānā́*, especially *yáva* "barley" which had been farmed in the Indus Valley long before the Indo-Aryans entered the area (Wojtilla 2003: 39, 41–42). The R̥gveda shows a reasonably robust vocabulary for agricultural objects and implements: plow (*lā́ṅgala, sī́ra*), plowshare (*phā́la*), plowman (*kīnā́śa*), threshing floor (*khála*), sickle (*dā́tra, sŕ̥ṇī*), sheaf (*parṣá*), and so forth. A number of these agricultural words do not have Indo-European etymologies, and therefore likely reflect the encounter of Indo-Aryans with peoples more dependent on agriculture than they, although at which period and whether in Central or South Asia these encounters occurred is not certain. During the period of mobility, the Indo-Aryans searched for fresh pastureland for their animals, which brought them into

The Rigveda. Joel P. Brereton and Stephanie W. Jamison, Oxford University Press (2020).
DOI: 10.1093/oso/9780190633363.001.0001

conflict with one another and with other peoples controlling or seeking land. They also directly appropriated resources from their rivals by raiding cattle and crops. Since the periods of settlement and mobility were tied to the agricultural and pastoral cycles, they likely occurred at regular times of the year. This pattern is even directly reflected in later Vedic literature: Taittirīya Brāhmaṇa I.8.4.1 reports that the major tribes of the period, the Kurus and Pañcālas, become mobile during the cool season. The periods of mobility contributed to the movement of the Indo-Aryans farther east and deeper into South Asia. The bulk of the R̥gveda reflects locations in present-day Afghanistan and the Punjab, the area of the Indus River and the "five rivers" that are its tributaries; by the end of the R̥gvedic period, the geographical horizon extended at least to the Ganges River, which is mentioned in one late R̥gvedic hymn.

Social organization

Indo-Aryan society was made up of various large and small groups. Witzel (1995a: 313) gathered the names of approximately 30 such social groupings from the R̥gveda. The smallest social segment was the household (*gr̥há, dám*), which was presided over by the head of the household. In the R̥gveda, however, one word for "houselord," *gr̥hápati* refers to the household's divine head, normally the god Agni in his role as the household fire, rather than to a human. Both *dáṃpati* "lord of the house" and *dámūnas* "master of the house" are used of both divine and human heads of households, although when it refers to humans, the former appears only in an elliptical dual *dáṃpatī* meaning both the "lord and lady of the house." The *víś* is the next largest social division. There has been some difference of opinion concerning just what constitutes the víś. Some scholars see it as a "settlement," a group of households living and moving together; others envision it as a "clan," which shares a common lineage. Most likely it is both: the víś comprised a clan, which lived together under a "clanlord," the *viśpáti*, who in the R̥gveda was again often Agni, the god of fire, although humans and other gods are also called clanlords. The households and the clans were likely the most stable social groups. During times of settlement, clans may have lived in loose affiliation with one another, although still governed by an authority above the level of the clan that acted to keep the peace among the clans. Larger social divisions consisting of various clans are called *kr̥ṣṭí*s and *carṣaṇí*s, both of which refer to the boundaries of one kind or another that defined a group of clans. Another, sometimes synonymous, term for such larger collectivities was *jána* "people" or "tribe." Lineage, whether real or imagined, was one basis for these social formations, but it is also true that social groups could enter into voluntary alliance or alliance through marriage with one other. In times of mobility and especially in times of battle, clans banded together in tighter alliance to defend themselves and their herds or to secure the pasturelands or harvested crops they needed.

In describing the social system of the R̥gvedic period, we have said nothing about the social categories of *varṇa* "class" and *jāti* "caste," which marked the social orders of the post-R̥gvedic periods. Later *dharma* (roughly "legal") texts define a social system of four hierarchically ordered "classes"—*brahmin*s, *kṣatriya*s, *vaiśya*s, and *śūdra*s, together with a fifth category consisting of those born outside these four varṇas (Manu X.45). There is only one hymn in the R̥gveda in which this system is approximated. That hymn is R̥gveda X.90, the justly famous *puruṣa sūkta* "The Hymn of the Man," which organizes humans in a hierarchical order of *brāhmaṇá, rājanyà* "ruler," *vaíśya* "freeman," and *śūdrá* "servant" (R̥V X.90.12). There is no fifth category. These four varṇas, as they came to be called later, were not stable categories, nor in the course of Indian history did they play the same role in describing social reality, let alone defining it. Therefore, we cannot assume that a brāhmaṇá or a rājanyà in the late R̥gvedic period was equivalent to a brahmin or kṣatriya in any other period. But later writers saw their varṇa systems in the

R̥gveda, and it is likely that R̥gveda X.90, which is a relatively late composition, was placed in the R̥gveda in part to provide a constitution for an ideal Indian social order. But its descriptive relevance for all but the latest period of the R̥gveda is doubtful. What we observe in it is the process by which the clans and tribes of the R̥gvedic period eventually gave way to social categories that cut across and reconfigured them.

One R̥gvedic expression for the whole of the Indo-Aryans was the "five peoples," the *páñca jánāḥ*. Four of these five peoples are usually paired: the Yadu people with the Turvaśa, and the Anu people with the Druhyu. The fifth people were the Pūrus, who were connected to another group that may have formed a subtribe of the Pūrus, the Bharatas. Although they may have followed the other four tribes into the Punjab, the Pūrus and the Bharatas came to dominate them. Overlapping lines of three Pūru and three Bharata rulers are particularly prominent in the R̥gveda. Among the Bharatas these kings were Atithigva, his son Divodāsa, who may have led the Bharatas across the Hindukush, and Divodāsa's son or grandson, Sudās, whose prominence is reflected especially in the hymns of Vasiṣṭha, the poet of Maṇḍala VII. Among the Pūrus, the principal rulers were Purukutsa, Trasadasyu, and Tr̥kṣi. Whatever may have been the connection between the Bharatas and Pūrus, they became rivals. Aside from mythological battles, the most famous conflict mentioned in the R̥gveda is the "Battle of the Ten Kings," which is described by Vasiṣṭha, especially in VII.18 but also in VII.33 and 83. According to Vasiṣṭha's account, the battle took place on the Paruṣṇī River, the modern Ravi River, and marked the victory of the Bharata king Sudās over an unnamed Pūru king and his many allies, who included the Turvaśas, Druhyus, and Anus. At least in Vasiṣṭha's telling, therefore, this battle would have marked the dominance of the Bharatas over the other Vedic tribes.

The designation "five peoples" is a recognition of the common cultural ancestry of the Indo-Aryan peoples. Other names also signify the totality of the Indo-Aryans and point to other bases for their unity. One such term is *mā́nuṣa*, a derivative of the word *mánus*, a word that means "man." Additionally, however, *mánus* (also *mánu*) became the name of a particular man, Manu(s). In the later tradition this Manu was the first man, but in the R̥gveda he is the first sacrificer, and therefore the cultural ancestor of the Indo-Aryans. In R̥gveda IV.26 and 27, the poet Vāmadeva describes how Manu sent a falcon to heaven in order to steal the soma. Once the soma was obtained, Manu could then perform the Soma Sacrifice, which defined the R̥gvedic peoples. The term *mā́nuṣa*, which etymologically might have meant "related to man," was interpreted to mean "son" or "descendant of Manu." In calling themselves *mā́nuṣa*, therefore, the R̥gvedic peoples were asserting that they defined themselves by descent from the one who first performed sacrifice to the gods. Their possession and performance of the sacrifice marked them as different from other peoples. The R̥gveda describes people of other cultures in a variety of ways, but among them are that they are "without sacrifices" and that they do not follow the "commandments" of gods, including the commandments that govern the rituals: III.4.7 "Reciting the truth, they [=the seven priests of the soma rite] speak just the truth, reflecting upon their commandments as protectors of the commandments." The R̥gveda shows evidence that other peoples whom the Indo-Aryan migrants encountered in South Asia could be grafted onto the Indo-Aryan community by also performing sacrifice. The R̥gveda mentions sacrificers or generous patrons whose names do not appear to be Indo-Aryan, such as Śaṇḍa, Br̥bu, Araṭva Akṣa, and Balbūtha Tarukṣa (Witzel 1995a: 326). Such names suggest a process that brought various peoples into Vedic culture by giving them access to the ritual tradition. We would expect intermarriage with other peoples would bring women into the Vedic fold, but at least some males also adopted Vedic culture and its defining cultural idioms.

Another designation for the whole of the Vedic peoples was "Ārya," which probably meant those who were "civilized," that is, those who followed the customs and obligations of the Vedic peoples. The Āryas had their opposite in the Dasyus, or Dāsas, who were the cultural "other." Just exactly who these others were is uncertain. Generally, scholars have seen them as peoples who were in South Asia before the Indo-Aryans migrated there, but at least one scholar, Asko Parpola (2015: 92–106) has argued that they represented earlier waves of migrants to South Asia antecedent to the peoples who produced the R̥gveda. Whoever they were, these peoples were rivals for land and other resources, and therefore the R̥gveda represents them as enemies of the Āryas. In particular, the warrior god Indra defended the Āryas against their Dāsa or Dasyu foes, whether they be human or demonic. Addressing Indra, for example, Bharadvāja says: VI.18.3 "It was you who tamed the Dasyus, and who alone vanquished their communities for the Ārya." One reason that Indra helps the Āryas is that it is the Āryas who offer soma (V.34.6, IX.63.5). Therefore, according to R̥gveda I.51.8, Indra should distinguish between Āryas and Dasyus, punishing "those who follow no commandment," namely the Dasyus, and making them subject to him "who provides ritual grass," the Ārya sacrificer. Because of their dedication to the gods, the poets ask them to give light to the Ārya, which implies open spaces for settlement and herding (I.17.21, II.11.18, VII.5.6) and deny that light to the Dāsa. This light is linked to the light of the sacrificial fire, and therefore, addressing Agni Vaiśvānara, Agni "who belongs to all men," the poet says in I.59.2 "You did the gods beget as a god, Vaiśvānara, as light just for the Ārya." Agni Vaiśvānara is the sun, the universal fire, but it is also a ritual fire and a communal fire that signifies the union of the Ārya clans (Proferes 2007: 46–47), and therefore this fire should extend the dominion of the Āryas across all the land. Since the Āryas are associated with the light, which should be theirs, it is not surprising that the Dāsas or Dasyus are associated with darkness. So then, how should we understand verses such as R̥gveda I.130.8 "Indra aided the Ārya sacrificer in battles, affording a hundred forms of help in all contests—in contests whose prize is the sun. Punishing those who follow no commandment, he made the black skin subject to Manu" or VII.5.3 "The dark clans went breaking ranks, leaving their supplies, from fear of you. . . . You drove the Dasyus away from their home, o Agni, giving birth to broad light for the Ārya"? Did the Āryas see what we would call a *racial* divide between Āryas and Dasyus, as many interpreters have suggested? We believe that importing into the R̥gveda the idea of "race," which is a much later concoction, is at best misleading and that the opposition between the darkness of the Dasyus and the light of the Āryas is principally an ideological one, as Hock (1999b) has argued in his careful study of this issue. If skin color was involved in the opposition between Āryas and Dāsas, it was probably incidental to the more general associations with the light of the sun and the sacrificial fire and to the "broad light" of the areas through which Āryas might move freely. Finally, we need also note again that the poets of the R̥gveda describe conflict not only between Āryas and Dāsas but also between Āryas and other Āryas and Dāsas. The poet asks for success in battle over both in X.83.1 "Might we be victorious over Dāsa and Ārya with you [=Battle Fury] as yokemate," and similar are II.1.19, IV.30.18, X.38.3, 102.3. Both Dāsas and Āryas can be "obstacles" to the life and prosperity of the poet and his people, and therefore the poets ask that Indra smash them as he smashed the great Obstacle, Vr̥tra, as in VI.33.3 "You, o champion, smite both kinds of enemies, the Dāsa and the Ārya obstacles," and likewise, VI.22.10, 60.6, VII.83.1, and X.69.6. Other Āryas could be just as much rivals for land, crops, and cattle as were Dāsas or Dasyus.

Kingship

The leadership of the Vedic communities was invested especially in the *rā́jan* [/*-rā́j*], which we translate as "king," although, with reason, some scholars have hesitated about that translation and preferred "chieftain." No translation really captures the range or nature of the office, for rājans apparently ruled over a variety of social groups or confederations. A rājan might govern a number of clans or a tribe or an alliance of tribes. Likewise, the responsibilities of a rājan might vary depending on the purpose for which a confederation or alliance had been formed and for which the rājan ruled. And finally, the process of appointing a rājan may also have differed depending on the magnitude of the grouping over which he ruled and possibly also the period of R̥gvedic history.

Kings governed both in times of settlement and in times of mobility, but there are varying opinions concerning whether there was a single king who governed both during times of settlement and times of mobility, or whether different kings were appointed during different times or even whether there were complementary rulers at the same time. One reason for this uncertainty is that we are forced to reconstruct the society of humans through the stories of gods. There are various gods who are called kings, principally Indra, Varuṇa and Mitra, Soma, and Agni, all with very different divine profiles. Do these different gods correspond to different humans and to different kings? Or do they represent different sides of kingship? The characteristic rule of Varuṇa, which involves judgment, punishment, and the timely rain necessary for agriculture, makes most sense during the period of settlement. The rule of Indra concerns war, victory, open spaces, and winning cattle and therefore conforms to the period of mobility, battle, and raiding. The language of the R̥gveda distinguishes between the kingships of Varuṇa and of Indra. Typically, Varuṇa is called a *samrā́j*, "universal king," implying that he governs an array of clans, tribes, or peoples to maintain relative peace among them. Indra is called a *svarā́j*, a "king over his own" or an "independent king," because he commands a particular group or alliance that stands in opposition to other groups. While it is possible that there were two kings, one after the model of Varuṇa during the period of settlement and peace and the other after the model of Indra during the period of mobility and battle, we think it more likely that Varuṇa and Indra represented different functions of kingship that were invested in a single human. Its evidence is not unequivocal, but Ṛgveda IV.42 points to a single king. The hymn was composed for the consecration of the Pūru king, Trasadasyu. There both Varuṇa and Indra are invoked, and in our understanding, the hymn presents Trasadasyu as a king who represents both Varuṇa and Indra. This interpretation accords with later royal consecrations, in which a king was crowned as the human embodiment of both Varuṇa and Indra. Thus, whether ruling over a large or small social segment, a king was tasked with keeping the peace between the communities within his rule during settlement and with leading those communities into battle or into new lands during times of mobility.

It is also difficult to reconstruct the means by which a king was appointed. Both the Ṛgveda and Atharvaveda speak about a king being chosen by the clans he governs: Atharvaveda III.4.2 "Let the clans choose you for kingship. Let the five divine directions now (choose) you." The "five divine directions" may refer to divinities above and in the four directions, but especially in this context, they may also allude to the five tribes that comprise the Vedic peoples. But the question remains whether this "choice" of a king was really the selection of a king (Proferes 2007: 16–17) or simply an acclamation or acknowledgement of a king (Schlerath 1980: 204). That there is a lineage of Bharata kings and Kuru kings indicates that at one level of kingship, there was a regular succession of rulers, which would support the idea that this choice was a formal one. Another possibility is that the king was selected from among a number of competitors, for just as there is an ideology of choice, so also there is an ideology of contest in the appointment of a king. In royal rites of the post-Ṛgvedic period, there are various ritualized contests. The Vājapeya, or the rite of the "Drink of Victory," includes a horse race. The Rājasūya, or the rite of "Royal Consecration," includes the ritual enactments of a victorious raid for cattle and other goods and of the king's victory in a dicing game. At least in its origins, the Aśvamedha, the "Horse Sacrifice," required a demonstration of sovereignty. A horse is set to wander for a year, and the king shows his authority by defeating any challengers in the lands through which the horse moves. But it is unlikely that the leaders of clans or tribes actually chose a king as a result of such contests. Rather, the king's victory was a formal demonstration of his ability to lead and to protect the people he governed. However a king gained sovereignty, it was also possible for him to lose sovereignty. Atharvaveda III.3, for example, is a hymn to bring back a king who has been driven from power and exiled, and it is likely that also in the period of the Ṛgveda a king who failed in his responsibilities as king could be displaced. These responsibilities may have included not only leadership in times of settlement and mobility but also the general prosperity of the tribes and clans. Kingship is associated with the rain, for example, and therefore a king whose rule did not result in seasonable rains may have been vulnerable to replacement. Despite the fluidity and possible uncertainty of governance, however, the system successfully allowed the Vedic peoples to assert sovereignty over increasing areas of north India and laid the foundation for the larger polity led by Kuru rulers in the post-Ṛgvedic era.

Mundane daily life and the depiction of women

One could read swathes of the Ṛgveda and come away with the sense that the only occupations followed (besides priest and poet) were warrior and stockbreeder, but the text gives us occasional hints of a more varied range of pursuits. One hymn (IX.112) lists a series of possible professions: carpenter, physician, and smith among them, and the artisan who fashions chariots is often presented as a model for the poet fashioning a hymn, as we will see. An itinerant peddler or merchant figures briefly and enigmatically in V.45.6, and I.125 treats a figure called the "early-comer" who seems to be a tramp poet/priest offering his services door-to-door (or settlement-to-settlement). The text also has a curious fascination with the thief, for which there are several words (*táskara, tā́yu, -tr̥p, -máthi*) and who figures in similes, as in V.15.5 describing Agni as "hiding your track like a thief." Hunting and snaring of birds also merit some mention, as in III.45.1, where they hope that other sacrificers will not keep Indra from their sacrifice: "Let no one hold you down, as men using snares do a bird." But the tasks of daily life—hauling water, cutting wood (though see X.146.4), cooking, and so forth—and the people who performed them are quite recessive in the text.

If this is so for males, it is considerably more pronounced for women, who are visible only in the roles related to their stage in life. We often meet beautiful and seductive young women, since the goddess Dawn is regularly compared to them. But there was obviously considerable anxiety for the unmarried girl, especially one without a brother to help in the husband-finding. As in later orthodox Hinduism, the only satisfactory path for women was marriage. In I.124 (translated in full in the Appendix) Dawn is first described as "exulting in her spotless body" (verse 6) but immediately after is compared to "a brotherless (girl) who goes right up to men" (similarly, IV.5.5). Young women are several times depicted as going to festive gatherings (I.124.8, etc.), quite possibly to find eligible partners, or to a rendezvous (I.123.9), but in I.167.3 "a young woman roving in secret, going to men in a public hall" seems to refer to a less respectable or happy pursuit. The plight of the woman "who grows old at home" (*amā-júr*) is clearly pitiable (e.g., VIII.21.15), and the text also touches obliquely on a girl who has a child out of wedlock (V.2.1). Still, the happy girl newly engaged to a worthy bridegroom is also given due space, as in X.27.12 "the maiden, gratified all around by an admirable (gift) worthy to be chosen, from a bride-seeking man from among the young bloods. She becomes a fortunate bride, when she is well-adorned. She wins herself an ally [=spouse] in public." In an oft-repeated simile the wife is depicted as "richly dressed, ever eager for her husband"

(I.124.7, etc.). But the existence of two charms against co-wives make it clear that for some wives, competition for male attention continued after marriage. And the chilling simile "as a single common husband does his wives, Indra has dragged down all the strongholds to submission" (VII.26.3) does not cast a favorable light on such marriage. On the status of the widow, see p. 60.

In discussing different types of R̥gvedic hymns, we will also touch on pregnancy charms and charms against miscarriage; pregnancy and childbirth were obviously dangerous states for women. The fraught birth of Indra—he chose to exit from his mother's side—is related in the dramatic hymn IV.18. In that hymn his mother's apparent abandonment of her newborn is obscurely described, though depictions of motherhood are generally tender, as in II.38.5, where "the mother has set out the best portion for her son," or the comparison of the soma-pressing stones to "playful (boys) jostling their mother" (X.94.14). In the very late R̥gveda, we see a new role for the wife, that of ritual partner to her husband, a major ritual innovation in that period (see Jamison 1996, 2016b, 2018).

Despite the limitations of their roles, the women depicted in the R̥gveda, especially in the *ākhyāna*, or dialogue hymns, tend to be strong, spunky, and outspoken, as indeed they are throughout Classical Indian literature. We will meet irrepressible, tough-talking dialogue partners like Yamī, Lopāmudrā, and Urvaśī (see p. 161); to this number we can add others, like Mudgalānī (X.102), who takes over her husband's losing chariot and as charioteer drives it to victory, or Apālā (VIII.91), who even as a young maiden performs a private soma rite for Indra (a ritual that was of course off-limits to lone females, especially young girls), attracts his attention, and wins boons from him.

6
Ritual

Overview

The Ṛgveda is primarily a liturgical text; the individual hymns collected in it were composed to be recited as the verbal (or, more accurately, *a* verbal) portion of a ritual performance that also involved the physical offering of foodstuffs, to put it in its simplest form. Though some of its hymns, especially in the Xth Maṇḍala, do not appear to have the tight connections to ritual performance that we find elsewhere in the text—for example, the hymns speculating on the origins of the cosmos or of human beings—they are relatively few and are segregated in particular parts of the text—and, in fact, we cannot be completely certain that they did not have a place in ritual.

We can be even more precise about the ritual connection: as already noted, almost all the hymns in the Ṛgveda were destined for the Soma Sacrifice, the multipart ritual in which a deified drink known as soma was offered to the gods. This was the most solemn and elaborate of the non-royal rituals. What soma the substance was is much disputed, and already in the middle Vedic period, and indeed perhaps in the Ṛgvedic period, substitutes were employed, possibly because the original substance was difficult to obtain. It was made from a dried plant, which was first soaked in water and then pressed to produce a yellowish juice, which was then mixed with water and often also with milk. Unadorned it was apparently quite bitter. As already noted, the purification and mixing of the soma juice provide the occasion for the 114 hymns of Maṇḍala

The Rigveda. Joel P. Brereton and Stephanie W. Jamison, Oxford University Press (2020). © Oxford University Press.
DOI: 10.1093/oso/9780190633363.001.0001

IX extravagantly celebrating those ritual actions and praising the juice-become-god.

What did Ṛgvedic ritual look like and how do we know? Here we are on both firm and shaky ground. We know what followed it—the śrauta rituals of the middle Vedic period, exhaustively detailed in both the *brāhmaṇa*s (prose exegetical texts, some of which are not too much younger than the late Ṛgveda) and in the *śrauta sūtra*s (manuals that codified ritual practice toward the end of the Vedic period). The rituals described by these later texts contain much that can also be found in the Ṛgveda: names of priests, names of offerings, the layout of the ritual ground, and particular procedures employed in praise and offering. Much of what has been written about Ṛgvedic ritual starts with the later material and backprojects it by locating correlates in the Ṛgveda. In some sense there is no other way to proceed: the systematic treatment and richness of detail offered by the later texts provide a context in which to situate the less organized and more enigmatic information in the Ṛgveda.

The Soma Sacrifice in later Vedic texts

What then do these later texts tell us about Vedic ritual, and, in particular, about the Soma Sacrifice, the dominant ritual in the Ṛgveda? In the later Vedic tradition, there were Soma Sacrifices of various lengths. The simplest form was a one-day sacrifice called the Agniṣṭoma, the "Praise of Agni." The soma rite of whatever form began with three fires that were used in the daily Agnihotra rites and in monthly rites at the new and full moon.

To the west was the round Gārhapatya Fire, or "Householder's Fire," which was used especially in the preparation of the sacrificial offerings. To the southeast of the Gārhapatya was the half-moon shaped Dakṣiṇāgni Fire, the "Southern Fire," which was apotropaic, keeping at bay evil forces—typically conceived as coming from the south—and which also received offerings to the ancestors. And, finally, to the east was the square Āhavanīya Fire, the "Oblation Fire," into which most offerings were poured. The shapes of the Gārhapatya and Āhavanīya Fires represented earth and heaven respectively, so that ritual movement from west to east toward the Āhavanīya represented the progression from the realm of humans toward the world of the gods. Between the Gārhapatya and Āhavanīya Fires was the Vedi, which was a depression or elevation covered with grass in which sacrificial implements and oblations were laid. (It should be noted that, despite superficial similarity, the word "Vedi" is entirely unrelated to "Veda" and the English adjective Vedic.) In the Soma Sacrifice and in other more elaborate rites, a Mahāvedi, or "Great Vedi," was constructed to the east of this sacrificial ground. The Mahāvedi then became the place to which the soma plant was brought and the soma prepared and the location of a new Āhavanīya Fire into which the soma oblations were poured. The sacrificial area, or *yajana*, then had the shape shown in figure 6.1.

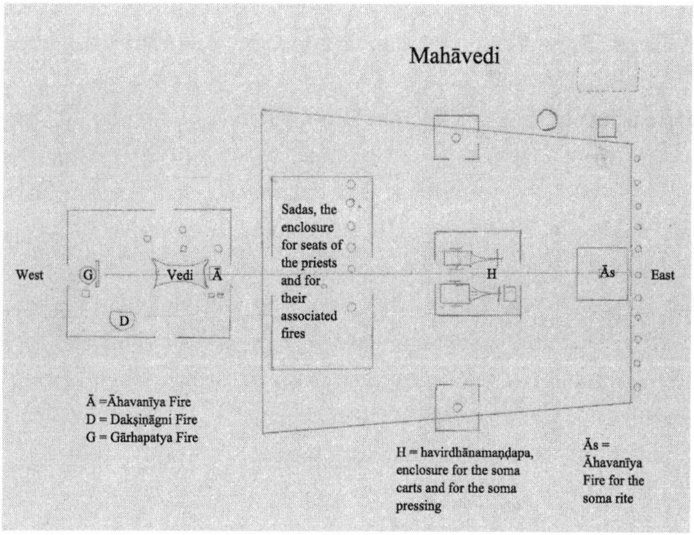

Figure 6.1. The Ritual Ground for the Soma Sacrifice

Before the principal day of the Soma Sacrifice, there are several days of preliminary rites such as the consecration of the Sacrificer, offerings of ghee (clarified butter) and rice cooked in milk, the formal purchase of the soma plant, and the laying out of the new Vedi. The actual soma oblations takes place on the last day of the Soma Sacrifice. That final sacrificial day centers on three "soma pressings," in which the soma juice is extracted and offered in the morning, at midday, and in the evening. In the first two soma pressings, the preparation of the soma juice begins when the priests pour water on the stalks of the soma plant and crush the stalks. After several rounds of crushing the stalks, collecting them, and crushing them again, the stalks and their juice are placed in a vessel from which the soma juice and water are poured across a woolen filter to remove any debris. The soma is then offered at various points in the order of rites. Some oblations just use the filtered soma; in others the soma is mixed with milk or grain. In the Evening Pressing, the preparation of the soma distinctly and interestingly differs. Instead of pounding fresh soma stalks, the priests use left-over soma juice prepared in the other two pressings and soma extracted from already crushed stalks, to which milk is added to increase the volume.

Each of the pressings shows a similar structure defined by a repeated ritual sequence. In each of these sequences, after the soma juice is pressed, priests first fill the cups from which the soma will be offered with soma juice. Then there is a chant, or *stotra*, whose texts are taken from the Sāmaveda but which originate in the Ṛgveda, and a recitation, or *śastra*, essentially an anthology of Ṛgvedic verses. The oblation of the soma into the fire follows the recitation, and the ritual sequence concludes in the priests' drinking the soma that remains in the cups after the offering. In the Morning and Midday Pressings there are five such sequences of chant, recitation, offering, and consumption; in the Evening Pressing, two.

In the Morning Pressing the sequences are dedicated to Indra and Agni, to the Viśve Devāḥ (the "All Gods"), to Mitra and Varuṇa, to Indra, and to Indra and Agni. In addition to these, there are soma oblations to Indra and Vāyu, to Mitra and Varuṇa, and to the two Aśvins. In the Midday Pressing there are single sequences for Indra together with the Maruts and for Great Indra, which are followed by three sequences for Indra. Finally, in the Evening Pressing the first sequence is dedicated to the All Gods and the second to Agni together with the Maruts. The Evening Pressing also includes soma oblations to the Ādityas, Savitar, and Agni together with the Wives of the Gods. There is a great deal of other ritual activity surrounding these sequences and oblations. In each of the pressings, offerings of butter and other foodstuffs and various other rituals are interwoven throughout the pressings. Naturally enough, these many rites require many priests. The śrauta texts call for 16 or 17 priests (*ṛtvij*s) for the performance of even the simplest Soma Sacrifice. These priests are divided into four groups: priests led by the Hotar, who are responsible for the Ṛgvedic recitations; priests led by the Adhvaryu, who carry out the ritual actions; priests led by the Udgātar, who perform the ritual chants; and the Brahman priest, who oversees the rite and rectifies any ritual deficiencies that might occur.

There are now a number of documentaries and films dealing with Vedic sacrifice and with the Soma Sacrifice in particular. The modern documented performances of these rites do not necessary conform in every detail to the descriptions given in the śrauta texts, and this is likely true for all performances in the past as well as the present. But they are remarkably close, especially considering that 2,000 years distance us from these śrauta texts. Perhaps the most informative of these films remains *Altar of Fire*, which is available at https://www.youtube.com/watch?v=RYvkYk7GvJ0 (accessed November 2019). The rite in this film, which was performed in 1975, was an Atirātra or "Overnight" Soma Sacrifice with an Agnicayana. The "Overnight" Soma Sacrifice, in which the pressing day begins early in the morning and continues until the morning of the following day, is also known to the Ṛgveda. The

Agnicayana is a variant of the Soma Sacrifice that requires the construction of a brick altar on which the Āhavanīya Fire is placed. This form of the Soma rite is attested in the middle Veda but not in the R̥gveda.

Changes between R̥gvedic ritual and middle Vedic ritual

Unfortunately, we cannot take the extraordinarily detailed treatments of śrauta ritual as roadmaps for what we find in the R̥gveda: it is clear that there were a number of changes, often quite significant, between R̥gvedic and classical śrauta ritual, despite the superficial agreement in terminology and overall practice. We have already noted one major change: the free composition of new hymns for every ritual performance (or rather for every significant new performance) gave way to a fixed liturgy created by excerpting from and combining the older freely composed materials, as was just noted in the description of the śrauta Soma Sacrifice. Although the verbal portion of the ritual remained very important, the role of those in charge of this verbal portion had profoundly changed, from creative poets to rote reciters. The exuberance so evident in the R̥gvedic poets was tamed, and their position at the intellectual pinnacle of their society much reduced. The ritual and social dynamics must have changed, too, giving more prominence to other priests involved in the performance and altering the king-poet patronage relationship, though it is likely that poets still produced secular royal panegryic to glorify those kings.

Moreover, as we also noted, at the end of the period of free composition, an ecumenical, pan-Vedic liturgy was created, replacing the individual clan traditions and the bardic families that supported them. It is clear from the R̥gveda that, though all the clans shared a basic ritual structure focused on the Soma Sacrifice, there were differences in the details of their performance. These differences got ironed out in the post-R̥gvedic period. For example, in classical śrauta ritual the Midday Soma Pressing is dedicated to Indra and the Maruts; some R̥gvedic priestly families (notably the Bhāradvājas of Maṇḍala VI) also attest to this joint dedication, but for others Indra alone is the dedicand. The incorporation of the Maruts into Indra's Midday Pressing is in fact dramatized in the first Maṇḍala in a series of dialogue hymns (I.165, 170–71) depicting the reconciliation of Indra and the Maruts. A careful reading of these hymns allows us to witness the types of adjustments required to create a unified ritual out of divergent clan traditions and to see the kinds of mechanisms developed to justify this change. With the standardization of the ritual and the disappearance of free composition, the locus of ritual authority had shifted, and individuals and individual social groups no longer had the freedom to put their own stamp on the general ritual template.

And, leaving aside the deep rupture that the abandonment of free composition must have caused, there are other indications that R̥gvedic ritual differed in details and indeed in some serious structural matters from the later codified ritual. For example, while it is clear that already in the R̥gveda the performance of solemn ritual required three fires to be established, the standard names of those three fires (Āhavanīya, Gārhapatya, Dakṣiṇāgni) do not appear in the R̥gveda, though the names are found, and found together, in the next oldest text, the Atharvaveda. The very shape of the Soma Sacrifice may also have been different. In the classical śrauta ritual, the soma is pressed three times on the central day of the sacrifice. However, at least certain R̥gvedic clans seem to have had only two pressings; for example, in V.77.2 strong disapproval is expressed for sacrificing at evening. The Third Pressing, which takes place in the evening, would then be an innovation in particular circles, an innovation that then spread and was adopted into the ecumenical ritual. Even the required personnel seem to have changed. Classical śrauta ritual requires the Wife (Patnī) of the Sacrificer (Yajamāna) to be an active participant in all the solemn rites, but there is evidence that the intrusion of the Wife was an innovation in the late R̥gveda and was staunchly opposed by conservative ritualists. The positive evidence for the Patnī in the R̥gveda is confined to a few verses in a single hymn in the somewhat aberrant VIIIth Maṇḍala (VIII.31.5–9), and reading between the lines of a number of other late R̥gvedic hymns allows us to glimpse the theological resistance to introducing a female into the pure realm of the sacrifice. (See Jamison 2011, 2016b, 2018.)

Thus, while the most crucial materials for evaluating R̥gvedic ritual are provided by the voluminous accounts of classical śrauta ritual, dated to some centuries after the R̥gveda, these accounts cannot be naively backprojected into R̥gvedic times: too many fundamental principles had changed.

Pre-R̥gvedic ritual

So, that is what followed R̥gveda ritual. What preceded it? Here again we have some evidence, though it is less direct. As we noted, (Vedic) Sanskrit and indeed all the Indo-Aryan languages are closely related to the Iranian languages, and in their older stages Indo-Aryan and Iranian share not only many linguistic features but also numerous cultural, social, and religious ones. The oldest attested Iranian language is Avestan, in which the earliest texts of what later came to be known in the West as Zoroastrianism were composed. Although even by the time of the oldest Avestan texts (whose dating is comparable to, though probably somewhat younger than, the R̥gveda), the religion had undergone a number of changes, a ritual culture shared with early Vedic can be discerned. It was centered on a fire cult and with strikingly similar vocabulary and even ready-made superimposable poetic phrases. One of the most prized offerings was *haoma*, a word sound-for-sound identical with Vedic *sóma*, and haoma was both an offering and a deity, as in Vedic. There are numerous other lexical equivalences, for example, the Avestan *zaotar* priest and the Vedic *hótar* priest, names for various offerings, both physical (e.g., "oblation": Avestan *āzūiti* = Vedic *ā́huti*) and verbal (e.g., "song" Avestan *gāθā* = Vedic *gā́thā*), etc. Even more than these agreements in vocabulary and in ritual procedure, the high value placed on recondite poetry and elaborate verbal formulations and the similar poetic techniques and phraseology employed to produce them testify to a shared sensibility at the heart of their religious practice.

Thus, both Avestan and R̥gvedic ritual must have developed out of the same prehistoric system. Yet again, there are significant differences, chief among them that Avestan ritual was centered on a single fire, whereas all R̥gvedic solemn ritual presupposes a system of three fires (though, as noted, without the names they would soon bear). As it is unlikely that Avestan ritual simplified a multi-fire model, the three-fire system must have developed between the Indo-Iranian period and the time of the R̥gveda. How and why this happened is a matter of some mystery, but it seems to have been connected with the disjoining of family-centered life-cycle rites (what are later called *gr̥hya*, or "domestic," rituals, collectively described in the so-called gr̥hya sūtras) from the more public, community-centered rites that go on to form the śrauta ritual system (see Jamison 2019). One chief distinction between gr̥hya rituals and śrauta rituals is the number of fires, one for gr̥hya, three (or more) for śrauta.

Utilizing both the older Indo-Iranian evidence and that of the classical śrauta system and evaluating the often oblique evidence offered by the R̥gveda in light of these chronological poles, we see a ritual system that shares much with both but cannot be reduced to either and that is itself not unified across the various portions of the text and is in a period of transition.

The Ṛgvedic ritual model

With this awareness of the uncertainties and inconsistencies of Ṛgvedic ritual, we can nonetheless lay out a fairly simple model of ritual performance into which most of the many variants can be fitted. The template is a hospitality ceremony and festive meal. The gods are invited to come to us, to our ritual ground, which has been prepared for their comfort, with sacred grass strewn on the ground to make seats for the divinities. The grass, *barhís*, has an exact cognate in Avestan *barziš* "cushion, pillow." The journey of the gods is often described in hymns—they are ordered to hitch up their chariots and drive down from heaven. We eagerly and anxiously await their arrival, for there is always the possibility that they will find someone else's ritual more appealing and stop there instead. Indeed, hymns often contain a plea or command for the gods to pass over the rituals of other peoples and come to ours. Once they are here, settled on the grass, we offer them food (melted butter [ghee], small grain cakes, and the like) and drink, especially the prized soma, as well as entertainment in the form of recitations and songs. Although the *pūjā* rites of the later Hindu tradition are very different in form and unlike Vedic rites are centered on an image or symbol of the god worshipped, these pūjā rites nonetheless share a similar foundation, since they too follow the acts and norms of hospitality. Creating the verbal entertainment for the gods is the role of the Ṛgvedic poet. Since the gods clearly like to hear about themselves, the hymns offered praise them and their exploits, but since the gods already know their own wonderful qualities, this praise has to be imaginatively and elaborately confected to appeal to the gods' poetic connoisseurship. As is often said in the brāhmaṇas, "the gods love the obscure." (This characterizes the function of the hymns within the ritual hospitality model; for discussion of the deeper purpose of these compositions, see Chapter 9) At the end of the celebration the gods are sent home—generally after what in modern philanthropic circles would be called "the ask." That is, toward the end of many hymns (and in the more intemperate hymns, throughout), we request benefits from the visiting gods, both material—gold, cows, horses, sons, etc.—and not—success in battle, long life, etc.

This reciprocity—oblations to be consumed and praise to be savored, in return for largesse and good fortune conferred—is at the heart of the interface between human and divine, and an awareness of its balanced economics is often visible in the hymns. The physical site for this reciprocal exchange is the ritual ground.

As the classical soma rites still evidences, the Soma Sacrifice was in the first instance a rite in honor of Indra. The first recipients of the Morning Soma Pressing are Indra and Vāyu, the Wind. This rite marked the coming of the day and of light. The Midday Soma Pressing is to Indra or to Indra and the Maruts and was associated with the coming of the waters. And the Third Pressing, for the families among whom it existed, was anciently dedicated to Indra and the R̥bhus, priests who became divine through their performance of the ritual. It appears to have been grounded in the welfare of the human sacrificer (and his wife, if she participated in the rite in this period) and priests. Other gods for whom other rites may have been performed appear to have been grafted into the soma rites already in the pre-Rgvedic period, which refashioned the Soma Sacrifice into a ritual for all the deities of the R̥gvedic pantheon. This evolution of the Soma Sacrifice, which further enhanced its status as the foremost of the Vedic rites, continued in the post-R̥gvedic period.

It should be emphasized that the ritual ground on which the R̥gvedic rites all take place is not a temple—not a permanent built structure—or even a piece of land permanently dedicated to that purpose. Rather, any appropriate piece of ground can be demarcated and sacralized for the purpose of ritual performance, and the preliminary acts in the ritual involve this creation of sacred ground, especially by laying out the three fires. This requires "taking out" the additional fires from one that is presumably always kept burning and placing them at the designated places on the ritual ground. The offering fire, especially, is taken to the east end of the ground and established there. The ability to make any place a place of ritual must have been extremely handy for a people in constant motion.

The gods thus serve as our guests, and the ritual shares many features with the ceremonial guest-reception of mere human guests. An important feature of the "guest" model is that it envisions and requires direct interaction between gods and mortals, on the mortals' turf—or rather on a space that has been rendered temporarily neutral through its sacralization—on earth, the human realm, rather than in the gods' world, heaven. The arrival of the gods is an epiphany in the technical sense. The poets crave this epiphany and fear its failure to materialize. It is especially Indra whose epiphany they anticipate, and the fear that he may not appear leads to the more general fear that Indra does not exist, a possibility expressly voiced in the text (e.g., R̥V II.12.5). We should also remark that this model entails considerable conceptual danger. The host-guest relationship is often depicted as fraught in ancient Indian literature, and how much more so when one party to the relationship is markedly more powerful than the other. The elaboration of Vedic ritual may be an attempt to control the divine forces that could potentially run riot.

Another, more recessive model of sacrifice competes with the guest model in the R̥gveda, especially in Agni hymns. In this model the offerings go to the gods in heaven, rather than requiring the gods to come to earth to receive them. The libations ascend on the smoke of the offering fire, an image conceptually close to the Homeric sacrifice, with the smoke of the Homeric hecatombs rising to the gods (e.g., Iliad 1.315–17). Agni, the ritual fire, is considered the mouth of the gods, the eater of the oblations destined ultimately for them. There seems to be no conflict in the minds of the R̥gvedic ritualists between these two models, and they are not exclusive to different groups of poets but can in fact occur in the same hymn. See, for example, the Agni hymn I.1, where the "guest" model dominates, with the gods' travel to the sacrifice explicit in verses 2 ("he [=Agni] will carry the gods here to this place") and 5 ("Agni will come as a god with the gods"), but the oblation's movement *to* the gods is alluded to in verse 4 ("O Agni, the sacrifice and rite that you surround on every side—it alone goes among the gods."). It seems likely that the "go to heaven" model is the older one, judging from the Homeric parallels; it is also more appropriate to a period in which one of the chief gods was Father Sky (Dyauṣ Pitar), a divinity whose mobility was presumably limited. But Dyauṣ Pitar's importance had waned already by the beginning of the R̥gvedic period, and the dominance of more peripatetic gods made a "come to the sacrifice" model more viable.

Who were the participants in the ritual? As we've just seen, the gods were crucially present at the performance; without their presence it would make no sense to conduct it. The human side was represented by a collection of priests and other stakeholders in the success of the sacrifice. To approach the question of who they were, it is useful first to consider the personnel of the classical śrauta ritual, in which there are clearly demarcated roles. The Sacrificer (Yajamāna) is the person who arranges and pays for the sacrifice; despite the English title he does very little of the actual sacrificing. He must be married, and as noted, his wife must also participate in the ritual. In royal sacrifices the Sacrificer is the king; in others he must have been a substantial member of the Ārya community with sufficient resources and time to devote himself to the demanding exigencies of śrauta performance. In order to be a śrauta Sacrificer with the three requisite fires, a man must "establish the fires" (*agnī́n ā́ √dhā*) in an initial ritual called the Agnyādheya; thereafter he is called an Āhitāgni ("one possessing established fires") and has the right—and the requirement—to perform śrauta sacrifices, starting with the twice-daily Agnihotra offering. Many who were technically eligible to establish fires would nonetheless have chosen not to embark on this arduous religious path, contenting themselves with the simpler rites and single fire of the gr̥hya or domestic cult. How momentous the decision it is to become an Āhitāgni and how much lifelong labor is required after becoming one are dramatically depicted for present-day Vedic sacrificers in Knipe 2015, especially chapter 6.

The Sacrificer arranges for the priests who carry out the sacrifice. Elaborate śrauta rituals like the Soma Sacrifice require the cooperation of a number of priests, representing the three ritual Vedas: the Hotar priest associated with the R̥gveda, the Udgātar of the Sāmaveda, and the Adhvaryu of the Yajurveda, along with their assistants. The representatives of the three Vedas were each responsible for the liturgical portions drawn from their particular Vedas, as well as for any associated actions. Action was especially the province of the Yajurveda's Adhvaryu, who did most of the physical work.

The situation in the R̥gveda appears to have been more fluid. The priestly titles Hotar, Adhvaryu, and Udgātar all appear in the R̥gveda (though the last only once), and, as was noted, much of the VIIIth Maṇḍala is composed in poetic forms later associated with the Udgātar, much of it incorporated into the Sāmaveda. A number of other priestly titles are found, and the apportioning of their functions seems roughly comparable to that found later. However, the strict segregation by Veda affiliation is of course not found, since the R̥gveda presumably predates the formal separation into Vedas. The kings mentioned in the *dānastuti* (praise of the gift) that ends many hymns must have been the equivalent of the royal Sacrificer later. But it is not clear whether in nonroyal rituals there was a separate Sacrificer without a priestly role (as in later śrauta ritual) or whether the Sacrificer was one of the priests—or indeed whether both were possible. A number of hymns mention a patron or patrons (*sūrí*), who appear not to have priestly roles but to confer benefits on the priest/poets—and to act as middle men, redistributing to the ritual performers part of whatever the gods have given them because of the correct performance of the sacrifice they patronized. The role of patron thus seems close to that of the later Yajamāna, but whether this was the dominant R̥gvedic model or there was also a model in which the role of Sacrificer was conflated with that of priest/poet cannot be determined. Moreover, what was the position of the poet, in whose first-person voice R̥gvedic hymns are composed and recited? Because free composition of hymns was no longer a feature of classical śrauta ritual, there is no equivalent role there to match that of the R̥gvedic poet, and we are on even shakier ground in evaluating his structural position. Was he, as often seems to be the case, a priest? In the R̥gveda, the *brahmán* is mentioned as one of the seven priests of the soma rite in II.1.2 and one of the four priests in X.71.11. According to the most likely analysis, the word *brahmán* means "formulator," and therefore these references to a brahman priest mean that the poet was one of active priests in the ritual. The poet often addresses himself, by name and in the second-person singular (e.g., "praise Indra!"), as well as exhorting a larger second-person plural group to praise the gods (e.g., "[you all,] praise Indra!") or to perform certain ritual actions (e.g., "press soma!"); he also often uses the first-person plural to refer to these same actions ("let us praise Indra; let us press soma"). These habits of address suggest that the poet formed part of a larger group of officiants and also acted as spokesperson for them. Thus in the R̥gveda there seems to be far less definition of and separation into rigid ritual roles than in later times; the same person may well have been priest, poet, and the equivalent of the later Sacrificer. Moreover, since the division into separate Vedas had presumably not yet occurred, the various priestly functions would not yet have been divvied up among distinct social groups adhering to particular Vedas and their branches. The same man might have, on different occasions, chanted the chanted portions (as Hotar) and sung the sung portions (as Udgātar), while also pouring the oblation into the offering fire (as Adhvaryu).

Other types of rituals in the Ṛgveda

Although most of the hymns in the Ṛgveda have clear association with the Soma Sacrifice, other rituals are also represented. These are generally known also from later materials, and in those later materials they have often been amalgamated as subparts of the paradigm Soma Sacrifice. One of these is the Pravargya, which involves an offering to the Aśvins of milk and ghee, heated to boiling in a particular ritual pot. Both the offering and the pot itself are called *gharmá*, literally "heat." The boiling over of the gharma-pot is an image of over-abundance. In śrauta ritual the Pravargya is part of the Soma Sacrifice, but in the Ṛgveda it appears to have been an independent rite with a slightly mystical aura. It may provide the background of some of the enigmatic verses in the riddle hymn (I.164, at least vss. 26–29), and it is referred to obliquely in the famous Frog hymn (VII.103.7–9).

Animal sacrifice, which also forms part of the later soma ritual, is present in the Ṛgveda, but is generally not very prominent. The paraphernalia and actions of the classical animal sacrifice—the post to which the victim is tied and the circumambulation of the animal so bound—are alluded to, but often not directly, but in similes. There is, however, a litany contained in the 10 so-called Āprī hymns (see p. 141), composed on a tight template of key words—an unprecedented compositional technique in the Ṛgveda—that in śrauta ritual accompanied the fore-offerings of the animal sacrifice, and at the end of each of these hymns the post for the victim is addressed and the sacrifice of the animal is alluded to in extremely veiled terms. For example, X.110.10 "Send the oblations downward to the fold of the gods at the proper season, having anointed them by yourself. Let the Lord of the Forest [=post for the victim], the Butcher, and god Agni sweeten the oblation [=sacrificed animal] with honey and ghee." One particularly important animal sacrifice, the royal Horse Sacrifice, is treated in two hymns in the R̥gveda, I.162–163, discussed immediately below.

The royal rituals mentioned above with reference to the śrauta system are represented, but not abundantly, in the R̥gveda, and are mostly confined to the younger parts of the text—quite possibly an indication that a robust concept of kingship was only beginning to take shape. The royal consecration rite, later known as the Rājasūya, a term first found in the Atharvaveda, which involves pouring water on the new king as a symbolic conferral of authority, has a foothold in the late R̥gveda. The short hymn (six verses) X.173, identified as "praise of the king" (*rājñaḥ stutiḥ*) in the Anukramaṇī, appears to contain verses appropriate to a royal consecration, with a more aggressive companion piece in the next hymn, X.174, which emphasizes the combative and confrontational aspects of kingship. Although these hymns designed for the royal consecration are fairly late, as we have already seen, the hymn IV.42, well-embedded in the Family Books, depicts the consecration of the famous king Trasadasyu.

The most elaborate of the royal rituals in the śrauta system is the Aśvamedha, or Horse Sacrifice, to be performed by a king to consolidate or display his power. In the classical śrauta version a stallion is sent forth to roam for a year, accompanied by armed troops who fight the kings of any territory into which the horse strays. When the horse returns at the end of the year, it is sacrificed, along with numerous other victims, with due pomp but also with almost unimaginably outlandish accompanying actions. At the climax of the ritual the chief wife of the king has sex (or simulated sex) with the just-slaughtered horse on the ritual ground, while the other queens and their female attendants circle around, singing and dancing and trading obscene jokes with the officiating priests. Two late R̥gvedic hymns (I.162–163) directly treat the Horse Sacrifice, although the later sexual extravaganza is either unknown to them or, more likely, delicately omitted from discussion. The first (I.162) describes the (literally) gory details of the sacrifice itself, while commending the sacrificed horse and all its gear to the gods. The second (I.163) lavishly lauds the horse and identifies it with the sun on its journey to the gods. The racehorse Dadhikrā of king Trasadasyu, praised in three hymns (IV.38–40), may also represent the sacrificed horse of Trasadasyu's Aśvamedha. The sexual activity of the classical Aśvamedha, which is elided in I.162–163, may be indirectly alluded to in the famous dialogue hymn X.86, in which the god Indra, his wife Indrāṇī, and Indra's monkey pal Vr̥ṣākapi engage in sexual banter.

In addition to the rituals that will be codified in the later classical śrauta system, the R̥gveda marginally treats rituals that will form part of the later gr̥hya, or domestic, ritual system, primarily life-cycle rites. The R̥gvedic treatments are almost exclusively found in late portions of the text, in Maṇḍala X, and often have parallels in the Atharvaveda. The funeral is treated in a series of hymns (X.14–18). Of particular interest are X.16, which concerns the cremation fire and the actual burning of the dead man's body, and X.18, which describes the funeral service, the burial, and the return of those still living to their lives. Verses 7–9 of X.18 have attracted special attention because they appear to depict the widow of the dead man, first lying beside the dead man and then being recalled to life and to remarriage: X.18.8 "Arise, woman, to the world of the living. You lie beside him whose life is gone. Come here! You have come into existence now as wife of a husband who has grasped your hand and wishes to have you." This passage suggests that, while the later institution of *satī*, or widow burning, is not attested in the R̥gveda, the ritual representation of the widow's ceremonial death (though followed by ceremonial rebirth) could have provided a model for a more literal enactment. Many of the verses in this group of hymns are found also in the Atharvaveda funeral hymns, XVIII.1–4. Another hymn, X.56, describes the ascent of the body of the deceased by means of the cremation fire and its transformation into an immortal body in heaven. On the R̥gvedic conception of what happens after death, see Chapter 8.

A long and episodic hymn, X.85, is devoted to the wedding. Many of its verses are found also in the Atharvaveda wedding hymns and are utilized in the gr̥hya sūtra protocols for the wedding ceremony. Pregnancy and birth, a major preoccupation in the later gr̥hya material, is barely represented in the R̥gveda. There are charms for safe childbirth (V.78.7–9, X.184), the latter of which follows immediately a brief dialogue between husband and wife attempting to conceive (X.183), and in a short series of hymns against disease we find one against the dangers of miscarriage (X.162).

7

The Gods

Overview

As is clear from the account of the ritual provided in the previous chapter, the gods are the focus of R̥gvedic religious activity—active participants in the ritual that mediates between the human and the divine, conceptually present as discerning and eager guests at the here and now of the sacrifice, receivers of praise and oblations, bestowers of all good things. As it is also clear from the description of the R̥gvedic text, almost all of its more than 1,000 hymns are dedicated to one or more divinities. The text is a vast compendium of divine praise poetry, and the poets endlessly dilate on the qualities and exploits of the gods, address them directly, commanding and cajoling, and use all their verbal skills to conjure up the divine world and its inhabitants and to persuade the gods to do mortals' bidding. This chapter will discuss the different kinds of deities that inhabit the R̥gvedic world and the natures of these gods, first in general and then individually.

Perhaps the most surprising feature about the R̥gvedic gods, for people used to the interactive pantheons of Classical (Greek and Roman) and Germanic mythology—or to the developed narrative mythology of the Sanskrit epics and purāṇas—is the lack of a unified pantheon and indeed of a single model of divine figure. To put it contrastively, in Homer, for example, the gods are all recognizably of a human type, with a human shape and human desires, emotions, and behaviors. They also interact with each other—feasting together, quarreling with each other, taking sides,

The Rigveda. Joel P. Brereton and Stephanie W. Jamison, Oxford University Press (2020). © Oxford University Press.
DOI: 10.1093/oso/9780190633363.001.0001

playing tricks—and the riches of Greek mythology are essentially narratives of this interaction among the gods and of their interference in human affairs. The Greek gods of course have vastly more power than their counterparts on earth, but they are like greatly enhanced versions of human beings and society projected on a heavenly screen. The collection of Vedic gods is very different, consisting of various distinct types of gods, with limited interaction among the types, and a dearth of mythology except for a few gods and a few divine situations. What Vedic gods hold in common is the ritual, whereas what Greek gods hold in common is their internal social structure.

Vedic gods can be classified by what kinds of forces or phenomena they are most closely correlated with. We can begin with the forces of nature. Earlier Western accounts of Vedic gods, building on indigenous treatments like that of Yāska, divided all Vedic gods into three categories associated with the three cosmic regions—heaven, midspace, and earth—and within these categories were gods associated with the cosmic forces localized in those areas. This overarching nature-mythology paradigm has long since been discarded, along with the arbitrary pigeonholing of some gods in niches of nature into which they fit uneasily at best. But it cannot be denied that a number of gods do represent natural forces, and their names are often identical to the common nouns that express the same natural forces they represent. These include Sūrya "Sun," Vāyu "Wind," Parjanya "Thunder(storm)," Uṣas "Dawn," and Dyaus and Pr̥thivī "Heaven and Earth," not to mention the ubiquitous Agni "Fire." So, for example, the word *sū́rya* can be used both of the sun as a natural phenomenon and of the Sun as a divinity with abilities to perceive and to act characteristic of an animate being and with at least a rudimentary mythology or set of narratives and personal qualities. But the distinction between natural phenomenon and divinity is far less sharp for Vedic India than for the modern West: the Sun is still recognizably the sun, and the qualities and abilities he has are recognizably solar, though sometimes extended into spheres outside of strict physical nature. Thus, the Sun is often called the eye of Mitra and Varuṇa, which sees all the good and bad behavior of humans. This divine conceit has a natural basis: the sun is more or less eye-shaped, of course, and as it daily crosses the sky, it has a constant view of the earth on which all human activity plays out.

A second type of divinity includes those defined by the social sphere in which they operate. The most prominent deities in this category are the three principal Ādityas: Mitra, Varuṇa, and Aryaman. These gods represent the different principles that define social relations, and they ensure that human beings act according to these principles. As the gods of nature have functions within the social world, so these gods of the social world also have functions within the natural world. Mitra and Varuṇa are associated with the sun, and Varuṇa also governs the waters, granting them to those who uphold the principles he represents, withholding them from those who do not. In this way the processes of the visible world become the assurance of the reality of the principles of the social world.

Like the first class of gods, another group of gods have names that specify their activities. Several of these are agent nouns, principal among them being Savitar, the "Impeller," who compels cosmic entities as well as humans and other living beings to action or sends them to rest; for example, IV.53.3 "Savitar has stretched forth his two arms, at his impulsion causing the moving world to settle down and impelling it forth through the nights." And Tvaṣṭar, the "Fashioner," a skillful workman who fashions forms, including those in the womb, as in this little birth-charm: X.184.1 "Let Viṣṇu arrange the womb; let Tvaṣṭar carve the forms. Let Prajāpati 'Lord of Offspring' pour out the semen; let Dhātar the 'Placer' place the embryo in you." On the basis of this last activity Tvaṣṭar becomes especially associated with females, including female divinities like the Wives of the Gods. In this group we can also include fairly minor figures like Viśvakarman "All-Maker," Prajāpati, and Dhātar.

The two most celebrated gods in the Ṛgveda, aside from Indra, belong to yet another category, that of ritual elements, though each might also be classified in the first group of natural forces and substances. These are Agni and Soma. As already mentioned, the name Agni is also the common noun for fire (*agní*), and like *sū́rya* the word is used interchangeably and sometimes simultaneously for both the phenomenon and its divinized counterpart. The difference is that, given the model of Vedic ritual with its focus on fire, this divinized Fire is first and foremost the ritual Fire, the recipient of the oblations and the divine representative found in every household. Though lowercase "fire," as it were, can be used of non-ritual fires, Agni the god is characteristically the ritual fire. Soma the deified ritual drink is even more bound to the ritual context. Although Soma the god is invested with cosmic kingship and a vast realm in which to exercise it, he is entirely identified with soma the substance, which substance has no existence outside of the ritual.

A number of other gods are hard to classify and others cross the categories described above. This applies to the most prominent god in the Ṛgveda, Indra, the great warrior and the most longed-for guest at our sacrifices. Nearly a quarter of all Ṛgvedic hymns are dedicated to him, the greatest number for any god. He is that rarity among Ṛgvedic gods, one without a speaking name, and he embodies neither natural elements nor social forces. He is also the only god who has a truly developed mythology.

A group of gods closely associated with Indra are the Maruts, whose name also lacks a synchronic (or indeed diachronic) etymology. These gods, undifferentiated among themselves of uncertain number, combine the categories of the natural and the social: they are the personification of the thunderstorm, far more vividly and more commonly than Parjanya, with lightning, thunder, and rain all among their attributes. But they also represent a social factor, the Männerbund, an association of rampaging young men, temporarily operating outside the social bonds of the society they belong to.

Another set of that are gods hard to characterize are the two Aśvins, a pair of undifferentiated deities. They do have a speaking name—"the Horsemen, the Horse-possessing"—although the relation of this designation to their functions, principally to heal and to rescue, is not fully transparent. Moreover, the "Horsemen" designation is a secondary one; they have an alternative and apparently older name: Nāsatya (*nā́satya*), which has an Avestan counterpart, though it refers to a single being and is the name of a demon, and they appear to have even deeper roots in prehistory, corresponding to the Greek Dioskouroi (likewise a secondary designation, literally "Zeus's boys").

Those with an interest in later Hinduism will have noticed the absence of mention so far of two of the most prominent gods in the later period, Viṣṇu and Śiva. Both are present in the R̥gveda but are not particularly conspicuous, as will be discussed later in this chapter. Viṣṇu is generally associated with Indra as his sidekick or assistant and has little mythology of his own. His name has no evident meaning or connection to external substances or forces. Śiva is not found under that designation: *śivá* "kindly" is a euphemistic epithet later applied to the god Rudra. In fact, this epithet is regularly used of numerous other gods in the R̥gveda (not to mention substances like food [I.187.3]) and only once, in a late hymn (X.92.9), of Rudra. While the principal gods of the R̥gveda fade into decorative insignificance in later periods, Viṣṇu and Śiva come to prominence. Neither the eclipse of the old R̥gvedic gods nor the ascendancy of these originally marginal ones could be predicted from the R̥gveda alone; the seeds of change are invisible. Treatments of R̥gvedic divinity that begin with the later period and backproject into Vedic times inevitably distort the picture.

Another misleading backprojection involves the eternal enmity and competition between two groups of supernatural beings, the Devas and the Asuras. Already in the middle Vedic period we find a mythological cycle, consisting of narratives and fragments thereof, in which the gods (Devas) find themselves in perpetual conflict with their almost equally powerful negative counterparts the Asuras—with the narratives almost invariably introduced across the range of Vedic prose texts with the formula "The Devas and Asuras were contending." Although the Devas always prevail in any particular story, it is generally a bare victory and the Asuras live to fight another day. This conflict continues to be prominent in the post-Vedic religious landscape, as in the well-known story of the churning of the ocean of milk, in which the two moieties fight over the treasures churned up, found, for example in the great epic poem of India, the Mahābhārata. According to the middle Veda, the Devas and Asuras were both offspring of the god Prajāpati. In the Mahābhārata the conflict between these two groups of divine siblings has been transposed into a battle between two sides of the same human family.

An apparent mirror image of this paired opposition is found in Old Iranian in the Avestan texts, where *ahura*, the direct cognate of Sanskrit *ásura*, is the title of the head of the pantheon, Ahura Mazdā "Lord Wisdom," and the *daēuuas* (exact cognate of Sanskrit *devá*) are the enemies of all that is good. This apparently neat correlation had led many scholars to assume that the **daiva / *asura* opposition can be reconstructed for Indo-Iranian times and that Iranian has simply flipped the values. That **dei̯u̯o* can be reconstructed as the Proto-Indo-European word for "god" makes it almost certain that it was Iranian that would have made the change. However, the chronologically intermediate R̥gveda makes this polarized superimposition difficult if not impossible to maintain. The term *ásura* is common in the R̥gveda, usually in the singular, as a positive title "lord"; it is often used of divinities, including many who are also called *déva*, sometimes in the same passage. See, for example, VIII.25.4, where Mitra and Varuṇa are praised simultaneously as *déva*s and *ásura*s (and similarly, V.42.9 of Rudra) or III.55 with the refrain ending all 22 verses "Great is the one and only lordship (*asuratvám* 'asura-ship') of the gods (*devá*)." Only in the late Ṛgveda do we get any hints of the enmity between Asuras and Devas that will become prominent in the next stratum of texts; see X.157.4 "when the gods came, having smashed the Asuras" (and compare X.53.4 "Might I [=Agni] today devise this . . . , by which we gods will overcome the Asuras"). It should be noted that a close reading of one hymn, X.124, that has traditionally and repeatedly been used as evidence for Ṛgvedic Deva/Asura enmity does not support this interpretation, and so an important prop for the identification of this enmity in the Ṛgveda disappears (see Brereton 2016; Jamison 2016a). In our view, the Vedic opposition between Devas and Asuras is not ancient but late. For further discussion of *ásura* in the Ṛgveda, see the careful study of Hale 1986.

The most comprehensive grouping of gods is the category known as "all the gods" or the "All Gods" (Viśve Devāḥ), which is not really a unified category, although the Anukramaṇī identifies the Viśve Devāḥ as the divinity of a large number of hymns. The term, both in its usage in the text and in its application to a hymn type, is employed in a number of different senses. On the one hand, it is a handy way to refer to the whole divine community, to ensure that no god has been left out of a generic eulogy or request for aid. In this usage the gods are not treated as individuals but as an undifferentiated group, opposed to mortals or, later, the Asuras (as just mentioned). This group ultimately becomes conceived of as a sort of corporate entity, the All Gods. On the other hand, many Viśve Devāḥ hymns do not encompass the whole group, but name a series of individual gods, each one often allotted a single verse in a list hymn (e.g., VI.49). Here the phrase "all the gods" is a way of indicating that the hymn is not targeting a single god, as in the majority or Ṛgvedic hymns, but selecting a number of gods. And finally a number of hymns with the Anukramaṇī designation "all gods" actually have very little to do with the gods at all, but contain meditations on the mysteries of the cosmos, of the sacrifice, or of the powers of poetry and ritual speech (see, e.g., I.105 or the notoriously obscure V.44).

The striking difference between the roster of R̥gvedic divinities and their characteristics and behavior and those found even in middle Vedic, not to mention the post-Vedic religious landscape treated under the rubric of Hinduism, is yet another indication that R̥gvedic religion is sui generis and that comparisons between it and earlier and later systems must be made with great care.

The major gods

Indra

As the preeminent god of the R̥gveda, Indra has a variety of roles. But Indra is first a warrior, upon whom depend the protection and prosperity of his worshippers. His weapon is the *vájra*, the mace. In later tradition, when Indra was reduced to a storm god, the vajra became a thunderbolt, but in the R̥gveda it was a weapon, which could be thrown at an enemy or smashed down upon him, and the principal means by which Indra asserted his power.

The foremost story of Indra in the R̥gveda is the narrative of the battle between Indra and Vr̥tra. The story is mentioned often, but the hymn that comes closest to a sustained narrative of it is R̥gveda I.32. According to the story, Vr̥tra was a gigantic cobra, who was coiled around a mountain that enclosed the waters. In order for life to exist Vr̥tra had to be destroyed. Indra battled the serpent, alone, according to some hymns, or with the help of the Maruts or other gods, according to others. After a furious battle Indra killed Vr̥tra with his mace and smashed open the mountain, releasing the waters. This myth is occasionally merged with others, so that not only the waters but also the cattle and the sun emerge from the mountain. The name Vr̥tra means "obstacle," and one of the characteristic epithets of Indra is *vṛtrahán*, which can mean either "smasher of Vṛtra" or "smasher of obstacles." There is little difference between these two interpretations, however, since Vṛtra is the paradigm of all obstacles. To evoke Indra as the smasher of Vṛtra, therefore, is to evoke him as the god who smashes all obstacles. In the first verse of I.32, the poet begins, "Now I shall proclaim the heroic deeds of Indra, those foremost deeds that the mace-wielder performed: He smashed the serpent. He bored out the waters. He split the bellies of the mountains." The reason that the poet proclaims these heroic deeds is not just to remember what Indra accomplished but also, by stating these truths about Indra, to make these truths real again. As he did before, Indra will once again smash the obstacles that Vṛtra represents and will once again make life possible for human beings. The narrative of the destruction of Vṛtra was associated particularly with the Midday Soma Pressing, which is dedicated to Indra alone or to Indra and the Maruts.

The Vala myth is the second great narrative of Indra and a complement to the Vṛtra story. According to this myth a group called the Paṇis captured the cattle and kept them trapped in the Vala cave. Indra opened the Vala cave and released the cattle and, with them, the dawns. Remarkable in this story is that Indra does not defeat the Paṇis and free the cattle by using his mace, but rather by using the power of the truth in the songs he chants. That truth is his knowledge that the cattle *are* the dawns and by knowing that truth, he releases both cattle and dawns. Accompanying him and joining him in his chant are groups of priests, the Aṅgirases, sometimes along with other priests—the Navagvas or the Daśagvas. In this narrative, therefore, Indra is a priest-king rather than a warrior-king as he is in the Vṛtra story. In his role as priest-king, Indra is also called *bṛ́haspáti*, the "lord of the sacred formulation." The god Bṛhaspati, therefore, is often Indra himself in the Ṛgveda, but already there Bṛhaspati can also sometimes be a separate divinity alongside Indra. Gradually, as Indra and the Vedic king, who personified Indra, progressively lose their priestly functions in the late Ṛgveda and in the later Vedic tradition, Bṛhaspati increasingly stands apart from Indra.

The accounts of the Vala story are even more fragmented than those of the Vṛtra story, but a narrative of one episode occurs in X.108. That hymn tells how Indra sent his dog Saramā to the Paṇis to tell them to release the cattle. Saramā warns the Paṇis that if they do not, Indra himself will come and take the cattle. The Paṇis obviously failed to heed Saramā's warning, since Indra and the Aṅgirases themselves do finally free the cattle from the Paṇis.

As the Vṛtra story is connected with the Midday Pressing, so the Vala story was associated with the Morning Pressing, which takes place with the appearance of dawn. In the Ṛgvedic period the *dakṣiṇā*, the reward to the priests for performing the sacrificial rite, was often the gift of cattle. In the classical soma rite this reward was given at midday, but in the Ṛgveda it was given at the Morning Pressing (cf. X.107.1). The cattle that come to the priests thus reflect the advent of the cattle and dawns in the world. For a full discussion of both the Vala myth and the figure of Bṛhaspati in the Ṛgveda, see Schmidt 1968.

Although the two major mythological narratives with Indra as protagonist are the Vṛtra and the Vala victories, he figures in many other episodes—too many to mention here—which are often fragmentarily attested and poorly understood.

We may start with his parentage. Although the identity of Indra's mother is not clear, in the occasional mentions of her she is a vivid character—as in the snatches of dialogue between Indra and his mother in the famous birth hymn IV.18, where she tries to persuade him not to pursue an unnatural exit from her womb. Elsewhere she offers him soma to drink directly after his birth, soma that he stole from his father, named as Tvaṣṭar (III.48; also IV.18.3). And in an even more enigmatic bit of dialogue (VIII.45.4–6 ≅ VIII.77.1–2), she seems to reassure the just-born Indra that he will ultimately prevail against all his enemies. As just noted, Indra seems to participate in a rivalry with his father. Indeed, in VIII.18.12 the poet asks

Indra who made his mother a widow and answers this rhetorical question by then asking, "What god was merciful toward you when you destroyed your father, having grasped him by the foot?" The unnatural birth and the rivalry with the divine father are of course well-nigh universal attributes of "the hero"; the many prodigious feats attributed to Indra just after his birth are also typical of heroic biography.

Two minor but intriguing myths pit Indra against the two most important forms of celestial light, the Sun and Dawn. We find the merest allusions (primarily IV.30.8–11) to a puzzling episode in which Indra crushes the cart of Dawn and she runs away. Alluded to just a bit more (primarily V.29.5, 9–10; V.31.11, I.121.13) is the chariot race in which Indra bests the Sun, apparently by tearing the wheel off the Sun's chariot. This latter myth is somehow connected with one that is better attested, though hardly better understood, in which Indra and a sidekick Kutsa drive on the same chariot, drawn by the horses of the Wind, to the house of Uśanā Kāvya (a name with a shadowy attestation also in Avestan mythology) to receive some aid or advice, preliminary to slaying Śuṣṇa, the often-mentioned opponent of Kutsa.

Indra has a number of other named adversaries. In one striking whiff of a narrative, Indra, aided by Viṣṇu in some versions, shoots a boar named Emuṣa, enabling him to acquire a special mess of rice porridge hidden in or behind a mountain (see especially VIII.77; also VIII.69.14–15, I.61.7). This myth is further developed in the middle Veda, according to which the boar guarded the goods of the antigods, the Asuras. Indra killed the boar, and as a result the gods gained the wealth of the Asuras. Another myth with more presence in later texts involves Indra's slaying of Namuci by beheading him (e.g., V.30.7–8). In the later versions Indra accomplishes this by trickery, and part of the trick (using the foam of the waters as weapon) is already mentioned once in the R̥gveda (VIII.14.13). The names of other victims of Indra include Śambara, Pipru, Dhuni and Cumuri, and Varcin, inter alia. The details of these battles are too sketchy to provide much in the way of narrative mythology. It is worth noting, however, that the enemies of Indra include both those with Ārya and with non-Ārya names.

Like a number of other gods, Indra has his characteristic draught animals, and his are especially prominently featured in the text. His pair of fallow bay horses (*hárī*) convey him everywhere, especially to and from the sacrifice. They have their own food offered to them at the sacrifice (roasted grain; see, e.g., III.35), and hymns were even devoted to a libation made when the pair were hitched up for the return journey after the sacrifice (see I.61–63). The mention of the fallow bays is sufficient to signal that Indra is present in the context, and *hárivant* "possessing the fallow bays" is a standing epithet of Indra.

Agni

As was noted earlier, the word *agní* is both the common noun meaning "fire" and the name of the god who is deified fire. As with *sóma*, it is often difficult to draw the line between these uses. As we have seen, the sacrificial system of the R̥gveda (and later Vedic texts), like that of the cognate Old Iranian Avestan texts, is focused around the ritual fire. The sacrificial ground is defined by the presence of sanctified fires, oblations are made into them, and the gods and priests gather round them. Thus, first and foremost, Agni is the god always present at ritual performances and the immediate recipient of offerings. He is the most prominent of the R̥gvedic gods after Indra, and all the Family Books and most of the smaller bardic collections open with their Agni hymns.

Agni as ritual fire is both recipient of oblations in his own right and the conduit of oblations destined for other gods. He is therefore regularly called the mouth of the gods and acts as the mediator between the human offerers and divine recipients. The flames and especially the smoke of the fire carry the oblations to heaven, and as the one who brings the offerings to the gods, he takes on the role of a priest. But also, perhaps more often, Agni serves as a means for the gods to come to earth to the sacrifice: Agni is said to be the conveyor of the gods many, many times in the text. (On these two conflicting ritual models, see pp. 54–55). He is a mediator in another sense also, because he is a god who nonetheless dwells intimately among mortals. For mortals he is both ally and messenger to the more distant gods. However, since he is not one of us but a divinity, he is also viewed as and often called our guest.

Another ritual role of fire extends to the organization and cohesion of the Ārya communities. Agni was present as the divine guest in the hearths of every household. In addition, other fires represented the clans (*viś*) and the different tribes or peoples (*jana*) who comprised the Āryas. R̥gveda X.69 provides probably the clearest expression of the ritual amalgamation of clan fires in a single tribal fire, which embodied both the union of the clans and the king or chieftain under whom they united. In X.69 the king who led the united clans was Vadhryaśva, a deprecatory speaking name meaning "possessing gelded horses," and the central, tribal fire was called the "son" or "descendant of Vadhryaśva" (vss. 5, 9, 12). Fire could thus simultaneously symbolize both the dispersal of the Ārya peoples into many different households and clans *and* their cultural and social unity. The pattern of life during the time of the R̥gveda alternated periods when clans and peoples were allied in a common effort and periods in which they were dispersed. The diffusion of ritual fires and their fusion likely were markers of these different periods. For further discussion, see Proferes 2007, especially chapter 2.

The poets emphasize both the divine aspects of Agni and his purely physical form, often intermingling references to different forms of fire in the same hymn. As a god he is often identified with the sun, the celestial form of fire: blazing hot, shining bright, and appearing at the same time of day, namely dawn when the sun rises and the ritual fire is kindled. But the fire on our sacrificial ground is also clearly kin to the fire on our domestic hearth; indeed in later śrauta ritual the fire from which the other ritual fires are taken out is called the Gārhapatya or "Householder's Fire." Agni is therefore also praised for his contribution to daily life and the pleasures of home and family.

The potentially destructive aspects of fire are not forgotten, however. Many of the most inventive descriptions in Agni hymns are of the wild, uncontrollable rampages of forest fire, spreading across the land and "eating" everything in its path. Humans seek to harness this destructive power of fire, to turn it against our enemies and other threats to our safety, and Agni, sometimes with the epithet *rakṣohán* "demon-smasher," is urged to turn his relentless flames against opponents we name.

The paradoxical nature of physical fire also provides some part of the god Agni's personal qualities. That fire is fueled by plants, especially wood, contributes to the belief that Agni lives concealed within the plants and ultimately within the waters that nurture the plants until he is finally born from them. The connection between fire and waters is also evident in the identification of Agni with a minor divinity going back to Indo-Iranian times, Apāṃ Napāt, the "Child of the Waters." Originally he was probably a separate deity, a glowing fiery being concealed and nurtured in the waters, perhaps configured in part as lightning. But the single Ṛgvedic hymn dedicated to Apāṃ Napāt, II.35, gradually merges Apāṃ Napāt with Agni by attributing Agni's functions and form to him, until in the final verse Agni emerges fully in the poet's address to him.

The creation or birth of the ritual fire from the kindling sticks, his parents, is a major subject in Agni hymns, with intricate descriptions of the first stirrings of flame and smoke as the friction of the kindling sticks produces sparks that finally catch. The just-born Agni is depicted as a tender babe, who quickly grows to become stronger than his parents and to devour the plants from which he was born. The kindling of the fire marked the beginning of the sacrificial day, and such attention to the birth of Agni reflected the significance of this ritual moment.

Many aspects of Agni are expressed through the variety of names and epithets applied to him. Agni is Jātavedas as the fire established at the beginning of the rite that continues to its end. As an unbroken presence in the ritual, Agni Jātavedas also oversees the succession of generations, ensuring that a family's lineage will continue. Agni Vaiśvānara, the "Fire related to all men," is the fire become the sun. As the sun, this fire sees everything and governs everyone. This form of Agni is especially associated with the king, who like the sun stands above and reaches all beings. Agni is also Tanūnapāt and Narāśaṃsa. One or another of these names—or sometimes both (I.13.2–3)—appear in the Āprī hymns, which are recited in an animal sacrifice, and they both occur outside of the Āprī hymns as well. The word *tánūnápāt* describes Agni as the "son of himself," and *nárāśáṃsa* as the one "who embodies men's praise" of the gods. As Agni Kravyād, the "flesh-eating fire," Agni is the fire of the funeral pyre. This fire is both welcomed and feared (see especially X.16), but he is ultimately the means by which the dead can be transformed and transported to the realm of immortality. Another deity, Mātariśvan, is sometimes identified as Agni himself, but he is more properly the one who brought the fire from heaven.

Agni participates in almost no narrative mythology, in strong contrast to Indra. Besides the very sketchy account of Mātariśvan's theft of fire from heaven, there is one, ritually connected, tale—that of Agni's flight from the sacrificial ground and his self-concealment in the waters, to avoid his ritual role as bearer of oblations to the gods. The gods find him in his hiding place and coax him back by promising him a share of the oblations. This myth is treated most fully in the late sequence X.51–53, but there are glancing mentions of it elsewhere. The story may have in part been generated by the conflation of Agni with the figure Apāṃ Napāt "Child of the Waters."

Soma

Like Agni, Soma is both a god and a crucial ritual substance, and the boundary between them is not always clear. As discussed, the juice of the soma plant, pressed from the plant and elaborately prepared, is the chief offering of the most important complex of R̥gvedic rituals, the Soma Sacrifice. This sacrificial substance and its ritual preparation go back to the Indo-Iranian period, since Avestan attests to the substance *haoma*, an exact cognate to Sanskrit *sóma* and to its pressing and offering (see especially the Hōm Yašt, Yasna 9–10, which is an Avestan hymn in praise of the haoma). In both traditions the substance is also deified.

One of the perennial problems in R̥gvedic and Avestan studies has been the identity of the soma plant or its Iranian equivalent, the haoma plant. In the R̥gveda the effect of soma juice on both humans and gods is described by the verbal root √*mad*, roughly "exhilarate" or "elate." By these translations we mean that the soma juice invigorated those who drank it and heightened their senses in some fashion. We could be more precise about the effect of soma if we knew from what plant it was extracted. Early speculation that the soma juice was an alcoholic drink of some sort clearly missed the mark, since the preparation of soma does not allow for fermentation and √*mad* does not mean "intoxicate," if that implies drunkenness and not just transport. Of the substantial number of possibilities proposed in more recent times, four now dominate the discussion. The first is that the soma plant was a stimulant, and the most frequent candidate for that stimulant is one or another kind of ephedra. Although not original to him and defended by other scholars, the interpretation of soma as ephedra was argued with particular plausibility by Harry Falk (1989, 2002–2003), largely on the basis of internal evidence in the R̥gveda. Also in favor of this hypothesis are the use of ephedra in Zoroastrian ritual even in modern times and the discovery of traces of ephedra at various sites of the ancient Bactria-Margiana Archaeological Complex, a culture with apparent connections with Indo-Iranian culture, as was discussed in chapter 2. Neither of these discoveries confirms the ephedra hypothesis, and there have been and continue to be many critics of it.

The principal objection to the ephedra hypothesis is that it is a stimulant, and the R̥gveda, it is argued, attests visionary experience through drinking soma. Stuhrman (2006), for example, cites the hymns' light imagery and the unexpected associations made by the poets to argue that these are best explained as reflexes of hallucinogenic experience. Or again, there are a few hymns that might be explained as reflecting a hallucinogenic-inspired vision. The best example is X.119, the *laba sūkta*, or the "Self-praise of the Lapwing," in which the poet takes on the identity of a bird who experiences flight (vss. 2–3), who sees the Ārya peoples as specks far below (vs. 6), and whose wing stretches over the world (vs. 7). All these images are interspersed with the refrain: "Have I drunk the soma? Yes!" For an analysis of this hymn and defense of its hallucinatory inspiration, see Thompson 2003. The most famous proposal for a plant that might inspire hallucinogenic vision was made by Gordon Wasson (1968), who identified the soma plant as the *amanita muscaria*, the fly agaric mushroom. This proposal has fewer defenders than it once did. Wasson's argument for the mushroom depended in part on the descriptions of soma in the R̥gveda, but the soma is the juice of the soma plant, not the plant itself, and the little evidence we have for the plant suggests it had twigs. Moreover, the procedures to prepare the soma juice in Vedic ritual, which involve pounding the soma plant stalks, are unnecessary for a mushroom, and Wasson's view that the preparation of soma involves urination is wholly without support in either Indian or Iranian texts.

Flattery and Schwartz (1989) offered another approach to the problem. They argued that previous attempts to identify the soma/haoma plant had overvalued the Vedic evidence and undervalued the Iranian. On the basis of the latter, their candidate for the soma plant was *peganum harmala*, Syrian rue, which can induce dream states. Such states do not easily accord with the likely sense of

√*mad*, however, nor go very far in explaining hymns that might reflect an experience of soma.

Most recently Matthew Clark (2017) has argued that the original soma plant was not one plant, but a combination of plants. They could be used to make a preparation that was an analogue of ayahuascas, drinks compounded in the Amazon region that have entheogenic or psychedelic properties. Clark has identified a number of plants mentioned in the Veda that could have been used to create such a concoction. But there is no direct evidence in the R̥gveda that multiple plants were used in the preparation of soma. Indeed, since the nineteenth century, a number of scholars have argued that R̥gvedic *aṃśú* is the name of the soma plant. Nor does the theory explain why substitutes for the soma plant or plants came to be used in the late R̥gvedic or middle Vedic period.

This is not an issue that we can resolve, and we would leave it aside if we could. But the identification of soma affects the interpretation of some hymns and particularly the interpretation of the various and frequent forms of the root √*mad*. In general, we find more textual evidence to support the interpretation of the soma juice as a stimulant than as a hallucinogen. That soma was a stimulating substance seems clear from its constant mythological application: Indra must drink soma before confronting his opponents, especially Vr̥tra, and before going into battle. It provides him with the invigorating strength to defeat the forces arrayed against him. Moreover, visionary poetry does not require visionary experience, at least not the kind that need be induced by entheogens. Our view of the hymns is that they are careful, often intricate compositions that attest to the skill and imagination of the poets. To explain what is strange and cryptic in these hymns by pharmacology can inhibit the effort to see the underlying logic and intention of the hymns. While there is much that remains obscure in the R̥gveda, interpreters of the text have been able to make progress by the simple assumption that the hymns do make sense and that the poets did know exactly what they were doing and carefully crafted the hymns rather than producing them through streams of consciousness while in an altered mental state.

While the identity of the soma plant or plants may be an unsolvable mystery, the R̥gveda does tell a great deal about the religious meaning of the soma juice and the identity of the god Soma. The "Soma Maṇḍala" of the R̥gveda, Maṇḍala IX, contains 114 hymns dedicated to Soma Pavamāna "Self-purifying Soma." These hymns focus entirely on a single ritual moment, the straining of the juice by pouring it across a sheep's fleece to trap the impurities and into vessels prior to offering it to the gods. These actions are often presented metaphorically, with Soma conceptualized as a king making a royal progress across the filter and into the cups, a progress that can be compared to the conquering of territory. Or Soma is the Sun in his journey through the cosmos. Or, quite often, Soma is a bull racing to mate with a herd of cows, who represent the milk with which the juice can be mixed. Soma is thus regularly presented as having agency in the many descriptions of the purification of the liquid.

Besides this dynamic deification especially characteristic of the IXth Maṇḍala, there is little narrative mythology involving the god Soma. The most important tale is the theft of Soma from heaven, where he was confined in a citadel guarded by an archer called Kr̥śānu. A falcon stole him from there and brought him to earth, successfully evading serious injury from Kr̥śānu's arrow, to deliver him to Manu, the first sacrificer. This exploit is mentioned a number of times in the text but is most fully described in IV.26–27. The episode is then further developed in post-Vedic literature in the story of Garuḍa, the eagle who stole the soma from heaven in order to rescue his mother but who ultimately returned it to Indra.

Though one characteristic of Soma in later texts, a commonplace already in middle Vedic, is his identification with the moon, this equation is attested only in the very late R̥gveda. It is found clearly only in the wedding hymn (X.85), whose first verses depict the wedding of Soma and Sūryā, daughter of the Sun. The bridegroom Soma in this hymn takes on lunar qualities, which are distinguished from his identity as an earthly ritual substance. In the first hemistich of verse 5, for example, the waxing and waning of the moon are cryptically described as the draining and increasing of the soma juice: "When they take their first drink of you, o god, after that you swell up again." The second hemistich of this verse, in which the moon explicitly appears, is the reveal: "Vāyu is the guardian of Soma. The moon is the model of the years." Vāyu is the god of the wind, which blows through the midspace, and above it, the ever-changing moon, implicitly Soma, is the image of the passage of time.

Aśvins

The Aśvins, the two "Horsemen," are old Indo-Iranian or even Indo-European deities that have been incorporated into the soma rite. They are also called Nāsatyas, a name of obscure meaning and etymology, found already in an ancient Near Eastern Mitanni treaty dating from the fourteenth century BCE (in the form Na-ša-at-ti-i̯a) and in the cognate in Old Iranian, Nā̊ŋhaiθya. It is the older name of this pair, with the lexically transparent *aśvín* "horseman" originally an epithet. The Aśvins are connected with the honey, *mádhu*, and while soma comes to be called "honeyed" and "honey," the madhu was likely in origin a different offering to the Aśvins. They also receive the hot milk offering central to the Pravargya rite, an originally independent rite eventually integrated into the soma ritual. The Aśvins themselves were thus secondarily attached to the soma rite as part of a pre-R̥gvedic ritual consolidation that brought the principal Vedic gods into the soma rite, even those who earlier received different offerings in separate rites. Because they are a pair, the Aśvins find a place particularly in the morning soma offerings, which in the R̥gveda and still largely in the later period were dedicated to pairs of deities: Indra and Vāyu and Mitra and Varuṇa along with the two Aśvins. Reflecting their association with that Morning Soma Pressing, the Aśvins appear in the early dawn: they come at the break of dawn (I.157.1, VII.72.4), follow the chariot of Dawn (VIII.5.2), or accompany the dawn (X.61.4). However, they also receive the last soma offerings in an Atirātra or Overnight soma ritual, which ends in the morning of the day following the principal soma-offering day. Even if they were secondarily grafted onto the soma rite, that graft was a strong one. In addition to their presence in several episodes in the Soma Sacrifice, they are the fourth most frequently invoked deities in the Ṛgveda after Indra, Agni, and Soma.

As "Horsemen," the Aśvins are chariot riders and drivers, rather than riders on horses. Their chariot is an object of special attention for the poets. It is often threefold, with three chariot-boxes, three wheels, three turnings (I.118.1–2), and three wheel-rims (I.34.2). The sacrifice with its three soma pressings is compared to a chariot, so the Aśvins' threefold chariot may represent the sacrifice. Their chariot is also swift—"swifter than a mortal's thought" (I.118.1) or than the wink of an eye (VIII.73.2). Their chariot is drawn by various animals, including bulls, buffaloes, and horses, but also by birds (I.119.4), geese (IV.45.4), or falcons (I.118.4). Pulled by these many different draught animals, their chariot flies to many places and makes the Aśvins present in many spheres: in heaven, earth, and the sea, among plants, and at the peak of a mountain (VII.70.3). They and their chariot circle the whole earth (I.20.3, 46.14, 117.6, IV.3.6, X.39.1, 41.1, 106.3). The Aśvins' speed and mobility are essential for them, for they are gods who save people from dangers and difficulties in various places and circumstances.

The story of the Aśvins that the poets mention most often is their rescue of Bhujyu, the son of Tugra, whom his father had abandoned in the sea (e.g., I.116.3). Among their other deeds of rescue, they brought Rebha up from the waters, when he was bound, confined, and left for dead (I.112.5, 116.24, 119.6). They saved Atri from an earth cleft (V.78.4) and from threatening heat (I.112.7).

They found Viṣṇāpū, who was lost, and restored him to his father, Viśvaka (I.116.23, 117.7). They not only rescue those in distress, they also heal both people and their animals. They restored the youth and vigor of Cyavāna, who had grown old (I.117.13, 118.6, VII.71.5), and the sight of Ṛjrāśva, who had been blinded by his father (I.116.16, 117.17, 18). They replaced the lost foot of the mare Viśpalā with a metal shank (I.116.15) and made the cow of Śayu give milk (I.116.22, 117.20, 118.8). They also create families. They brought Kamadyū, the daughter of Purumitra, to be a wife for Vimada (I.116.1, 117.20, X.39.7, 65.12) and gave a son to Vadhrimatī, a speaking name that describes her as a woman "whose husband is a steer" (I.116.13, 117.24, X.39.7, 65.12) and therefore childless. Not only do they arrange marriage or bring a child to a marriage, they themselves also wed or woo Sūryā, the daughter of the Sun. While sometimes the husband of Sūryā is Soma (X.85) or Pūṣan (VI.58.4), elsewhere she chooses the Aśvins as her husbands (I.119.5, IV.43.2, 6, VII.69.3–4) and rides with them on their chariot (I.116.17, VIII.8.10).

What the Aśvins do has been relatively uncontroversial. Why they do it has been a more difficult problem, and both traditional and contemporary scholarship has offered a variety of interpretations of the Aśvins. Already in the third century BCE Yāska cited three different explanations of the Aśvins as personifying aspects of the natural world—heaven and earth, day and night, and the sun and the moon—and one additional interpretation, attributed to the *aitihāsika*s or "historians," that the Aśvins were "two virtuous kings." Earlier than Yāska, the Taittirīya Saṃhitā identified the Aśvins as the "two Adhvaryus of the gods" and as "two physicians" (Hillebrandt 1902: 381). The views of nineteenth-century and early twentieth-century scholars often echoed the theories that the Aśvins represented a pair of natural phenomena. Of these theories, perhaps the most influential and enduring has been that the gods represent the morning and evening stars (see, for example, Gotō 2009).

But such naturalistic interpretations have been largely abandoned. Early on, scholars observed their similarity and therefore possible genetic relationship to the Greek Dioskouroi. According to such scholars, both the Aśvins and the Dioskouroi ride or drive horses; both are young men (*koũroi* in Greek, *yúvānā* in Sanskrit); both are sons or, in the case of the Aśvins, perhaps grandsons of Heaven (*divó nápātā*); both rescue people in trouble; and both are twins. Focusing on the last characteristic, Zeller (1990) sought to show that the Aśvins' character and acts are determined by their being twins. So, for example, she explains their concern with sexuality and rescue as partly due to their birth. According to her interpretation, the Aśvins have one mother but two fathers, one who is mortal and the other immortal. Because they have two fathers, she argues, they themselves are endowed with a greater sexual potency, and because one of their fathers is mortal, they are closer to humans and inclined to help them. Along somewhat similar lines, Oberlies (1993) suggests that the Aśvins as twins represent the reconciliation of opposites. They are gods of the intermediate sphere, who facilitate movement between spheres: between childlessness and birth, death and life, old age and youth, non-marriage and marriage, and so forth. While these explanations of the Aśvins are extrapolated from R̥gvedic evidence, they are not expressed in the text. The circumstances of the Aśvins' births are not very clear in the R̥gveda, and while their being twins can be inferred from late portions of the R̥gveda, there is little direct evidence that this was their defining feature.

Maruts

The Maruts are a troop of male gods. Though they lack individual identities, they are quite prominent as a group: over 30 hymns are dedicated to them alone and several more to them in conjunction with Indra, and they are frequently mentioned elsewhere. Their character has both naturalistic and social aspects. On the one hand, they are the embodiments of the thunderstorm, especially of the monsoon, and many of their aspects reflect this natural phenomenon: like lightning, they are brilliant and flashing (VI.66.10–11), bedecked with ornaments and glittering weapons (I.64.4, V.54.11, VII.57.3); like thunder, they are excessively noisy on their wild chariot journeys (I.37.10, 13, 38.10, 14), causing the earth to shake with fear (I.37.8), bending the trees and even the mountain (I.37.7, 39.5); like thunderclouds they are shape-shifting and sometimes clothed in gray (V.52.9); and they are accompanied by floods of rain (I.38.8–9, 64.6, 85.5). The terror they inspire is more than balanced by the fructifying rains they bring. All these physical aspects of the Maruts often inspire the poets to vivid and imaginative language: I.64.8 "Like lions the discerning ones keep roaring, beautifully marked like mottled deer, granting all possessions. Animating the nights, urgently they join together with their dappled mares, with their spears—those who have a snake's fury in their strength."

As a social phenomenon, the Maruts represent the Männerbund, an association of young men, usually at a stage of life without significant other social ties (such as wife and children), who band together for rampageous and warlike pursuits. The violence of the thunderstorm is akin to the violence of these unruly age-mates, raiding and roistering. It is likely that Vedic society contained and licensed such groups among its young men, given the frequent warfare depicted in the R̥gveda, and the divine Maruts provide the charter for this association and behavior.

The Maruts are not, however, entirely without social ties. Their parentage is clear, though the manner of their birth problematic and disputed—and often alluded to as a mystery. Their mother is a dappled cow, Pr̥śni, who can display androgynous characteristics and behavior; their father is Rudra, and they are often themselves referred to as Rudras. Moreover, they have a female companion, Rodasī. When the word *ródasī* appears in the dual number, it refers to the two world-halves, but as a singular (and accented *rodasī́*),

Rodasī is the name of the Maruts' consort, a beautiful young woman who accompanies them on their chariot. Their normal location in the midspace between the two world-halves is presumably responsible for her name.

Perhaps the Maruts' most important companion is Indra, for whom they serve as a sort of posse: *marútvant* "accompanied by the Maruts" is one of Indra's standing epithets. Their major role in dynamic mythology was to provide support and encouragement to Indra before the Vr̥tra battle, an episode also treated in Vedic prose narratives. But, according to R̥gveda I.165, 170, and 171, a set of striking hymns that comprise a dialogue among Indra, the Maruts, and the seer Agastya, Indra disputed the extent of their aid at that time. In these hymns Indra and the Maruts argue over their respective rights to a sacrifice offered by Agastya; Indra asserts his entitlement to it in part because he claims the Maruts abandoned him to fight Vr̥tra alone, though elsewhere in the R̥gveda (and later) there is no doubt about their supportive role in that combat.

This mythological contretemps has its reflection also in ritual, in fact in a ritual change occurring during the R̥gvedic period. Although in some of the Family Books Indra alone is the recipient of the offering at the Midday Pressing, in Maṇḍalas III and VI, in scattered mentions elsewhere, and in the classical śrauta ritual, the Maruts share the Midday Pressing with Indra. The tense negotiations among Indra, the Maruts, and the sacrificer Agastya suggest that the change in recipients of the midday oblation was a contested topic for R̥gvedic ritualists and the inclusion of the Maruts needed and was given mythological underpinning.

Aditi and the Ādityas

As a group, the gods called Ādityas generally represent the powers that order human society. This function is most evident in the three principal Ādityas: Varuṇa, Mitra, and Aryaman. In addition to these three, however, there are minor deities who are also called Ādityas—Dakṣa, Bhaga, and Aṃśa—and a number of other gods, such as Savitar and Sūrya, who may be called Ādityas when they exercise functions like those of the major Ādityas.

The Ādityas are sons of the goddess Aditi, whose name etymologically means approximately "without binding." Normally she represents specifically freedom from the bondage that comes from offense against the gods. She thus stands for "offenselessness" or "innocence." So, in VII.51.1 the poet asks the Ādityas to place their sacrifice "in guiltlessness (*anāgastvé*)" and "in *aditi*-ness, offenselessness (*adititvé*)." That is, the Ādityas should protect the sacrificers from any error that might offend the gods. Thus Aditi embodies obedience to the principles of right behavior that her sons represent. Even in the R̥gveda, and more emphatically later on, the motherhood of Aditi becomes central to her identity, and she becomes a mother to other deities or to the gods generally.

The most prominent of the Ādityas is Varuṇa, whose name is related to *vratá*, which comes to mean a "vow," but in the R̥gveda implies "commandment" or a governing principle, whether voluntarily assumed or imposed. Varuṇa therefore is the god of commandments or the god of authority. While all the major Ādityas are kings, Varuṇa in particular represents the authority of the king. In IV.42, as in the later Rājasūya, the human king becomes both Varuṇa and Indra; that is, as Varuṇa, the king is a judicial authority governing the actions of his subjects, and as Indra, he is a leader in war. The divine acts of Varuṇa were often reflected in the functions of the R̥gvedic king. Like the king, Varuṇa watches over his subjects by means of his *spáśaḥ*, his "spies" (e.g., I.25.13). One of the responsibilities of the king was to ensure the prosperity of his subjects by providing sufficient water for animals and crops. Therefore, the divine king Varuṇa brings rain (V.85.3–4) and controls the waters, causing them to flow according to his commandment (II.28.4). As the king orders the human world, so

Varuṇa orders both the human world and the world at large: the moon and stars appear and disappear according to his commandment (I.24.10), and he makes a place and a path for the sun in the sky (I.24.8, V.85.2, VII.87.1, 5). The king maintained the social order by punishing wrongdoers, and, likewise, poets fear Varuṇa's anger and his fetters (*pā́śāḥ*), with which he binds those who violate his commandments (e.g., I.24.15, 25.21). Varuṇa is the master of the truth that governs the actions of things, as the king must be as well (II.28.6). Given that his kingship complements Indra's, we might have expected Varuṇa to have had a greater presence in the R̥gveda than he does. However, the R̥gveda emerged primarily from the soma rite, and the soma rite belongs to Indra. In the R̥gvedic period there probably were other rites dedicated to Varuṇa or to Varuṇa and other Ādityas—there is such a rite in the classical tradition—but these left little trace in the R̥gveda.

In most of the hymns in which he is invoked, Varuṇa is closely connected to Mitra, with whom he shares most of his royal functions. Unlike *váruṇa, mitrá* is used as a common noun as well as the name of the god. A *mitrá* was an "ally" or an "alliance," and Mitra is therefore the god of alliances. While Varuṇa governs relations in which one person has authority over another, Mitra governs relations defined by mutual obligations. These two kinds of relationships overlap with one another, so the functions of Mitra and Varuṇa often coincide and the two gods are often paired. Only one hymn, III.59, is dedicated to Mitra alone. As the god of alliances, Mitra governs peace agreements between different people, ensuring that they will take their proper places (III.59.1, 5; cf. VII.36.2) and remain in them (III.59.6). When other gods have functions similar to Mitra's, they may be identified with him. In particular, Agni is called Mitra (e.g., III.5.4) or creates a *mitrá*, an alliance, when he appears at dawn (X.8.4). The alliance to which such passages refer is the sacrificial alliance between gods and mortals. Humans offer truth and praise in their hymns and soma, milk, ghee, and the like as their oblations. In this way, they empower the gods, and the gods in turn provide what is necessary for human life.

The last of the major Ādityas is Aryaman, the god of the cultural norms of the Āryas. He therefore represents a third social principle, the customary rules that govern relations among Vedic tribes and peoples. This principle was essential in a society where the authority of the ruler would not have penetrated deeply into the daily lives or the households of his people. Among the spheres in which custom determined behavior was marriage, which created a new social bond between unrelated families, and therefore marriage fell within Aryaman's governance. While we describe Aryaman as the god of customs, Thieme (1938, 1957) and other scholars following him have preferred to see Aryaman more narrowly as the god governing the rules of customary hospitality. In the absence of a state, the Vedic peoples needed to expect Ārya strangers to recognize and to act according to the customary norms of hospitality. Such norms were critical in creating the possibility of relations among Āryas and therefore in unifying them. Aryaman does not often appear apart from Varuṇa and Mitra and shares their broader roles in maintaining the natural as well as the social world.

Although relatively minor presences, three other gods, Bhaga, the god of Fortune, Aṃśa, the god of the Share, and Dakṣa, the god of (priestly) Skill, are also called Ādityas. Bhaga ensures that people will receive an appropriate portion of the goods of life. He is often linked with Aryaman and with the expectation of prosperity in marriage. Aṃśa ensures that people will receive the share of goods owed them, and therefore he is concerned with inheritance. In both cases, the two gods bring goods to people according to their behavior and family identity, and that function brings them within the sphere of social principles represented by the major Ādityas. Like the major Ādityas, Dakṣa is also concerned with right behavior, but in his case, it is the skilled actions of sacrificers. For further on the Ādityas, see Brereton 1981.

Savitar

Sometimes linked to the Ādityas and especially to Bhaga is the god Savitar. He is the god who "impels" or "compels" beings—and these can include mortals, gods, animals, and objects. He especially acts at the beginning of night, when he sends beings to rest, as in IV.53.3 "Savitar has stretched forth his two arms, at his impulse causing the moving world to settle down and impelling it forth through the nights." The words "impulse" (*sáviman*) and "impelling forth" (*prasuván*) in this verse derive from the root √*sū* "impel" as does the name Savitar, and therefore the verse illustrates the correspondence of the god's action and his name. In this verse Savitar stretches out his arms as a gesture of command (see also II.38.2), but Falk (1988) reasonably suggests that his outstretched arms, together with his brilliance, also represent the Milky Way. Savitar's association with the night extends also to his chariot: "bright-beamed Savitar" mounts his chariot, which is "covered over with pearls, having every beauty, with golden yoke-pins, lofty" (I.35.4). His chariot thus reflects or embodies the starry night, which golden-eyed (vs. 8) and golden-handed (vss. 9, 10) Savitar brightens, even in the absence of the sun (vs. 7). Because he is associated with the night, Savitar is also connected with the generation of offspring, who would be conceived during the night. Savitar not only sends the world to rest at night, but he also commands the beginning of the day when he impels beings to action once again. Thus R̥gveda IV.53 ends with the prayer that Savitar will continue to drive us forward: vs. 7 "Let him quicken us through the nights and the days. Let him speed wealth that brings offspring." The memory of Savitar's night-time command is preserved in the later Soma Sacrifice, for the soma offering to him is made at the Evening Pressing. But later tradition, recognized already by Yāska (Nirukta 10.32), understands Savitar to be another name for the sun.

Sūrya

If the Milky Way is the celestial embodiment of Savitar, Sūrya, the Sun, comes close to being that of Mitra and Varuṇa. The Sun is their eye, for his gaze is wide (VII.35.8) and falls on everyone (I.50.2). The Sun watches over the good and evil deeds of humans (VI.51.2, VII.60.2–3) and, so the poet hopes, declares the innocence of the sacrificers to Mitra and Varuṇa (VII.60.1, 62.2). The Sun is the felly that rolls toward Mitra and Varuṇa (V.62.2) or the chariot that the two gods set in heaven (V.63.7). Since he is so closely linked to the Ādityas, he himself is called an Āditya (I.50.13, 191.9, VIII.101.11). His link to the Ādityas is also a link to the king, who oversees his subjects the way that the Sun oversees all beings (X.121; and Proferes 2007: 140–141).

However, Sūrya is not connected exclusively with the Ādityas. He is a form of Agni, both Agni Vaiśvānara and Agni Jātavedas, and the face of Agni. He is represented by Soma as well, whose course across the purifying woolen filter is compared to the track of the sun (IX.10.7; see also Oberlies 1999, especially 164). Many verses to the Sun center particularly on his rising, as he follows the Dawn across the sky: I.115.2 "The Sun approaches the gleaming goddess Dawn from behind, like a dashing youth a maiden." Because the Dawn can be the daughter of the Sun, as well as his wife, however, the Sun's pursuit of the Dawn can suggest incest. Needless to say, such a negative view of the Sun has no place in hymns that praise the Sun, but the theme appears in the cryptic story of Svarbhānu, who wounds the Sun for his act of incest. The story is hinted at in the Ṛgveda, especially in V.40, and further developed, although still obscurely, in the middle Veda. The details are worked out in Jamison (1991: 133–303). Various gods, not only the Ādityas (IV.13.2) or Mitra and Varuṇa (V.63.4), but also Varuṇa and Indra (VII.82.3), Agni (X.3.2), Soma (VI.44.23, IX.86.22), and Indra and

Viṣṇu (VII.99.4), are said to have given birth to the Sun, to have caused him to rise to heaven, or to have established his brilliance. A constant is that the rising Sun brings the promise of prosperity and joy, especially after the anxieties of the night: X.37.4 "The light with which you thrust away the darkness, O Sun, and the radiance with which you rouse up every moving creature, with that drive away from us every want of nourishment, every lack of oblation, drive away disease, away the bad dream."

A number of images depict the movement of the Sun after he rises and as he journeys through the heavens. The Sun flies through the air on a chariot pulled by seven horses (V.45.9) or seven mares (I.50.8, 9, IV.13.3), or the Sun is a wheel pulled by only one horse, Etaśa (VII.63.2). The Sun himself is the "reddish eagle" (V.77.3) or a falcon (V.45.9), or he flies like a falcon (VII.63.5). However, there are relatively few narratives concerning the Sun. One repeated but mysterious story is that Indra stole or tore off the wheel of the Sun. He did so in order to help his ally Kutsa in Kutsa's battle against Śuṣṇa (I.130.9, 175.4, IV.30.4, V.29.10). What exactly Indra accomplished by doing this and how this helped Kutsa remain unclear.

Uṣas "Dawn"

Dawn is one of the few female divinities in the R̥gveda and the most prominent among them. Twenty-one hymns are dedicated to her alone (every maṇḍala but II, VIII, and of course IX containing at least one), many of them displaying high poetic artistry and beauty of imagery, and she is mentioned hundreds of times in the text. She also has an Indo-European pedigree, her name being cognate with the Greek goddess Eos and the Latin goddess Aurora.

The femininity of Dawn is one of her defining characteristics. She is generally depicted as a beautiful young woman, flirtatious and scantily dressed. In one of the most attractive hymns of the

Ṛgveda, the Dawn arising up from the eastern ocean is compared to a young woman rising from her bath: V.80.5 "Like a beauty who knows her own body, she has stood up erect like a bather for us to see. Thrusting away hatred and the shades of darkness, Dawn, the Daughter of Heaven, has come here with her light." Since she embodies the first light of day, she is gleaming and covered with bright ornaments, and as in the verse above, her appearance thus strongly contrasts with that of her dark sister Night, a much less prominent goddess, though the ceaseless alternation of Dawn and Night is often remarked on. Her dispelling of the darkness and of fears of night is much appreciated, as she awakens and rouses everyone to their daily activities. Dawn is also, not surprisingly, associated with the god Sun, Sūrya, who is often depicted as following her as her suitor or husband. She is also said to be the mother or possessor of cows—the cows being the milky sky and rays of light at early dawn (see Watkins 1987 and 2009 for the Indo-European trope of "the milk of the dawn cows").

Her associations are not all positive, however. Because she heralds every new day, she reminds men of the unstoppable passage of time and of the aging process, as well as of the generations of men who used to view the dawn but have passed away. Dawn's daily rebirth as an ever-young beauty presents a cruel contrast to the human condition of change and decay: I.92.10 "Being born again and again, though ancient, always beautifying herself to the same hue, the goddess, like a successful gambler with the best throw who diminishes his opponent's stake, ever diminishes the lifetime of the mortal as she ages him." The poets also often reflect on the paradox that each Dawn is new but each is the same as the one before and the one that will come after.

The characteristics of Dawn mentioned above are reflections of the universal nature of dawn, but she also displays culturally specific qualities relating to Vedic ritual. Dawn ushers in the sacrificial day, especially the kindling of the ritual fire preparatory to the early morning rites, and the interplay between the natural sources of light—dawn and the sun—and the man-made one—fire—is often described as complex and co-determined. Moreover, Dawn is regularly associated with wealth and its distribution to the sacrificial participants, and she is urged to give generously to them. This association between wealth and dawn has no naturalistic source but arises from the fact that in R̥gvedic ritual the *dakṣiṇā*s or "priestly gifts" were distributed to the priests and poets at the early morning rites.

Despite the vividness of her depiction, Dawn participates very little in narrative mythology, though there is a briefly alluded to (primarily IV.30.8–11) and extremely enigmatic tale in which Indra smashes the cart of "evilly angry" Dawn, and she runs away. Why Indra should turn against this emblem of benevolent femininity is unclear, but the story is also associated with Indra's stealing the wheel off the Sun's chariot, and both may have to do with the perturbation of regular temporal sequences for a purpose that remains obscure.

For the full translation of one of the finest of the Dawn hymns, see I.124 in the Appendix.

Vāyu/Vāta "Wind"

As his name indicates, Vāyu is an ancient god of the Wind, although verses to Vāyu that refer to the phenomenon of wind are somewhat rare and oblique. For example, the roar of Vāyu (X.100.2) echoes the sound of the wind, his hundredfold (I.135.3) or thousandfold (I.135.1) team reflects the wind's speed, and Vāyu gave birth to the Maruts, who personify thunderstorms, especially the monsoon storms, from the belly of heaven (I.134.4fd). He arrives at the sacrifice together with dawn (I.134.4abc), which likely reflects the rising of the wind at the beginning of the day. Such characteristics show Vāyu's close connection to the wind, even though the wind as natural phenomenon is not normally called *vāyú*.

The most prominent characteristic of this god is that Vāyu is the first of the gods to receive the soma on the soma-pressing day: I.134.6 "You, Vāyu, with no one ahead, have first right to the drinking of these soma drinks of ours—you have the right to the drinking of these pressings" (also I.134.1, VII.92.1; cf. II.11.14). The soma he drinks is "clear," that is, unmixed (VII.90.1–2). But Vāyu also arrives with Indra on the same chariot (VII.91.5), and the two of them share the first drink of soma (I.135.4). Just how both Vāyu and Vāyu and Indra have the first drink of soma is unclear, but following a suggestion of Oberlies (1999: 155), perhaps Vāyu's first drink reflects soma's symbolic descent through the midspace as it is filtered, and the first drink of Vāyu and Indra is the first soma libation.

The ordinary word for the wind is *vā́ta*, and unlike Vāyu, the god Vāta closely reflects the character and activity of the wind. He goes shattering and thundering, raising the dust (X.168.1); he moves through the midspace and is the companion of the waters (X.168.3). The symbolic features of Vāta likewise reflect the wind. Vāta is the breath *(ātmán)* of the gods (X.168.4), and as the lifebreath, he is the father, brother, and companion of the man whom he makes live (X.186.1–3). Like the Sun and the Dawn, therefore, Vāta, the Wind, is completely transparent to the natural phenomenon to which his name refers.

Heaven and Earth

One of the most remarkable and satisfying phrasal equations across the older Indo-European languages is that of Vedic *dyaúṣ pitā́* "father Heaven" with Greek Zeus Pater and Latin Jupiter, thus attesting to a deified paternal Heaven for Proto-Indo-European as well as the older daughter languages. Ironically perhaps, the Vedic god, the meaning of whose name is still transparent and additive, is far less important in the Vedic pantheon than his correspondents in the Classical languages, where the original semantics have become attenuated or have disappeared entirely.

In the R̥gveda Heaven as a divinity is generally paired with the female Earth, who is frequently referred to as "mother," with the two a complementary parental pair. They are normally grammatically joined in a dual compound (*dyā́vā-pr̥thivī́*), and several hymns are dedicated to this couple. If Heaven and Earth are the archetypal parents, who are their progeny? This is mentioned less than one might expect, but in a few hymns it is clearly stated that the gods are their children (I.159.1) and especially the Sun (I.160). A less beneficent aspect of Heaven's fatherhood is found in a myth, obliquely but vividly referred to a few times in the R̥gveda (I.71.5, 8; X.61.5–7) and told more clearly in Vedic prose (though with the god Prajāpati substituting for Heaven)—namely his rape of his own daughter. Complicating their conception further, Heaven and Earth are also called "mothers," as well as "father and mother," or even "sisters" because they were born together, as in III.54.7 "Jointly but kept apart, with their ends at a distance, they have taken their stand in a fixed place, ever wakeful. And though they are sisters and young women, they are called opposing names." Perhaps this metaphor owes something to the gender fluidity of the word for heaven, *dyaús*, which can be grammatically feminine as well as masculine.

Heaven and Earth also give shape to and encompass the cosmos, providing a safe enclosure within which life can flourish. The separation of the two to create this space is the primal cosmogonic moment, and Indra's accomplishment of this separation by propping them apart is often celebrated.

Tvaṣṭar

The meaning of Tvaṣṭar's name is fully transparent: he is the "Fashioner," the skilled artisan who has created both objects and living beings. Most significantly, Tvaṣṭar fashioned Indra's distinctive weapon, the vajra or mace, for him (I.32.2, V.31.4, VI.17.10, X.48.3), and he carved a cup for the gods to drink the soma, which then the R̥bhus made into four cups (III.60.2, IV.33.5, 35.2, 3, 36.4). His artisanship was not restricted to things, however, for it is Tvaṣṭar who "adorned all the creatures with their forms" (X.110.9) and who knows all living things (IV.42.3). Perhaps because he fashioned living beings, he more broadly takes on the role of father. He is the father of Indra (III.48.2–4), whom Indra displaced and from whom Indra stole the soma (III.48.4). Indra is even said to have killed his father to obtain the soma. Tvaṣṭar is also sometimes called the father of Agni (III.7.4), and he is the god who has begotten offspring (III.55.19; cf. III.4.9). His role as a father perhaps explains his close relationship with the Wives of the Gods (I.22.9, 161.4, II.1.5, 31.4, 36.3, VII.35.6), with whom he is ritually joined. There have been scholarly attempts to locate Tvaṣṭar in the natural world, but he is better understood to be, like Savitar, a deified agency, which can then appear in various roles.

R̥bhus

In at least some forms of the R̥gvedic Soma Sacrifice, the three R̥bhus have a significant role as principal soma recipients in the Evening Pressing. But despite that role, they have a limited presence in the R̥gveda itself and an even more diminished one in the post-R̥gvedic period. Only 10 hymns are dedicated to the R̥bhus, together with one other that invokes the R̥bhus along with Indra. Nonetheless, despite their decidedly low profile in the R̥gveda, their principal actions emerge clearly. The R̥bhu hymns repeatedly return to five great deeds for which the R̥bhus are famed. They took a soma cup made by the god Tvaṣṭar and fashioned it into four cups (III.60.2, IV.33.5, 35.2, 3, 36.4). They made a chariot, sometimes identified as the chariot of the Aśvins (I.20.3, 111.1, 161.3, IV.33.8). They created the two fallow bay horses of Indra (I.20.2, 111.1, III.60.2, IV.33.10,

34.9, 35.5). They fashioned a cow, or made a cow give milk, or carved up a cow (I.20.3, 110.8, 161.7, 10, IV.33.4). And lastly, they rejuvenated their aging parents (I.20.4, 110.8, 111.1, IV.33.3, 35.5, 36.3). Significantly, as a result of these creative acts, the R̥bhus are said to have attained immortality or to have become gods. As such, the R̥bhus are models for priests, who attain "deathlessness" through the soma rite. In the Agniṣṭoma, on behalf of all the priests the Hotar priest recites R̥gvedic verses beginning with the mantra VIII.48.3 *ápāma sómam amŕ̥tā abhūma* "We have drunk the soma. We have become free from death" (Caland and Henry 1906: 216–217).

Their skillful acts are priestly, and their great deeds reflect ritual acts or, more specifically, ritual acts at the Evening Pressing. The four soma cups they created are the cups of the four principal soma drinkers: Indra and the three R̥bhus themselves. As mentioned, the Aśvins' chariot can represent the sacrifice, and therefore the chariot they made could be the sacrifice in general. The creation of the fallow bays of Indra is reflected by a special soma offering in the Evening Pressing that marks the departure of the two horses of Indra. The cow over which they work may represent the soma stalks from the previous soma pressings, which are pressed again at the Evening Pressing. Understanding the stalks to be cows can explain the different ways that the R̥bhus treated the cow. In re-pressing the soma stalks and mixing the juice with milk, R̥bhus make them once again into cows that give the soma juice as their milk or cause these cows to release their milk. Or in beating again these already mangled stalks, they are "carving up" the cow. Their last deed, the rejuvenation of their parents, is mysterious, but it might represent the return or "rejuvenation" of the Aśvins at the end of the sacrifice in an Atirātra or Overnight rite, or it might reflect the rejuvenation of the sacrificer and his wife, since the fertility of the sacrificing couple is a theme of the Evening Pressing in the later soma rite. Or this might be yet another R̥gvedic mystery resistant to solution. For a detailed discussion of the acts of the R̥bhus and their possible meaning, see Brereton 2012.

In all but a faint trace, the Ṛbhus disappear from the later soma rite. In the Evening Pressing, where they were principal soma recipients in some priestly traditions, they no longer received any soma oblation at all. They are recalled in a chant in the Evening Pressing, named the *Ārbhavapavamānastotra*, "the Chant of the Ṛbhus for the Self-Purifying Soma," which is sung following the mixing of the soma juice with milk. But the underlying verses for the chant are soma verses from the IXth Maṇḍala and therefore do not mention the Ṛbhus at all.

Pūṣan

Although Pūṣan is a minor god in the Ṛgveda, with only eight hymns dedicated to him alone and several more shared with more prominent divinities (Indra and Soma), his idiosyncratic characteristics and the special diction used in his hymns attract more than his fair share of attention. Of the bardic families, only the Bharadvājas of Maṇḍala VI favor this god: they dedicate five hymns to him (VI.53–56, 58) with another one to Pūṣan and Indra (VI.57) and a significant portion of the composite hymn VI.48. The three other hymns exclusive to him are found in the later portions of the Ṛgveda, Maṇḍalas I and X.

The characteristics ascribed to Pūṣan are humble and somewhat countrified: his draught animals are goats, his tools and also his weapons are generally an awl and a goad (VI.53.5–9), his food of choice is porridge (VI.56.1), and the skills he deploys for us are especially the protection of the roads and the finding of lost articles, particularly cattle: VI.54.1 "Pūṣan, lead us together with one who knows, who will direct us aright, who will say 'just here it is.'" The level of discourse is often colloquial and lively, though he is occasionally celebrated in a register more appropriate to loftier divinities.

One striking feature does not fit this profile: Pūṣan in several passages is said to be the husband or consort of Sūryā, the daughter of the Sun, who is the archetypal bride in the R̥gveda, and he is also said to be the lover of his sister and the wooer of his mother (VI.55.4–5), though this apparent incest provokes no blame. The tangled family relations thus alluded to are not treated in any detail, so we are left with only tantalizing clues.

Viṣṇu

In the middle Veda, Viṣṇu became a central figure as the embodiment of the sacrifice itself and therefore of a power that can exceed even the might of the gods. In Classical India, of course, he finds an even great destiny since for many Hindus, he becomes the supreme divinity. There is little sign of those futures of Viṣṇu in the R̥gveda, which contains only a half-dozen hymns dedicated to Viṣṇu or to Indra and Viṣṇu (I.154, 155, 156, VI.69, VII.99, 100). Viṣṇu often appears alongside Indra, especially in his battle with Vr̥tra (IV.18.11, VI.20.2, VIII.100.12), but he is also Indra's ally generally. When paired with Indra, he is the subordinate partner in the R̥gveda (e.g., I.85.7), in direct contrast to the Mahābhārata (XIII.135.30) and later texts, in which he has become *atīndra*, the one "surpassing Indra." As we might expect, he is associated with the Maruts (V.87.4), who are also allies of Indra.

Characteristic of him are his three strides or three steps. With these strides Viṣṇu encompasses the earth, and with his third step he disappears into a realm where none can follow (I.155.4–5). Or he enters into heaven where there is the "wellspring of honey," the source of soma (I.154.5), or into the highest cattle-pen (III.55.10). He is therefore the god who is wide-ranging (*urugāyá*) and wide-striding (*urukramá*). The purpose of his strides is to create space and a place for people to live and move (I.155.4, VI.49.13, VII.100.4). This purpose could explain Viṣṇu's close connection with Indra in the fight with Vr̥tra, since Vr̥tra represents what confines and hinders and Viṣṇu's strides what opens and frees. So close is the connection between the two gods that the two gods together create open spaces: VI.69.5 "O Indra and Viṣṇu, this deed of yours is worthy of admiration: in the exhilaration of soma you two strode widely; you made the midspace wider; you spread out the realms for us to live." Because of his strides, Viṣṇu extends to far places, even to the mountains where he dwells, and he encompasses all living beings (I.154.2). These strides of Viṣṇu in the R̥gveda anticipate the strides that Viṣṇu takes as Vāmana, the dwarf avatar of Classical Hinduism, by which he reclaims the world from demonic control. This avatar of Viṣṇu has roots in the middle Veda, in which Viṣṇu as the sacrifice is a dwarf (Śatapatha Brāhmaṇa I.2.5.5), through whom the gods are able to obtain the whole world. However, there is no direct evidence that Viṣṇu already has the form of a dwarf in the R̥gveda.

It is not clear whether Viṣṇu attained his later prominence because of his characteristics in the R̥gveda or because of religious developments outside of the R̥gveda. His expanding the world, making life possible, and charting the way to heaven all could form bases for his post-R̥gvedic status. Even the mystery of his name may have contributed to it. Unlike the names of most R̥gvedic deities, the name Viṣṇu is obscure. The most likely analysis is that it derives from *ví* + *sā́nu*, meaning approximately "he whose back is spread apart." But even if correct, it is not enough for us to know with certainty what determines the character of Viṣṇu. Perhaps it signals a connection to the later dwarf avatar, or perhaps not. Or perhaps such lack of a definition that plainly sets Viṣṇu within the world was part of what placed him beyond the world and beyond the other gods. Or again, there may be another clue in one hymn, I.156, by the ever-complex and often mystifying poet Dīrghatamas. According to this hymn, Viṣṇu governs other gods and assumes the identity of a number of them, including Mitra, Tvaṣṭar, Indra-Br̥haspati, and especially Agni. In thus overlaying Viṣṇu and Agni, the hymn might look forward to Viṣṇu's middle Vedic role as the embodiment of the sacrifice, and in enveloping other gods within him or his sphere, it might look forward to Viṣṇu's superiority to other gods. But such identifications are not unique to Viṣṇu, and the hymn is too isolated to know if it reflects the course of his development or not. At the end, therefore, we are left with possibilities but no certainties about the roots of Viṣṇu's later status.

Rudra

Although Rudra, under his euphemistic epithet Śiva "the kindly one," has an extraordinarily great future in Classical Hinduism, in the R̥gveda he has a very circumscribed role. There are only three complete hymns dedicated to him (I.114, II.33, VII.46) and two hymns dedicated to Rudra and Soma (I.43, VI.74). He has two major and complementary characteristics: on the one hand, he is fierce and malevolent, with an often inexplicable anger that needs to be appeased; on the other, he is a healer, who controls the remedies for disease. These two characteristics appear in the same hymns, although the poets prefer to emphasize his more benevolent side. Through most of R̥gveda I.114, for example, the poet asks for and anticipates Rudra's favor in response to his praise: vs. 1 "These poetic thoughts do we proffer to Rudra, the powerful one with braided hair . . . so that he will be luck for our two-footed and four-footed, so that everything in this settlement will be flourishing, free of affliction." But in two later verses (vss. 7–8), the poet anxiously begs Rudra not to harm his parents, his children, or his animals, thus acknowledging Rudra's ability to bring affliction on exactly those whom the poet hopes the god will prosper. Why he has this double character is not clear. Like Viṣṇu, Rudra's name is not transparent and therefore does not offer much help in understanding him. The traditional interpretation of his name, which already appears in the middle Veda (e.g., Śatapatha Brāhmaṇa VI.1.3.10), derives it from the root √*rud*^{i} "cry." This etymology is not historically sustainable, although linking Rudra to a frightening howl catches his ominous side.

The distinct character of Rudra is reflected in his unusual appearance and presentation: his hair is braided and knotted in the form of a cowrie shell (I.114.1); he carries a taut bow and sharp arrows (VII.46.1, cf. II.33.10–11, V.42.11, X.125.6); he wears gold ornaments (II.33.9) and shines like gold (I.43.5). He is young and ferocious: the flame-red (*aruṣá*) "boar of heaven" (I.114.5), or the one "pouncing like a terrifying wild beast" (II.33.11), or the red-brown (*babhrú*) bull (II.33.5, 8, 15).

One approach to understanding the distinctiveness of Rudra is to begin with his association with the Maruts, who play a much larger role in the R̥gveda than he. Rudra is the father of the Maruts (I.114.6, 9, II.33.1), who are called *rudrá*s (I.39.7, 85.2, V.54.4, 87.7) or *rudríya*s "sons of Rudra" (II.34.10, III.26.5, VII.56.22, VIII.20.3). And not surprisingly, given this familial relationship, Rudra and the Maruts share some of the same characteristics. Like Rudra, the Maruts also wear flashy dress, and, like Rudra, they are healers (II.33.13), though their healing is through the waters they bring (V.53.14, VIII.20.25–26). Rudra is "turbulent" (*tveṣá*) (II.33.8, 14), as are the Maruts (I.38.15, V.53.10, 58.3, VI.48.15), who are "turbulent sons of Rudra" (I.38.7). Rudra's wildness, his unpredictability, and his link to the Maruts suggest that Rudra is also associated with a group or groups outside the normal social orders of clan and settlement. According to a number of scholars (see especially Falk 1986 and Heesterman 1993), the character of Rudra as well as the Maruts might reflect sodalities of young men who had not yet established their own households and who had therefore not yet assumed their ultimate social roles. Such a connection could help explain the status of Rudra as an "outsider" divinity, who plays a necessary role but who stands apart from other deities who were integrated into the more normal patterns of settlement and movement.

8
Eschatology

The reader may have noticed that in our survey of the religious system of the Ṛgveda we have mentioned nothing about Ṛgvedic conceptions of death and what happens after death. This is particularly striking because, among ideas most closely associated with Classical Hinduism, there are two interrelated concepts of what happens after death. First, a person who has not attained the ultimate state of salvation enters a process that results in rebirth. According to one typical formulation, the realms of rebirth range from the god Brahmā to a blade of grass. That is to say, a person could be reborn as any life form whether it be plant or animal, divine or demonic. Second, the form of rebirth is not randomly achieved but is the result of *karma*, a word that means "action" but in this context refers to the "consequences of action." Actions in the moral universe create appropriate outcomes: a life of meritorious actions results in a good rebirth, one of demeritorious actions in a bad rebirth. Neither of these concepts is present in the Ṛgveda, although it is possible to see elements in the text that may have contributed to their development.

Much of what we can say about Ṛgvedic eschatological ideas comes from the latest portions of Ṛgveda, especially Maṇḍala X, although there is some material also in Maṇḍalas I and VIII. The Family Books, Maṇḍalas II–VII, say little about death, let alone what happens after death. A verbal form from the root √*mṛ* "die" is attested only once in the Family Books, the derived noun *mṛtyú* "death" also appears only once, and both these verses (VII.104.15 and 59.12 respectively) are later attachments to their hymns. Other

The Rigveda. Joel P. Brereton and Stephanie W. Jamison, Oxford University Press (2020). © Oxford University Press.
DOI: 10.1093/oso/9780190633363.001.0001

hymns indirectly mention death in their hope that one will not die, as for example, II.27.14 "Might I reach the broad light that is free of fear, Indra. Let the long darkness (of death) not reach us," and VII.89.1 "O King Varuṇa, let me not go to the house of clay!" In the last example, "the house of clay" is earth, in which the dead are buried. Similar too is II.29.6, addressed primarily to the Ādityas, "Rescue us from falling into the pit, you who are worthy of the sacrifice." Because this verse refers to a "pit" (*kartá*), some scholars have taken it as referring to a sort of underworld afterlife. Were they correct, this verse would suggest that there is a parallel between the R̥gveda and the dismal world of the dead, which Odysseus encounters in book XI of the Odyssey, and that the R̥gveda continues an early Indo-European concept of the afterlife. But *kartá* here and in its other attestations more likely refers to the grave and not to an underworld.

That is to say, there is little evidence for a subterranean world of the dead or a hell for evildoers. But what about somewhere more encouraging? Is there the possibility of a more promising destiny? Again, the Family Books alas do not say much. Their hymns mention ancestors alongside the gods (e.g., III.55.2). These ancestors can help in invoking and propitiating the gods in the sacrifice (VI.52.4). Such passages show that at least some of the dead continue to be part of the ritual lives of their descendants. The hymns also mention deified ancestors, such as the Aṅgirases and the other priests who help Indra open the Vala cave and free the cattle. Or again, the R̥bhus, who appear to have once been mortal, attained the status of gods through their sacrificial skill. In general, however, the deathlessness of the gods stands in contrast to the mortality of humans. The gods possess immortality, while human beings' lives continue by means of the succession of generations: IV.54.2 "For you first impel immortality to the gods, who are worthy of the sacrifice, as their highest share; right after that, o Savitar, you reveal your gift: lives following in succession for the sons of Manu."

Because the older parts of the Ṛgveda say little about death, it is difficult to determine what may have been the expectations for an afterlife. There are various possible reasons for the silence of the Family Books about what happens after death. Perhaps talk of death was inauspicious and therefore excluded from Ṛgvedic poetry. But at least part of the explanation is that most hymns of these maṇḍalas were composed for the soma ritual, and the essential aim of this ritual was prosperity in this life. Offspring, cattle and other forms of wealth, freedom of movement, success in battle, and health and long life are the typical aims of this ritual and the poetry embedded in it. As far as the Family Books are concerned, the Soma Sacrifice does not concern life beyond this world. But in somewhat later parts of the Ṛgveda there is evidence that the Soma Sacrifice can bring not only prosperity but also immortality. The latter half of the last hymn of the IXth Maṇḍala, the collection of hymns to the "Self-purifying Soma," opens into a vision of heaven. The poet, Kaśyapa Mārica, who probably represents a later generation of poets, asks that Soma to place him there "where the inexhaustible light is, in which the sun is placed," there "in the immortal, imperishable world" (IX.113.7). Kaśyapa repeatedly asks Soma to "make me immortal" (vss. 8–11) there. Similarly, the priests of the soma rite declare in VIII. 48.3 *ápāma sómam amŕ̥tā abhūma*, "We have drunk the soma; we have become immortal." Complicating our understanding of this verse and of the Ṛgvedic view of death and life after death generally is that *amŕ̥ta*, "deathless" or "deathlessness" and here translated "immortal," can also mean "conferring life." It is therefore not always clear whether it describes immortality or signifies freedom from untimely death, living a full lifetime. It surely does mean "immortal" in connection with the gods (e.g., II.1.14, III.21.1, 26.3, 28.5, IV.1.10, 35.8, V.42.5, 57.8, VI.15.18, VII.4.5, 17.4), and as remarked earlier, normally humans are excluded from such immortality. But in verses like VIII.48.3 it appears to have this meaning also for participants in the sacrifice. Perhaps then the soma rite was understood to bring immortality even in the earlier parts of the Ṛgveda, but at the very least, later poets bring the attainment of immortality to the fore in a way that older poets did not.

It is especially in hymns from Maṇḍala X that the poets tell us more about the possibility and nature of an afterlife. Among such hymns are those of the "Yama collection," Ṛgveda X.10–19, which prominently features Yama, the king of the dead (e.g., X.14.11, 15). The second part of the collection, X.14–19, was composed for funeral rites or likely connected in some fashion with such rites. According to the hymns of this collection, Yama, the son of Vivasvant, chose to become mortal "for the sake of offspring" (X.13.4), who would succeed him. That is to say, by becoming mortal, he brought about the succession of generations of mortals. As the first to die, he was the first to find the way to the world of the dead (X.14.2) and therefore became its ruler. A verse from the Atharvaveda represents the view shared by the late Ṛgveda: AV XVIII.3.13 "Who as the first of mortals died, who as the first went forth into this world—with your oblation serve him, King Yama, son of Vivasvant, who assembles the peoples." Yama now dwells along with the forefathers, who have joined him in the world of the dead. He also becomes not only the king of the dead, but the god Death himself (X.165.4), a role he continues to play still today.

The path that Yama took to the realm of the dead is a difficult one, and others who would follow it need the help of deities such as Agni (X.17.3), Savitar (vs. 4), and especially Pūṣan, the god of paths, who "will lead us along the least perilous (way)" both on earth and in heaven (vss. 5–6). Among the dangers on the path to the world of the dead are two "four-eyed and brindled" dogs (X.14.10), who guard the way to the forefathers. But despite the dangers, those who perform the rites correctly (X.16.4, 17.4) and who give "priestly gifts" to those performing the sacrifice (X.107.2) can attain the realm of the dead. This realm in which the ancestors live is in the middle heaven (X.15.14). Yama is also there, of course, and also Varuṇa (X.14.7); other gods are not mentioned but they may not be far away. R̥gveda X.135 is a puzzling hymn in a variety of ways, but it is dedicated to Yama and opens with a verse in which a son says that in death his father, who is also the lord of his clan, is now joining Yama and the gods: X.135.1 "The leafy tree at which Yama drinks together with the gods, toward there our clanlord and father follows along the track of the ancient ones."

There may have been several ways of representing the journey to the realm of the dead. In one of them, the cremation fire carries the dead to heaven, just as the oblation fire carries offerings to the gods. The body of the dead is placed into the fire, and Agni, in the following passage called Jātavedas, gives him over to the ancestors: X.16.2 "When you will have made him cooked, Jātavedas, then hand him over to the fathers. When he will go on this course leading to the other life, then he will lead forward the will of the gods." The deceased's destiny to join the world of the fathers here reflects the will of the gods. While there are various interpretations of R̥gveda X.56, in our view the hymn represents the cremation fire as a horse that conveys the dead to the world the ancestors. According to this hymn, as the body of the dead burns, it becomes the cremation fire, and therefore the fire is both the horse that conveys the dead and the dead themselves, who are conveyed. This is the complicated image behind R̥V X.56.2 "Let your body, o prizewinning horse, leading the body, establish a thing of value for us and protection for you. Unswerving, in order to uphold the great gods, you should exchange your own light as if for the light of heaven." The departure of the dead as offerings to the gods benefits the gods and the living as well as the dead, who, having become fire, are here compared to the light in heaven. This light of heaven might be a reference to stars, for, according to Oldenberg (1894: 564–565; and see also Oberlies 1998: 471 n. 89), there was an ancient belief that the souls of the dead, or at least the souls of heroes and sages, become stars. We would amend this view in one detail, however, since in the Ṛgveda, the dead are not disembodied souls but rather have assumed transformed bodies of light. One verse in the Ṛgveda may directly describe the ancestors as stars rather than simply compare them to heavenly lights. This is X.68.11 "The fathers have adorned heaven with constellations, like a dark horse with pearls." Elsewhere, the Ṛgveda says that the heavenly bodies of the dead are without flaw (Oberlies 1998: 501) and are bodies of light: X.14.8 "Having left behind imperfection, come home again. Let you of good luster join together with your body." The "good luster" of the dead is both their illustriousness and their visible luster.

In X.16.2, quoted earlier, the cremation fire transports the dead to heaven. In the very next verse, we have what appears to be a different way of understanding the fate of the dead. The poet addresses the dead, saying, X.16.3 "Let your eye go to the sun, your life-breath to the wind. Go to heaven and to the earth as is fitting. Or go to the waters, if it has been fixed for you there. Take your stand in the plants with your limbs." Here the various parts of the body of the deceased are translated into corresponding parts of the visible world. How exactly we are to understand the journey of the dead in X.16 is not clear. Perhaps the deceased is variously transformed, the physical limbs and faculties find their cosmic equivalents while the body of fire makes its way to the realm of the ancestors, or perhaps his faculties and the body are somehow reunited in the heavenly world (cf. Oberlies 2012: 334). The dispersal into the visible world echoes Ṛgveda X.90, which describes the Man whose body parts give rise to the visible and social worlds. It may be that offering the body of the dead into the fire makes him in some fashion equivalent to the Man. These ideas of the dispersal of the body into the macrocosm and of a journey of the dead to heaven will both continue in the later Veda and in the later tradition, even while concepts of rebirth and transmigration come to define the tradition.

In addition to the cremation of the dead, the R̥gveda also refers to burial. The practice of burial is best attested in one of the funeral hymns, X.18. The poet calls on the earth to receive the dead gently: X.18.11 "Arch up, Earth: do not press down. Become easy to approach for him, easy to curl up in. Like a mother her son with her hem, cover him, Earth." The earlier part of the hymn refers to cremation, so this verse likely describes the internment of the bones of the dead after cremation. Although the hymn speaks of the earth as providing shelter for the dead (vs. 12), the earth mound also appears to become a pillar that supports the life of the dead in the world of Yama (vs. 13).

The R̥gveda refers to the deceased by masculine pronouns and to the world of the ancestors as the world of the "fathers." What are we to conclude about the destiny of women? Is the masculine pronoun meant to refer to only males or to human beings? And would we read too much into the term "fathers" if we assume that only male ancestors inhabit their realm? There is not much in the R̥gveda that allows us to answer these questions. Yama's twin, Yamī, is never mentioned as inhabiting the world of the dead along with her brother, and this may suggest that she is not there. We can say that the wife of the deceased did not accompany her husband on the funeral pyre; there is no rite of *sati* attested in the R̥gveda. This is clearest once again in X.18. In the rite which this hymn accompanied, a woman, presumably the deceased's wife, mounts the funeral pyre, but then is called back to life: X.18.8 "Arise, woman, to the world of the living. You lie beside him whose life is gone. Come here!" But what is to become of her once she does die—about that the R̥gveda is silent.

While the R̥gveda does not attest the ideas of rebirth and karma in the forms developed within the later tradition, the idea that the dead assume a transformed body in the world of the ancestors perhaps intimates the notion of rebirth. But this conception is still a considerable distance from the development of the idea of rebirth in the later Veda. Middle Vedic literature also speaks of the possibility of "redeath" in the world beyond, which would then raise the question whether this redeath is also a rebirth into another existence. The R̥gveda does not say that the life in the world of ancestors is eternal, and perhaps it is not (cf. Ikari 1989: 161–163), but again, the R̥gveda is silent.

9

Ṛgvedic Poetry and Poetics

The purpose of Ṛgvedic poetry: the power of the word

Before treating the poetry in any detail, we should approach the general question: why were the hymns composed, what purpose(s) did they serve, and who were their composers, what social role did they fulfill? We have given some preliminary answers in this book, but they are not entirely adequate. We noted that the hymns provide the (or a) verbal portion of the multimedia performance that is the Vedic sacrifice. We further noted that these hymns serve as entertainment for the gods who come as guests to our sacrifice, and in that hospitality context they both flatter the visiting gods, by praising their deeds and qualities, and try to persuade them to reciprocate with gifts of material goods and nonmaterial benefits. For Vedic India the phrase "fine words butter no parsnips" definitely did not hold: our fine words of praise were expected to bring ample buttered parsnips in return.

This is all true, but we should not therefore consider the hymns to be merely the equivalent of background music at a banquet, a pleasant hum to which the gods can attend or not while supping on ghee, grain cakes, and soma. Nor should we think that because the praise hymn is a crucial element in the fundamental system of ritual reciprocity—human praise in exchange for divine gifts—that it can be reduced to its crass economic underpinnings. For both the humans and, as far as we can tell (or project onto them), the gods share an ideology about the power that inheres in the word.

The Rigveda. Joel P. Brereton and Stephanie W. Jamison, Oxford University Press (2020). © Oxford University Press.
DOI: 10.1093/oso/9780190633363.001.0001

Classical Indian culture in general invests the spoken word with extraordinary compulsive force. This is not the place to survey this topic across genres and across the millennia; a few examples should suffice. In the great epic, the Mahābhārata, many stories tell of words spoken in haste or ignorance that cannot be taken back and have long-term and widespread consequences. For example, Draupadī's unprecedented marriage to all five Pāṇḍava brothers resulted from a casual directive issued by her future mother-in-law in response to a misunderstood joke. On the other hand, the truly spoken word brings rewards: for example, in the other great Indian epic, the Rāmāyaṇa, Sītā enters and exits fire protected by the power of the truth she utters that she has never once been disloyal to her husband Rāma.

Thus, words can make things happen; to put it in modern terms, for Classical India discourse is full of speech acts (if we can somewhat redeploy this technical term). This type of verbal action can be clearly seen in the Atharvaveda, the second-oldest Sanskrit text. It contains numerous healing (and disease-causing) spells, charms to awake emotions (like love) in others, and so on. In most of these spells, the first-person speaker says something like "I have just cured your disease"; "I have just made you love me"; etc. Accompanied by physical gestures and the use of potions, amulets, and so on, the statement "I have just . . ." is a speech act—it effects the cure, causes the love, and so on, by the very fact of its pronouncement.

The Ṛgveda is full of similar "has just" statements, using the same type of verb form, the aorist of the immediate past. But many of these pronouncements would not seem, to our eyes, to concern actions in the control of the speaker: "the dawn has just dawned; the sun has just arisen." But from a Ṛgvedic point of view, the statement does have coercive force: in a hymn praising the goddess Dawn at the moment of dawn, the priests have, by their verbal formulation of that action "dawn has just dawned" (and the accompanying ritual procedures), caused the action to occur. (Of course, they would not test this power at midnight—there is no desire to alter the orderly functioning of the cosmos, just to keep it humming along. Nor would they want to set arbitrary challenges to test the power of their speech.)

The importance of words goes beyond even this ability to make things happen. Words mirror, indeed embody, reality, and poets seek to formulate the deep truths about reality—about the hidden relationships between things. One word for such truths is *r̥tá*, a resonant word that has been much discussed. Many scholars render it as "order" or "cosmic order," and such glossings are not wrong—but they fail to take into account the verbal aspect of *r̥tá*: order is order insofar as it can be expressed in words; words in some sense create the reality of the ordered cosmos. In other words, *r̥tá* is both "truth" in verbal terms and the "reality" that it expresses. R̥tá essentially defines what a being or object is and what it does, and it structures the relationships of beings and objects with other beings and objects. Moreover, "truth" is not a passive concept; it does more than reflect reality. By speaking these truths of essence and relationship, the poets could make the truths real and actual in the present. *Words create worlds.*

But the truths the poets seek are not obvious and easy to find. They must be sought amidst the welter of clashing superficial perceptions, and then deeply pondered and mentally shaped and the right verbal formulation found to express them. These formulations are called *bráhman*, a word that goes on to a glorious—and very different—career in later Indian religion and whose R̥gvedic meaning, like that of *r̥tá*, has been much discussed. In our view in the R̥gveda a bráhman is a verbal encapsulation of some aspect of *r̥tá*, and this verbal encapsulation is made by a sage poet, who uses his insight to penetrate to the hidden truth. Producing a bráhman requires both wisdom and verbal agility; the latter does not merely contribute embellishment, but, as we saw in our discussion of *r̥tá*, replicates the nature of the cosmic truth being formulated. One who achieves these formulations is called brahmán "possessor of the formulation," and the word brāhmaṇá, which comes to mean a priest and member of the highest social class (*várṇa*), is derived from these terms.

The poet

The word *brahmán* is far from the only Ṛgvedic word for poet; others focus on different qualities and skills. A common one is *kaví*, yet another word whose sense has been much debated. In later Sanskrit of course, the kavi is the poet par excellence and a derivative of this word, *kāvya*, is the term used for the most elaborate styles of verbal art in Classical Sanskrit. The association with intricate forms of poetry is certainly found in the Ṛgveda as well, but more prominent is the kavi's wisdom. He has access to esoteric knowledge; he is a sage, who transforms into words his insight into the enigmas of reality. The importance of knowledge for the Vedic poets is underscored by the variety of words for the poets' thinking and its articulation in the hymns. The poets speak of their *dhî* or *dhītí* "insight" or "vision," *matí* or *mánman* "thought," and *manīṣā́* "inspired thinking." The hymn and the understanding that gives rise to it are so closely related that the boundary between them becomes permeable, and the poets use words for thinking and knowing for the hymns themselves.

The origin of these insights, visions, and thoughts is sometimes ascribed to external forces—the gods give us visions, for example, which we then translate into words of praise to give back to them; see, e.g., I.61.16, an exhortation to Indra: "confer insight with all its ornaments on them [=poets]." But poets also produce their own insights from within themselves, as in this poet's address to his companions, V.45.6 "Come on! let us produce an insight, o comrades." Sometimes these result from states of excitement and inspiration. One of the words for poet, *vípra*, is derived from a verbal root that means "tremble," and this designation highlights the inspiration of the poet, the "trembling" caused by a state of imaginative frenzy, as in IX.71.3=X.11.6 "he trembles with his thought."

Another common designation of the poet is *ṛ́ṣi*, generally rendered "seer." The ṛ́ṣi is also characterized by knowledge and insight, but the word is especially used of legendary seers of the past and of current poets who aspire to that status. This connection across the generations highlights the role of tradition in shaping the poet and his practice.

The different words for poets just surveyed do not name different classes or types of poets, but simply focus on one or the other of the many qualities a successful poet must have. The various terms can be applied to the same poet, often in the very same passage.

The status of the poet

As should be clear from the foregoing, the poet was no mere wordsmith. Ṛgvedic poets understood their hymns to be new and creative formulations of truths about the cosmos and about the gods, and they held that these formulations and the accompanying rituals could make real, at the place and time of the sacrifice, the powers that govern human life and the world. These poets were, on the one hand, the foremost intellectuals of their day: their verbal formulations resulted from exacting and systematic mental probing of what lies behind the superficial world of disparate forms. But they also participated in the worldly power structure in a way that most modern intellectuals could never imagine. By modeling the deeper reality mentally, they unleashed and, to some extent, controlled the powers below the surface and, with luck, could channel it in favorable directions: their intellectual labor was not abstract and separated from the sociopolitical structure, which wanted to harness it to achieve its own ends.

As we have already seen, the composers of Ṛgvedic hymns were integrated in a priestly elite—were most likely at the pinnacle of this priestly elite—and were in a reciprocal and rewarding relationship with a patron or patrons, often a king. The priests, and especially the poet, ensured the success of the sacrifice sponsored by the patron. The economic model was triangular, with its base on the earth, its tip in heaven: the king sponsored the sacrifice; the poet and priests performed the sacrifice, pleasing the gods with praise and oblations; the gratified gods granted largesse to the king, who redistributed much of it to the poet and his cohort. Or, to use a different image, the process involved constant recirculation of a currency that was at times material (goods, livestock), at times intangible (praise, blessings), and that was sent from earth to heaven and back again.

On the other hand, the relationship between poet and patron was also direct and reciprocal. In a culture in which words were powerful and in which verbal reputation was a crucial component of power, the poet provided the king with the verbal ammunition he needed to maintain his position vis-à-vis the gods—and most likely with regard to humans too. It is extremely probable that the poet produced not only hymns of praise to divinities but also secular praise, eulogies, for his royal patron. In other words, he served as the ancient equivalent of a spokesperson and press agent, though of a superior sort and superior skill. This latter category of secular praise poetry (later known as *praśasti*, a word that also appears in the R̥gveda and sometimes in this secular sense) was not preserved because it was not sacralized and thus frozen in the way that the R̥gveda was and, perhaps more important, because each new king would want his own catalogue of praise and would be inclined to suppress that of his predecessors. (For further discussion see Jamison 2007: chapter 4.)

We can catch glimpses of it in the brief sections called *dānastuti*, or "praise of the gift," that end some hymns, in which the poet praises his royal patron and especially the gifts (cows, horses, women, gold, etc.) he bestowed on the poet in return for his poem—as in this elaborate example, with an astonishing (and indeed not at all credible) amount of livestock detailed. Note that the passage ends by stating that the king has made highest fame for himself by giving these gifts to the poet; that is, the satisfied poet will create the poetry that provides the king with this fame.

> VIII.46.21. Let him come here—any non-god who has taken as great a gift
> as Vaśa Aśvya [=poet] has taken from Pṛthuśravas Kānita [=king] at the dawning of this dawn here.
> 22. I have won sixty thousands in equine property, myriads, twenty hundreds of camels,
> ten hundreds of dusky mares, ten of those with three red spots, ten thousands of cows.
> 23. Ten dusky stallions, following wealth to fulfillment, straight-tailed, swift,
> skittish, have turned the felly homeward.
> 24. These are the gifts of Pṛthuśravas Kānita, the very generous.
> In giving a golden chariot, he has become the most bounteous patron.
> He has made his fame the highest.

We can also get an even briefer glimpse of what damage a poet could cause if he was displeased: some dānastutis do not in fact *praise* the gift, but rather belittle it—and accuse the patron of stinginess unworthy of the splendor of the praise produced by the poet who's been stiffed. Such is the finale of the hymn VIII.70, where the dānastuti seems to promise lavish praise to come, but the poet takes this back in verse 14 with a rhetorical question: will you really receive praise for a gift that consists of calves doled out in miserly fashion? The final verse specifies just how miserly: a single calf for three poets. In these verses the standard vocabulary of generosity (benefactor, patron, bounteous one) is deployed sarcastically, and the poet cleverly gives his criticism a gloss of praise.

VIII.70.13. O comrades, find the resolve: how shall we bring to success our praise of Śara,
who is a benefactor, a patron without restraint?
14. Will you be praised in any way by many seers provided with ritual grass,
Śara, if you will hand over your calves in just this way, one by one?
15. The bounteous son of Śūradeva, having grabbed hold of its ear, led a calf here to us three,
a patron leading a nanny-goat to give suck to three kids.

The extravagance of the gifts praised, however exaggerated that extravagance may be, is a strong indication of the thorough integration of the poet into the realm of power. As in modern society, his rate of pay is an index of his status. His crucial role in attracting the gods to the sacrifice of his patron and thus assuring the success of the sacrifice and the resulting flood of divine benefits makes him indispensable to the king and his retinue. All this defines the poet's status as quite different from our modern notions of a poet. But in recognizing his public prominence and influence on public affairs, we should of course not forget that he was indeed a poet, not (or not only) a cynical or conniving courtier, and his success depended on his long training, his skill with words, and his mental acuity and penetration. We might almost think of him as a combination of poet laureate and public intellectual, if both those roles were not so pallid and marginal in the modern world.

Homologies, semantic webs, secret names, and riddles

We can now dig a little deeper into the kinds of insights the poet is aiming for, the truths he is attempting to formulate. A particular habit of thinking provides much of the "deep structure" of

Ṛgvedic discourse. The Vedic mental universe is structured by a web of identifications or equivalences among elements in the ritual realm, in the cosmic realm, and in the realm of the everyday. These homologies play an enormous role in the thought of later Vedic texts, the brāhmaṇas and upaniṣads, where knowing the hidden connections between apparently disparate elements, particularly the equivalences between cosmic and ritual elements, gives the knower some power to control the cosmic by manipulation of the ritual. In these later Vedic texts, such types of equivalences have a technical name—*bandhu* "bond, connection" (a word of course cognate with English "bind," etc.)—and the difference between the cosmic and the mundane system of equations is pervasive enough to be distinguished by technical terms: the cosmic level is called *adhidaivam* or *adhidevatam*, roughly "concerned with the divine," while the mundane is called *adhyātmam*, roughly "concerned with the person(al)" or "the body." These two systems meet in and focus on the sacrifice, a controlled and orderly sphere of human activity, as a way of modeling the complex web of relationships that obtain in the two other realms, which are not under human control. The level of the sacrifice is called *adhiyajñam* "relating to the sacrifice." A good example of a system of homologies between the ritual and the cosmic is found at the very beginning of the *Bṛhadāraṇyaka Upaniṣad*, where the parts of the sacrificed horse of the Aśvamedha ritual are equated with cosmic elements and processes:

> The head of the sacrificial horse is really the dawn—its eye is the sun; its breath is the wind; and its gaping mouth is the fire common to all men. The body of the sacrificial horse is the year—its back is the sky; its abdomen is the intermediate region; its underbelly is the earth; its flanks are the quarters; its ribs are the intermediate quarters; its limbs are the seasons; its joints are the months and fortnights; its feet are the days and nights; its bones are the stars; its flesh is the clouds; its stomach contents are the sand; its intestines are the rivers; its liver and lungs are the

> hills; its body hairs are the plants and trees; its forequarter is the rising sun; and its hindquarter is the setting sun. When it yawns, lightning flashes; when it shakes itself, it thunders; and when it urinates, it rains. Its neighing is speech itself. (BĀU I.1, translation Olivelle)

Although the correspondences are not as systematically worked out and presented in the Ṛgveda as in those later texts, this way of thinking is just as pervasive in that text, though somewhat backgrounded: the poets assume that they share with their audience a web of associations, and this shared knowledge allows the poet to substitute one element for another without overt signaling.

We can illustrate this poetic habit with some (by no means all) of the stable associations of cows in the text. Some of these associations are found in the natural world. Thus, for example, the first rays of light at dawn are homologized to cows. The conceptual link here is both physical—cows are often reddish in color like early light—and behavioral—cows go out to pasture at dawn. See, for example, IV.52.5, where Dawn's rays are compared to "gushes of cows." In a further development the goddess Dawn is called "the mother of cows" (e.g., in the same hymn IV.52.2–3). Images of ruddy cows overrun the hymns to Dawn, as when she is said to "hitch up with her ruddy cows" (V.80.3) or when "her cows roll up the darkness and extend the light" (VII.79.2). Although of course real bovines can't roll up darkness, the referent—namely Dawn's first rays—understood by poet and audience—can participate in this image, an image that involves the further metaphor of a skin or cloth that can be both rolled up (as darkness) and stretched out (as light). This interweaving of two different, unrelated metaphors is hyper-characteristic of the Ṛgveda. Decoding this simple clause ("the cows roll up the darkness") requires knowledge of both sets of metaphorical associations and the ability to combine the two without mental discomfort.

Cows also have a ritual association: the milk mixed with the soma juice after it is pressed is envisioned as a herd of cows. Again the soma hymns are filled with depictions of the soma (as bull) running toward or mixing with "the cows," that is, the milk. The sexual polarity of the virile bull soma and the eager female cows is fully showcased in many of these passages. Of the literally scores of such passages in the IXth (Soma) Maṇḍala, we will cite only a few: IX.77.4 "The drop [=soma] rushes to the wide-open pen of cows"; IX.87.5 "These soma drinks have been sent surging toward bovine thousands (*gavyā́ sahasrā́*)"; IX.91.3 "The bull roaring over and over moves towards the gleaming white milk of the cow"; IX.93.2 "Like a young blood going to a maiden at the trysting place, he comes together with the ruddy cows in the tub." Once again, further metaphors elaborate on this image. For example, Soma is said to "clothe himself with cows" (e.g., IX.2.4, 8.5–6; more elaborately IX.69.45), that is, to enter the milk mixture and be enwrapped and engulfed by milk, or, as a steed, he is "groomed with cows" (IX.43.1) or "wreathed with cows" (IX.86.27), that is, bepoured and anointed with milk. The desired union of soma and the cows generates further images, as in this passage with two added similes (see also IX.93.2 quoted earlier): IX.32.5 "The cows have lowed to him, like a young woman to her dear lover. He has gone to them as to a contest that has been set." The first makes the sexual eagerness of the "cows" explicit; the second emphasizes soma's agonistic and competitive character. Note also that these cows standing for milk behave in bovine ways; e.g., they low and yearn for sex (as milk does not). The bull/cow dyad is made more piquant by the fact that soma itself is often identified as milk, milked out of the stalk by the pressing stones (e.g., IX.34.3), and the pressed soma drops on their journey are often themselves likened to cows (IX.68.1 "the drops flowed forth like cows").

Cows are also homologized to waters, as in this description of a storm: V.53.7 "The rivers have flowed forth like milk-cows." The equation of water and cows is particularly common with regard to the waters confined by Vr̥tra and released by Indra's killing of that demon. In the great Indra-Vr̥tra hymn I.32, the waters released by Indra's smashing of Vr̥tra "like bellowing milk-cows, streaming out, went straight down to the sea" (I.32.5; cf. I.174.4, etc.). Cows thus also have a symbolic presence in mythology. This is strikingly true, in a reverse way, of the other great Indra myth, the Vala myth, in which cows confined in the Vala cave are released by Indra/Br̥haspati. There the cows are narratively *cows*, stolen by the Paṇis and stashed away in the cave. But those cows are then homologized to the dawns and sometimes to the waters: the dawning of a new day can be likened to the freeing of the Vala cows. See, e.g., IV.1.13 (and cf. verses 16–17) "They [=the Aṅgirases] drove up those with a rock as their pen, the good milkers within the cave, the ruddy dawns being called to." This cow-dawn connection brings us full circle, but where in our first examples dawn's rays are called and portrayed as cows, here cows are portrayed as dawns.

We have not come close to exhausting the other metaphorical applications of the cow; others include cow as poetic inspiration, as poem, as the earth, as source of riches. Thus, any cow encountered in the R̥gveda could in fact be just a cow: real cows are among the most highly prized goods we seek from gods and human patrons. But she also has a high probability of standing in for something else, in the realm of nature, ritual, or mythology. And in many, many passages, more than one of the cow's values will be in play. The audience of the R̥gveda would be well aware of the cow's boundary-crossing capabilities and flexible enough to interpret each cow in the appropriate context.

Modern readers of the R̥gveda must try to internalize the many associations and identifications that formed the unconscious mental universe of the contemporary audience; otherwise almost every hymn in many of its parts will seem unintelligible or nonsensical. Other important homologies include that between the sun and the fire, especially the ritual fire (e.g., VI.2.6 "you [=Agni] shine with your body like the sun with its brilliance"); indeed some hymns, e.g., III.3, are covertly structured throughout by this identification between fire and sun. In general, the various parts and procedures of the ritual are regularly homologized with both cosmic and everyday elements. For example, the ritual itself, or the praise hymn specifically, is often identified with a chariot, and the crafting of poetry is homologized to chariot-making; see, for example, V.2.11 [=V.29.15] "I, the inspired poet, have fashioned this praise song as a clever artisan fashions a chariot." Whole hymns, e.g., II.31, are dominated by the identification of the ritual with a chariot. Soma is often identified with a bull, as we have just seen, but often otherwise with a horse, and the ritual preparation of the soma is equated with the grooming of this horse, as in IX.87.1 "Grooming you like a prizewinning horse, they lead you towards the ritual grass with reins." Or he is a bird settling into his nest (e.g., IX.72.5 "Like a bird sitting in the wood the tawny one [=soma] has taken his seat in the two cups") or a king embarking on conquest (IX.86.45 "Going in the vanguard, the king found in the waters displays his power"). The ritual ground itself is often identified with the cosmos, with the ritual fire a pillar connecting heaven and earth, and any movement on the ritual ground implicitly compared to a vast journey across or around the cosmos. Consider, for example, this passage of cosmic reach and ambition that really describes the very limited physical act of pouring soma juice across a filter and into the milk mixture: IX.68.14 "Clothing himself in a mantle that touches heaven, the one worthy of the sacrifice [=soma], filling the midspace, is fitted into the worlds. While being born, he has stridden along the cloud towards the sun." Here, the "mantle that touches heaven" may be the waters in which the soma stalks are soaked prior to their pressing; it "touches heaven" because the stream of liquid poured from above is envisioned as a conduit joining heaven and earth. As the soma juice spreads out across the filter, it "fills the midspace." The "cloud" along which he strides may be the filter; the sun toward which he strides is the bright white of the milk. Such piling up of complex identifications and metaphorical actions is commonplace not only in the Soma maṇḍala but throughout the R̥gveda, and the contemporary audience would have had the tools to decode these shifting associations without effort.

It is not possible here to list anything approaching all the important connections that underlie R̥gvedic poetry. But any reader of the R̥gveda must be alert to, and open to, this overall substitution principle, and also recognize that these homologies are not mere poetic embellishments, imagery for its own sake, but an implicit statement about the way things *really are*, the pervasive underlying connections unifying apparently disparate elements.

It is one of the poet's main jobs to find and articulate these hidden connections, as well as to identify the *real* or *secret* names of things known by other words in the exoteric quotidian world. The phrase "secret name(s)" occurs on a number of occasions and encapsulates the esoteric knowledge that is the province of the poet, as in VIII.41.5 "Who knows the secret names of the ruddy dawns, their hidden names, he is a poet who fosters the many poetic arts." (In this particular case the dawns' secret names are probably cows—bringing us back to the associations discussed earlier.) Discovering and articulating the hidden connections, learning the secret names—these mental and verbal activities give the one who succeeds at them power over the things themselves—to direct the actions of those beings whose secret names he knows, to manipulate cosmic forces by manipulating elements in the ritual or worldly realm by virtue of knowing the connections between these realms. This power of the hidden name is expressed in a passage like X.55.2 "Great is that hidden, much-coveted name by which you begat what has been and by which you will beget what is to be." Though the addressee in this passage is the god Indra, the implication is that anyone, god or mortal, with the knowledge of the hidden names could harness equivalent power.

Part of the training of a poet clearly involved learning how to recognize the esoteric underlying the everyday and how to draw associations between apparently unconnected elements—quite recherché associations often. These are often formulated as implicit questions—what we might call riddles—but we must recognize that in Vedic culture, as in many other ancient and medieval cultures, the riddle was not a trivial child's entertainment but a deeply serious way both to model the mysterious underpinnings of reality and to test and train aspiring poets. As we will see, a number of Ṛgvedic hymns are structured as a series of riddles—the most famous is the lengthy (52 verse) I.164—and often the answer or answers (many of these riddles can be read in multiple ways) elude us to this day. Some riddles, however, are easily solved, and indeed the answer is sometimes immediately supplied. These often turn on the deeds or characteristics of the gods, and the god's name is the answer—an elementary form of "secret name." A simple example, with no need for an answer key, is VIII.29.4 "A mace this one bears in his hand, set there; with it he keeps smashing obstacles" [=Indra], in a hymn that contains one such riddle per verse. The words used in this verse—"mace," "smash," "obstacles"—are almost exclusively associated with Indra. But X.48.10 presents a more challenging example: "Soma is visible in the one, even when it is within him; the herdsman exposes the other by its absence," characterized, as often in riddling expressions, by balanced indefinite referents and paradoxical formulations. The answer is not entirely clear, but it may refer to a good and successful man, who possesses soma, and a bad or unsuccessful one, whose lack of success is shown by his lack of soma (or vice versa). Besides indefinite reference and paradox, another formal characteristic of many riddles is numerology; the second verse from the riddle hymn, I.164.2, can serve as an example: "The seven harness the chariot with a single wheel. A single horse with seven names draws it. Triple-naved is the unaging, unassailable wheel, on which all these living beings rest"—a verse explained by the distinguished translator, Karl Friedrich Geldner, as referring to the sun's chariot as visible symbol of the year or of time. Many more examples could be adduced, on a sliding scale from the patently obvious (perhaps for initial training of a novice poet) to the insoluble and multilevel. This penchant for riddles and enigmas places the puzzle-to-be-solved at the heart of the intellectual and poetic enterprise.

Praise and request in the Ṛgvedic praise hymn

There is no single, universally applicable template to which all, or even most, Ṛgvedic hymns conform. At best we can state the uselessly vague obvious already alluded to: most hymns praise a god or gods, often with reference to their attributes and deeds, and explicitly or implicitly request goods and services from the divinities in return for this praise. This exchange is often effected during the sacrifice at which we hope they are present, either because they are part of the sacrificial paraphernalia (like Agni and Soma) or have come as invited guests. Scholars who have addressed the structure of the Ṛgvedic hymn—and there are surprisingly few of them—have not been able to progress much further than this, because they have been attempting to impose a structure on all (or most) exemplars, in the face of the dazzling diversity of the collection. However, one generalization that stands up relatively well is that the requests for goods and services *tend* to come toward the end of the hymn, while the earlier parts of the hymn *tend* to be occupied with other matters.

Within the extremely loose parameters just sketched, the poets take many different approaches, often emphasizing one element of the overall program while backgrounding or ignoring others. Indeed, sometimes even the "praise" portion of the overall genre "praise hymn" seems to have been entirely elided—though this is rare. In this section we will give a brief survey of the types of praise encountered in the hymns, no matter what their structure. These categories of praise can be found in any type of hymn, mixed in with each other and interspersed with other matters, and it is this promiscuity and diversity of praise that can give an impression of loose and episodic structure.

Praise of deeds: mythology

Praise can take a number of forms, but roughly falls into the categories of praise of deeds and praise of attributes—both of which are regularly found interspersed in the same hymn. Praise of deeds especially involves mythology, but as an organizing principle mythology is used less often than one might expect—for several reasons.

On the one hand, as was noted earlier, Indra is the only god with a robust and varied mythology, that is, a number of narratives in which he participates as a principal character. But even with Indra, though many Indra narratives get alluded to, very few get fully developed in the R̥gveda—primarily the Vr̥tra myth, in which he slays the serpent named Vr̥tra ("Obstacle") that had been confining the waters, and the Vala myth, in which he opens up the mountain cave named Vala that had been confining the cows. These two myths are so important in Indra mythology throughout Classical India that in the epic Indra is often referred to simply as *valavr̥trahan* "the slayer of Vala and Vr̥tra." Already in the R̥gveda the thematic parallels between these two myths and their equivalent importance in Indra mythology are recognized, to the extent that the two stories can be compared to each other (as in I.32.11, where the plight of the waters in the Vr̥tra myth is likened to that of the cows in the Vala myth), conflated, or intertwined (as in IV.16.3–8).

Other gods in the R̥gveda have at most one or two defining narratives—e.g., Viṣṇu, who is famous for his three strides that define the cosmos and who also has a part in a marginal Indra myth in which a boar is slain with an arrow.

The other reason that narrative seldom functions as a structural principle comes from the way in which mythology appears in the text. Stories are never told in a straightforward fashion, starting with the beginning and proceeding to the end by way of the middle. Instead they are simply alluded to, by the names of the protagonists (in Indra mythology, often his victims), by a catchword associated with the story (most prominently *áhann áhim* "he slew the serpent," encapsulating the Vṛtra myth), or, at most, by the depiction of a vivid episode selected from the narrative. A modern equivalent would be referring to a well-known fairytale by the character's name "Little Red Riding Hood," by the phrase "what big eyes you have, grandma," or by exclusive focus on the moment when the wolf eats the little girl with no mention of the preliminaries or the aftermath. In the Ṛgveda even hymns that contain a sustained account of a particular myth, like the famous I.32, which treats the Vṛtra myth in 14 of its 15 verses (all but the last, summary, verse), do not actually tell the story. In I.32 the hymn begins by announcing the killing, then gestures back to a few preliminary events, returns to focus again, and obsessively, on the moment of the killing, depicts what happens to the body of the slain serpent, and then returns once more to the fight, this time portrayed rather differently. A surprising finale sees Indra fleeing the scene, for reasons not given (nor yet understood millennia after the composition).

These myths do not have to be told in linear fashion because the audience—both human and divine—already knows the stories. The gods will not be pleased by a plodding recital of the events in order; they are intimately familiar with their own actions. They want the story refracted through art, through the mind of the poet—broken up into its components and reassembled with embellishments and vivid re-imaginings, with the spotlight focused on the divine protagonist. The shattered narratives that we encounter in the Ṛgveda make sense to their hearers because of the shared narrative culture of the audience, and they are necessarily shattered because of the aesthetic expectations of the same audience.

Still, we should not give the impression that praise of divine deeds is rare or muted in the R̥gveda. There are few Indra hymns that don't mention the Vr̥tra and/or Vala exploits, and many of his other victories are also recounted or alluded to. There is a veritable catalogue of demonic enemies, e.g., Śuṣṇa, Śambara, Arbuda, who seem only to exist to be smashed by Indra. His slaying of the boar Emuṣa, sometimes with the help of Viṣṇu, occupies a marginal place in the text, treated only in a few hymns in VIII and one verse in I, but it is vividly evoked (and taken up again in the brāhmaṇas). A competition with the Sun involving a chariot race is obscurely treated here and there, especially in the Indra hymns of Maṇḍala IV; Indra's troubled birth and his boyhood deeds are also frequently mentioned, with his birth especially brutally and enigmatically depicted in IV.18.

Other gods are at least partly defined by their exploits. This is especially true of the Aśvins, known for their daring rescues of named individuals left in the lurch (e.g., Bhujyu, plucked from the sea where his father had thrown him [I.116.3–5, etc.]) and their healing of the sick and the maimed (e.g., fitting the horse Viśpalā with a new foreleg when her original had been cut away [I.116.15, etc.]). Even the ritual gods Agni and Soma, whose usual roles are not particularly conducive to narrative, have at least one characteristic myth apiece: for Agni it is his flight from his ritual role as oblation-carrier for the gods, during which he concealed himself in the waters, hiding from the gods who sought to put him back to work. Alluded to occasionally throughout the R̥gveda, this story is dramatized in the dialogue hymns X.51–52. As for Soma, it is the daring theft of Soma from heaven by a falcon that provides him the most narrative focus (though he is only a passive participant in this story). Again there are allusions to this episode elsewhere, particularly in the Soma Maṇḍala, but the story only finds sustained, if sometimes baffling, treatment in IV.26–27.

Cosmogonic activities also often come in for praise. Indra, especially, is celebrated for having separated the two world-halves and placed the sun in the sky, thus creating both space and time, since the progress of the sun regulates day and night; cf., e.g., VIII.89 "then you [=Indra] spread out the earth, and then you propped up heaven" (verse 5), "you made the sun mount in heaven" (verse 7). But other gods, such as Soma and Mitra and Varuṇa, are often credited with the same sorts of deeds (e.g., IX.42.1 "[Soma] begetting the luminous realms of heaven, begetting the sun in the waters" and V.63.7 "You two place the sun here in heaven as your shimmering chariot," respectively), while Agni, due to his own physical characteristics, creates light (e.g., VII.5.6 "giving birth to broad light for the Ārya").

Praise of deeds need not be limited to mythological or primal deeds. The Maruts are the embodiment of the thunderstorm, and many hymns describe their violent and highly visible actions in this guise. The Marut cycle composed by the incomparable Śyāvāśva (V.52–61) is particularly remarkable in this regard, as in this little snatch (V.54.2–3): "Forth, o Maruts, go your forceful, water-seeking, vigor-increasing, horse-yoked, swirling chariots. They join with lightning; Trita bellows. The waters resound, swirling in their stream bed. With lightning as their might and stones as their missiles, the superior men, the Maruts, turbulent as the wind, shaking the mountains, though just with a desire to give water, roll hailstones in an instant—they with thundering onslaught, violent, overpowering." Likewise, though Agni hymns tend to focus on the ritual fire, a number reserve some portion for the devastating activities of an uncontrolled forest fire (e.g., VI.6). A few verses from this hymn show the force of the description:

VI.6.3 Sped by the wind, your flaming beams, o flaming Agni, spread out wide asunder.
Powerfully destructive, like the heavenly Navagvas, they conquer the woods, breaking them boldly—
4. Your flaming flames, o possessor of flame, which shear the earth—flames like unharnessed horses.

Then your flickering radiates forth widely, marshaling itself on the back of the dappled one [=earth].

5. Then the tongue of the bull keeps flying forth, like a cattle-raider's missile let loose.

Like the onslaught of a champion is the ardor of Agni. The fearsome one, difficult to obstruct, fragments the woods.

The activities of Dawn and of Savitar in rousing living creatures in the morning and, in the case of the latter, also settling them down at night also come in for celebration. In the first selection the variety of people Dawn rouses is emphasized: I.133.5–6 "The bounteous one has awakened them, for even one who lies crossways to move, for another one to seek wealth to his use, for even those who see only a little to gaze out widely. Dawn has awakened all the creatures. She has awakened one for dominion, another for fame, another to seek greatness, another to go to whatever his goal. Living beings are not alike in what they have in view. Dawn has awakened all the creatures." In the evening hymn dedicated to Savitar, II.38, all creatures and indeed natural forces like the wind are subject to his quieting, but the most striking verses treat human homecoming: II.38.5–6 "The domestic blaze of fire is dispersed prominently throughout the houses, one for each, for each one's whole lifetime. The mother has set out the best portion for her son, according to his intention which has been aroused by Savitar. Whatever was dispersed seeking gain has been gathered together. Desire for home has arisen in all who roam. Each and every one has come, abandoning unfinished work, following the commandment of the divine Savitar."

And of course the activities that we humans most rely on the gods for—protection from dangers and generous bestowal of good states and good things—are the ground base of praise in the R̥gveda.

Praise of attributes

Praise of attributes is probably more pervasive in the Ṛgveda than praise of deeds, and perhaps the most common type of attribute thus praised is power. Vedic Sanskrit contains numerous words for power, many barely, if at all, distinguished from each other. Even confining ourselves to a single type of grammatical stem, we can quick assemble *ójas, máhas, śávas, sáhas*. In fact, the translator is sometimes hard pressed to produce a suitable array of synonyms for such terms, even in a synonym-rich language like English: power, strength, might, force, greatness . . . The gods' power is manifested not only physically but also by qualities of mind and spirit—by will and intention, by energy and capability, by mastery and dominance. All prominent divine figures in the Ṛgveda are credited with these types of power, even the delicate beauty Dawn. With the possession of these types of power comes the ability to act with them—to compel humans, other divinities, and even cosmic forces to do the bidding of the one possessed of power and to acknowledge his (occasionally her) authority. Many many Ṛgvedic passages both describe a particular god or gods as powerful and depict the exercise of this power; e.g., VI.5.6 "o you possessing strength, thrust away our rivals with your strength." Even when the passage contains only the description, the possibility of such exercise is always in the background. Thus does praise of attributes shade into praise of deeds.

The other intangible attribute most often marked out for praise is mental acuity: wisdom, insight, and discernment. Numerous different gods, but perhaps especially Agni, are described as *vidvā́n*, "knowing, wise," *cikitvā́n*, "perceptive, discerning," *dhī̂ra*, "wise, insightful," and other such intellectual characterizations.

Praise of the physical attributes of gods varies considerably by god because a number of Vedic gods lack a physical presence. Chief among these are the divinities representing the social realm, the Ādityas. Even the principal Ādityas—Mitra, Varuṇa, and Aryaman—have no distinctive physical features. They are anthropomorphic and credited with appropriate body parts—face (Varuṇa's VII.88.2), an eye (see later in the chapter), arms (V.64.2, VII.62.5), and, marginally, feet (V.64.7)—but their bodies play little role in the discharge of their divine duties. Even body parts apparently ascribed to these gods are often metaphorical; for example, as noted, the sun is often called the "eye" of Mitra and Varuṇa (e.g., VI.51.1, VII.61.1, 63.1), but only because, as a god traversing the sky, he sees the activities of men and transmits this knowledge to Mitra and Varuṇa, not because he is a literal sense organ affixed to their divine bodies. Of gods whose names denote their functions, like Savitar, there will be just enough mention of physical features to allow the god to perform the function. Savitar "the Impeller," for example, has arms that he raises to set the world in motion (e.g., II.38.2, IV.53.3–4), but the rest of his body is generally irrelevant. He has golden eyes (I.35.8), a golden tongue (VI.71.3), and golden hands (e.g., VI.71.3), but it is the "golden" descriptor that is important here, indicating the gleaming radiance that suffuses him.

Gods of natural elements have the appearance of that element, though projected onto an anthropomorphic shape. The female Dawn is a beautiful woman, radiant, generously revealing her lovely body in the early light of day. Some of the most lyrical poetry in the RV is devoted to describing her feminine charms, as in the following passage (V.80.4–6):

4. She, the dappled one, becomes doubly exalted as she reveals her body in the east.

She follows along the path of truth, straight to the goal. Like one who knows the way, she does not confound the directions.

5. She, like a beauty who knows her own body, has stood up erect like a bather for us to see.

Thrusting away hatred and the shades of darkness, Dawn, the Daughter of Heaven, has come here with her light.

6. She, the Daughter of Heaven, facing towards men, lets her breast spill over like a fortunate young wife,

disclosing desirable things to the pious. The young woman has created light once again, as before.

But even in this passage Dawn's purposeful journey, her function as distributor of goods, and what we might call her moral compass are mixed in with the physical description. Sūrya the sun is not just a brilliant disk—though his disk shape clearly helps account for his being called the eye of Mitra and Varuṇa, as we saw above. But he is also a being with recognizable human aspects; he is the lover of Dawn who follows her; he has a chariot and horses that he drives; and so on.

The ritual and natural god Agni "Fire" is a special case. Perhaps because fire was always on view in daily life—and most definitely not human shaped—he is not generally anthropomorphized physically; the body parts with which he is most often credited, tongues (e.g., VIII.43.8) and hair (e.g., I.45.6), are ones that bear a strong physical resemblance to flames (compare English "tongues of flame" and the verb "lick" used of flames beginning to burn an object). It is, in fact, sometimes asserted that he lacks body parts, as in IV.1.11, where he is described as "footless and headless." Nonetheless, fire's appearance is a constant theme of Agni hymns: his ever-varying shape, from his first near invisibility at kindling to full upright blaze, the colors and shapes, the smoke, and the uncanny ability of a fire to seem alive and to display what seems like intentional action as it engulfs its fuel (a perception not limited to Vedic India, it should be emphasized). The kindling of the fire is regularly portrayed as a birth, with the kindling sticks his parents; during its growth and spread, it is portrayed as a youth in his prime; the interaction between the (male) fire and the (female) firewood is sometimes sexualized; and though the extinguishing of a fire is seldom portrayed, the graying of old age is sometimes implied, suggested by the gray ash of a dying or extinguished fire—so Agni is the one god with a full lifetime. He also has a notional mouth, by which he ingests the oblations to convey to the gods. Thus Agni's physical appearance is constantly described and praised, but though he is credited with human-type desires, intentions, abilities, and lifetime, he does not have a human appearance. The other principal ritual divinity, Soma, is in something of the same situation. He is often animatized—as a king, as a bull, as a horse, and so forth—but with regard to his intentions and actions, not his physical appearance. The physical descriptions of Soma are true to his physical being: a golden-yellow liquid.

It is not surprising that Vāyu "Wind" is not described visually, since wind does not have a visual profile, but it is perhaps surprising that the pair Heaven and Earth (Dyaus and Pr̥thivī) receive very little description. The most common (though indeed not very common) descriptor of Heaven is "lofty" (*br̥hánt)*, but this is a quality of the physical location, heaven, rather than its deified counterpart. Of course, the name for Earth incorporates her physical description, since *pr̥thivī́* (*/pr̥thvī́*) is literally the feminine form of a word for "broad, wide." She also displays "feminine" characteristics—yielding to the masculine onslaught of the thunderstorm, for example, but again receives almost no physical description. Though the Aśvins attract a number of adjectives, these descriptions are rather generic: these two gods are young, beautiful, and bright. Just as the Aśvins are not distinguished from each other in appearance, the pair of them are not sharply distinguished from the general run of gods.

The gods who merit the most vivid, indeed exuberant, physical description are the Maruts, the martial gods of the thunderstorm. Their unblemished youth and radiance, augmented by glossy unguents, and their varied equipment—bangles (quite possibly of animal bones), spangles, garlands, the brilliants attached to their breasts, their gleaming golden helmets, their glinting spears of lightning—all of this is ubiquitous in Marut hymns. This dazzling visual display is accompanied by thunderous noise and constant headlong and turbulent motion, engaging multiple senses at one time. Along with Indra, who is depicted with a body, arms, hands, lips, a beard, hair, as well as attributes like his mace, the Maruts seem fully realized anthropomorphic beings—perhaps enhanced versions of the Ṛgvedic warrior's aspirational self-image.

The praise of deeds and attributes is not, of course, done merely for its own sake—or even to express humble awe, wonderment, and delight at the glories of the divinities. Besides the function of praise as flattery, to inspire a counter-gift, the particular aspects the poets choose to praise are models for the behaviors and attitudes that they want the gods to display now. Indra's great victories over formidable enemies in the mythic and semi-mythic past should be repeated—for us—in the present, as he defeats the foes that we currently face. He should fight alongside us, indeed lead us into battle, and his previous victories are templates for what should come. One of the characteristic features of Ṛgvedic discourse is the constant oscillation between the past, especially the mythic past, and the present. Sometimes this modeling of present on past is explicit, as in this passage describing Agni's previous performance in the ritual and asking him to repeat it:

> III.17.2 Just as you performed the sacrificial role of the Hotar of the Earth, o Agni, and just as you observantly performed that of the Heaven, Jātavedas,
>
> so sacrifice to the gods with this offering.

But more often and more strikingly, it is covert and sometimes conveyed by the application of a phrase or clause to past and present simultaneously, aided by some structural ambiguities in Vedic grammar, such as the injunctive form of the verb (discussed later), or lexicon, such as the word *vṛtrá*, which is both the name of Indra's opponent in his most storied mythic exploit and a common noun meaning "obstacle." Thus, a passage like VIII.93.32 containing *vṛtrahántama* "best smiter of *vṛtrá*" can mean both "He who is known, now as before, as Indra, best smiter of Vṛtra" (in the mythic past) and ". . . as best smiter of obstacles" (in the present day as well as the past, mythic or not). Although this chronological blurring can be disconcerting to the modern audience, it would make perfect sense to the ancient audience, who saw actions in the present as re-creations of their counterparts in the past, enhanced and strengthened by their resonance with regularly repeated past acts.

It is also surely no accident that it is power that is most often attributed to the gods, for it is their power that we want to harness to our own ends. Praise of another type of attribute, only briefly mentioned earlier, falls into this same category of desired replication—that of generosity. The gods, particularly Indra, are often characterized as generous, bounteous, as profligate givers commanding great largesse to distribute. One of the stable epithets of Indra is *maghávan(t)* "the bounteous," to the extent that it can serve as an alternate name for him, but numerous other gods are called possessors and givers of goods. Needless to say, this praise of generosity is not disinterested: the god is expected to show that he possesses this quality by dispensing goods to us now.

The "ask"

We should begin by noting that Ṛgvedic poets have no compunction about baldly demanding what they want from the gods. They seem to feel no need for politesse or indirection, with the standard linguistic means being the direct, second-person singular imperative—"give!" or "help" or "come here!"—addressed even to the most powerful of gods, Indra. They do sometimes use seemingly deferential expressions, often referring to their own hopes and desires, such as "might we win or enjoy X" in the optative mood, but this often seems to arise from the impulse to poetic variation, rather than a real sense of humility. One result of this blunt approach is that the request portion of a hymn, especially when it comes toward the end of the hymn, is generally far less poetically elaborate and carefully wrought than the parts containing praise and description.

The actual requests involve both tangible goods and divine aid and services. The poets ask very frequently for wealth, which is often then further specified: livestock (cattle and horses especially) and gold being the most commonly desired. They also request offspring and descendants, often expressed as a desire for "heroes," which probably refers to strong and virile sons. They appeal to the gods for rain, refreshment and nourishment, and a good dwelling place (e.g., II.19.8). As for less tangible desires, they ask for protection and for help, especially help in battle, and this latter is often phrased as a request for the god (generally Indra) to inflict harm on our enemies, to help us overcome our rivals, and generally keep us out of the toils of hatred and hostilities and those who practice them. An oft-expressed desire is for the gods to lengthen our lifetime, especially to the canonical number of a hundred years (e.g., II.22.2), and to allow us "to see the sun" (e.g., II.33.1). As is appropriate for a people in need of pastureland and constantly advancing into new territory, they regularly ask the gods to "create wide space" (e.g., II.30.6) as they seek escape from the narrow environment that hems them in. Many of these requests are generic and directed to any or all gods; others are divinity specific: Indra's aid is more likely to be solicited in battle, while Varuṇa and the other Ādityas are asked to "loosen offenses," that is, to free us from the consequences of violation of divine commandments or other obligations (e.g., II.28.5, 7). They also ask for personal qualities, like wisdom and might (e.g., II.34.7). The various types of requests are not segregated but can jostle each other in an unordered list. Consider this multipart demand, in the last verse of an Indra hymn: II.21.6 "Indra, grant to us the best goods, the perception that belongs to sacrificial skill, and the possession of a good share, as well as a prospering of our riches, freedom from harm for our bodies, sweetness of our speech, and the blessing of good days for our days."

Although poetic artfulness seems not to have been prized in these solicitations, some do make their requests more subtly. An expression like "may we be charioteers of wealth" (II.24.15) avoids the crass imperative and introduces a beloved image, that of the chariot. Even more indirect is II.34.6 "Make for the singer a visionary thought that has prizes as its ornament." Here the poet asks the divine addressee (the Maruts in this case) both to inspire the poet's thought, which will produce his hymn praising them, and to make this vision good enough that it will be amply rewarded with wealth (probably from his human patron, not the gods directly). Alternatively, the request can be straightforward, but accompanied by a striking image, as in II.29.1 (addressed to the Ādityas) "put at a distance from me my offense, as one who gives birth in secret does her baby." Even more indirect are the requests implicitly embedded in praise, a type discussed in earlier sections—where the praise of a god's mythological exploits implicitly invites him to repeat them in the present day for our benefit, and the praise of a god's attributes (like might or generosity) implicitly urges him to mobilize them again for our benefit.

Structures and types of R̥gvedic hymns: some organizing principles

In the following section we turn to structure proper—the structures in which the various types of praise just discussed are embedded—and first pick out a few especially common tropes that can dominate single hymns—this is a representative, not exhaustive selection. After that we will discuss *formal* devices that provide structure to whole hymns. Our underlying assumption throughout is that hymns should be approached *as hymns*, not as mere unordered collections of loosely linked verses, despite the superficial impression noted above, and that it behooves the investigator to seek structure and coherence even when the hymn may seem on the surface to lack them.

Thematic organization

One common way to provide a through-line for a hymn is through the sacrifice, which, since it proceeds chronologically, can provide a similar organization of the hymn. In hymns that roughly conform to the sacrificial model, we can single out two salient aspects, which sometimes carry all or most of an entire hymn: the invitation and the journey. Many hymns begin with an invitation to the god to come to our sacrifice. Many other hymns focus on the god's journey to the sacrifice (e.g., III.35)—the hitching up of horses and chariot, the progress from heaven through the midspace and across the earth, often passing over other sacrificers on the way. Not surprisingly, the invitation and the journey are often combined in a single hymn. III.35, addressed to Indra, begins "Mount the pair of fallow bays being yoked to the chariot. Drive, like the wind, to our teams [=poetic thoughts]" (verse 1ab). It then immediately promises (1c) "You will drink the stalk when you have surged to us. Indra, hail!" In verse 5 the poet urges Indra to ignore the rival sacificers: "Let other sacrificers not stop your bullish, straight-backed fallow bays. Drive beyond them, each and every one." The preparations for Indra's arrival are described in verses 6–7. The epiphany of the god, his arrival at our ritual ground, can be the climax of the hymn (for a superb example of this genre, see the Marut hymn I.88, in which the Maruts arrive simultaneously with the poetic thought the poet was seeking for inspiration), or the actual sacrifice, with interaction of god and men, can follow. In the last verse of III.35 before the refrain (verse 10), Indra, now clearly in place, is urged to drink the soma and enjoy the sacrifice. This hymn entirely lacks both praise of the god and mention of any of his deeds or attributes.

The progress through the sacrifice, itself a kind of journey, is also a frequent organizational device. Sometimes this organization is quite precise, as in the hymns that follow an ordered series of oblations, like the Praügaśastra (I.2–3, II.41), the R̥tugrahas (I.15, II.36–37), and, especially, the Āprī litany of the Animal Sacrifice, 10 versions of which are found scattered through the R̥gveda (e.g., II.3, III.4). The Āprī hymns are especially interesting because of what they tell us about the process of composition. In each Āprī hymn the same set series of subjects or key words, one per verse, are treated in the same order, generally in 11 or 12 verses. The keywords include ritual personnel (e.g., Tvaṣṭar), qualities (e.g., "well kindled"), or equipment (e.g., ritual grass), but the wording of the verses in which they appear is variable, so the poet was free to improvise on this skeletal frame—though one must say that none of the Āprī hymns is poetically remarkable.

More often the ritual progress of a hymn is less formalized—e.g., the dawn sacrifice, first signaled by the approach of the goddess Dawn, the rising of the sun, the kindling of the ritual fire, and the first strains of poetic recitation, followed by the arrival of the gods who receive the offerings at the Morning Pressing, especially Vāyu, Indra, and the Aśvins, and the distribution of the priestly gifts, or dakṣiṇās. In the Dawn hymn VII.78, for example, Dawn is first seen in verse 1; in verse 2 the fire is kindled, and the poets begin to hymn her, while her journey continues through the rest of the hymn. We should note here, however, that just as mythological narrative is often scrambled and incomplete because the audience already knows the story, the progress of the ritual may be depicted in jumbled order, and well-known steps in ritual procedure (like the kindling of the fire or the mixing of soma with milk) are often shrouded in metaphor and figurative language—for the same reason: the audience well knows (and is indeed currently observing) how the ritual unfolds.

Although, as we have regularly noted, most R̥gvedic hymns contain both praise of the gods and appeals for their help and benefits, generally at least partially separated, some hymns consist only of requests and pleas to the dedicand(s), though some praise is often subsumed in the address to these gods. Such a hymn is III.24, addressed to Agni, which gets right to the point in the first pāda (the minimal metrical line, a subdivision of the verse; see discussion of meter later) of verse 1 "O Agni, overwhelm in battles," with every one of its five verses containing at least one imperative (though verses 2–3 order Agni to take part in our ritual for his own enjoyment), with only a bare minimum of flattering description—ending with (verse 5) "sharpen us to be endowed with sons." On the other hand, some hymns lack the request portion, focusing only on praise. The Indra hymn III.49 consists of four verses (exclusive of the clan refrain, verse 5) thick with flattering description of the god, but devoid of overt demands; however, much of the description, especially in the latter part of the hymn, centers on Indra's wealth and generosity, with the final verse of the hymn proper (verse 4) picturing him as "teamed with goods" and "a distributor of the share"—leaving little doubt about what our expectations are of such a bounteous figure. VIII.89, also dedicated to Indra, is even more purely a praise hymn, in which not only the human ritualist but also the Maruts are repeatedly exhorted to sing praises to Indra for the deeds enumerated in the hymn.

Formal organizational devices

Repetition

Let us now turn to formal means of organization. One of the simplest and most effective ways to impose structure is by repetition, a procedure that the poets constantly employ. It can be as straightforward as repeating the same word (often a personal pronoun such as "you" or the name or epithet of a god) at the beginning of every verse. Let us begin with what is probably the most boring hymn in the Ṛgveda—a competition in which there are remarkably few entries—VII.35. In the first 13 verses of this 15-verse hymn, every pāda begins with the indeclinable word *śám* "luck, weal" in the hardly varying formula "luck for us be X" (*śáṃ naḥ*, with the first-person pronoun) with X a god or gods, power, or sacrificial element. Since there are sometimes additional occurrences of *śám* within the pāda, there are, by my count, an astounding 67 examples of this word in the hymn; as a sample, consider verse 3:

> VII.35.3 Luck for us the Establisher and luck be the Upholder for us. Luck for us be the Wide-spreading (Earth?) with her own powers.
>
> Luck be the lofty World-halves, luck for us the Stone; luck let the easily called names of the gods be for us.

But even fairly strict repetition is usually more flexibly employed, providing a framework into which disparate material can be inserted. For example II.1 dedicated to Agni has 16 verses; of these the first 14 begin with a form of the 2nd-singular pronoun *tvám* "you," followed by the vocative *agne* "o Agni." In fact 54 pādas out of 56 open with a 2nd-singular pronoun, in addition to other pronominal forms scattered in non-initial position: there are seven forms of *tvám* in the first verse alone. Sanskrit grammar facilitates such patterned repetition because its elaborate case system allows flexible word order, and therefore whatever their grammatical function, key words can be positioned in initial position. Almost all of these verses involve identifications of Agni with another god or a social or ritual entity—a conceptual structure also built on repetition. But these identifications are richly detailed and together provide a web of associations of cosmic reach, thus avoiding monotony, as in this two-verse excerpt:

> II.1.4 You, Agni, whose commandments are steadfast, are King Varuṇa; you, wondrous to be invoked, become Mitra.
>
> You, as the lord of settlements who offers a common meal, are Aryaman; you, apportioning at the ritual distribution, god, are Share.

5 You, Agni, giving wealth rich in heroes to the one who does honor, are Tvaṣṭar—yours is kinship, o you accompanied by the Wives of the Gods and possessing Mitra's might—

You have given wealth rich in horses as the Impeller of swift horses [=Child of the Waters]. You of many goods are the troop of men [=Maruts].

The poets often introduce complications into their repetitive schemata. Sometimes a repetitive pattern takes awhile to become established in a hymn, with the first few verses providing several variants that settle down into a frozen pattern somewhat later; see, e.g., I.112, a long Aśvin hymn, which consists of a catalogue of the Aśvins' helpful deeds and miraculous rescues. The catalogue proper only begins with verse 5; the earlier verses, though superficially showing the same structure as the catalogue verses, with a verse-final refrain syntactically connected to a relative pronoun in the third pāda, have divergent, and challenging, content. Conversely, strict repetition earlier in the hymn may loosen up in the last verses. In II.1 just discussed, in the 15th verse the "you, o Agni" opening of the first 14 verses is distracted, with the vocative postponed till the second pāda, and in the last verse the opening 2nd-singular pronoun is dropped completely, leaving only "o Agni," which also opens the second pāda. The conceptual structure of the hymn also loosens up, with the identifications of the earlier verses giving way to more varied deployment of Agni syntactically.

A famous case of such patterned repetition is found in the first hymn of the Ṛgveda, I.1 dedicated to Agni. It is a nine-verse hymn. The first five verses open with a form of *agní-* in four different grammatical cases (verse 1 accusative *agním*, 2 nominative *agníḥ*, 3 instrumental *agnínā*, 4 vocative *ágne*, 5 again nominative *agníḥ*), what has been called a "versified paradigm." The sixth verse abandons this pattern—partially: its second word is the particle *aṅgá*, which scrambles the sounds of the god's name, while it is the *second* pāda that opens with a form of the name, the vocative *ágne*, with another echo in the epithet *aṅgiraḥ* closing the verse—reinforcing the sounds of the god's name while breaking the strict grammatical and lexical pattern. Such play on a god's name occurs in other hymns, e.g., V.85 (Varuṇa) and VI.18. Moreover, many cases of repetition consist not of a single repeated word, but of several (such is actually the case with II.1, where the pronoun *tvám* is followed by vocative *agne* "o Agni"), and the pattern may be established on the basis of grammatical *categories*, not simply words (e.g., PREVERB PRONOUN . . .).

Repetition also appears at the end of verses in the form of refrains. In some hymns every verse ends with a repeated phrase, which is often the length of a full pāda (e.g., III.55 "Great is the one and only lordship of the gods"; V.55 "As they drove in beauty their chariots rolled along"—both also being syntactically complete clauses), a hemistich (=two pādas), or even longer. See, for example, the three hymns VIII.35–37, in which only a portion of the verse varies, with the rest fixed. The first six verses of the seven-verse hymn VIII.36 consist of six pādas apiece, a total of 56 syllables per verse, but only the first pāda of 12 syllables has novel material. The rest is fixed: "O you of a hundred resolves, for exhilaration drink the soma which they fixed as your portion—you winning all battles, winning the broad expanse, entirely victorious amidst the waters, accompanied by the Maruts, o Indra, master of settlements," with the varying pāda containing material like (verse 4) "Begetter of heaven, begetter of earth." Refrains can also be shorter: for example, the famous refrain of II.12, "he, o peoples, is Indra," which occupies the last (post-caesura) six syllables of a triṣṭubh line. Sometimes the refrain is syntactically integrated into the verse in some parts of the hymn and not in others; in I.96 the first seven verses of this nine-verse hymn share a refrain, "The gods uphold Agni, the wealth-giver." This refrain is independent in verses 1–5, but in verses 6–7 it is a necessary part of the syntactic structure of the rest of the verse, as in 6cd "Protecting their immortality, protecting him, the gods uphold Agni, the wealth-giver."

Sometimes some or all subdivisions of the hymn have refrains; for example, in the tṛca hymn VIII.12 (33 verses) the last four syllables of the last pāda of each verse form a refrain, syntactically integrated in the verse, and each tṛca has a different refrain—e.g., verses 1–3 "for that we beg," verses 4–6 "you have waxed strong." Toward the end of the hymn the four-syllable refrain is expanded to a full 12 syllables, as in verses 25–27 "just after that your two beloved fallow bays waxed strong," which echoes the shorter refrain of verses 4–6. A special type of refrain is the family or clan signature: in some of the Family Books, many of the hymns end with a pāda that marks the hymn as a product of that bardic family, a sort of oral colophon—e.g., the Gṛtsamada refrain of Maṇḍala II "May we speak loftily at the ritual distribution, in possession of good heroes," found at the end of most, though not all, of the trimeter hymns of that book, and the Vasiṣṭha refrain "Do you protect us always with your blessings," ending most of the triṣṭubh hymns of VII.

In addition to repetition of a single word or phrase in every verse, or almost every verse, repetitions can knit one verse to another in a chain, a procedure we can call concatenative repetition or simply concatenation. There a word or phrase from one verse will be repeated in the next verse; then a different word from that verse will be repeated in the following one, and so on through the hymn (see, e.g., I.85, V.1, VI.55, X.84). In VI.55, a short Pūṣan hymn, the chain consists of "charioteer" (1c, 2a), "of wealth" (2c, 3a), "having goats for horses" (3b, 4a), "the lover of his sister" (4c, 5b). The last verse pair (5–6) does not show exact concatenation, but there is a phonological echo between *bhrā́tā* "brother" (5c) and *bíbhrataḥ* "bearing" (6c), showing the same type of loosening of the pattern discussed earlier. In such concatenative chains, the repeated word will generally function differently in its two occurrences; for example, the genitive "of wealth" in VI.55.2–3 depends on two different head nouns: verse 2 "we beseech the companion of wealth" and 3 "You are a stream of wealth." And it may be in a different grammatical form: "having goats as horses" in verse 3 is a vocative, but an accusative in verse 4.

Lists

Hymns are frequently structured as lists, with each verse representing a separate item in the list. This structural principle is well suited to All God hymns, many of which treat a series of gods, one per verse; see, e.g., VI.49, each of whose 15 verses describes and identifies one god or god group in what appears to be an unordered list. In this hymn all but two of the verses name the god in question. But when the name is withheld, the list form can shade into the riddle format; see VIII.29 discussed later as well as the more general treatment of riddles as a structuring device. The riddle as mode of thought was already treated earlier. Another common application of the list model is in the recounting of a series of divine deeds. A number of Aśvin hymns have this shape, with each verse treating a different (and often quite obscure) rescue or benevolent act performed by the Aśvins for a series of named persons (e.g., the Aśvins hymns of Kakṣīvant, I.116–19, or I.112, attributed to Kutsa, discussed earlier). See, for example, this action-packed sequence of two verses from I.117, with no lingering over the individual deeds:

> 7. You two, o men, gave Viṣṇāpū to Viśvaka Kr̥ṣṇiya, who was praising you.
>
> Even to Ghoṣā, living at home with her father, you gave a husband, though she was growing old, Aśvins.
>
> 8. You two gave a bright (body) to Śyāva Kaṇva of the great flood (?), Aśvins.
>
> That deed of yours is to be proclaimed, o bulls: that you bestowed fame upon the son of Nr̥ṣad [=Kaṇva].

Many list hymns are reinforced, their list shape called attention to, by syntactic parallelism and by repetition, as noted for I.112. For example, the famous Indra hymn II.12 consists of a series of definitional relative clauses ("[he] who . . .") recounting deeds and attributes of Indra, with each verse ending with a main clause refrain: *sá janāsa índraḥ*, "he, o peoples, is Indra." A specimen verse from this hymn shows how the repeated relative pronoun "who" punctuates the listed deeds:

> II.12.3 Who, having smashed the serpent, let flow the seven rivers, who drove up the cattle by uncovering Vala,
>
> who produced the fire between two stones, gathering the winnings in contests—he, o peoples, is Indra.

A list by itself is undramatic and has no built-in trajectory toward climax, but the Ṛgvedic poets are adept at finding ways to inject forward momentum into the static list pattern. For example, VIII.29 dedicated to the All Gods is a riddle hymn in which each verse refers to a different god or gods whose identity the audience must guess; the list builds on increasing numbers, from "one" (six verses) to "two" (two verses) to "some" (one verse), by way of "three" (once explicitly, once implicitly). The rising number leads toward climax, while the strict placement of each number in second position in the verse provides a rigid list skeleton.

Numbers

Numbers themselves can structure hymns. A simple example is the Aśvin hymn I.34, which is insistently dominated by the number 3: the Aśvins are urged to perform actions three times with equipment that comes in threes. A sample of this somewhat monotonous recital is verse 5:

> I.34.5 Three times bring wealth to us, Aśvins, three times to the divine conclave; and three times aid our insights.
>
> Three times bring good fortune and three times acclamations for us. The Daughter of the Sun mounted your chariot with its three standing places.

A more subtle use of number is found in the Aśvin hymn II.39. The Aśvins are always invoked as a pair; this hymn consists entirely of similes in which the Aśvins are compared to a series of paired items, some of which occur naturally in pairs (hands and feet, verse 5), some of which do not (messengers, verse 1; goats, verse 2). The word "two" does not occur at all in the hymn, but Sanskrit has a grammatical category of dual, used only for two entities, as opposed to the singular (for one entity) and the plural (for three or more). The dual is the most marked of the grammatical numbers, and the close-packed parade of dual nouns and dual verbs in this hymn makes its structural point without the use of the overt numeral. It is also noteworthy that the name of the Aśvins does not appear in the hymn until nearly the end (second half of verse 7 of an 8-verse hymn); the audience would intuit that the hymn concerned them simply by the constantly repeated dual. A taste of the hymn is given by verse 4:

> II.39.4 Like two boats, take us across—like two yokes, like two wheel naves, like a wheel's two cross-pieces, like its two outer-pieces, take us across.
>
> Allowing no injury to our bodies like two dogs, like two amulets (?) protect us from collapse.

Numbers and numerology play a large role in the enigmatic mysteries of Ṛgvedic cosmic speculation, and some hymns of this type are also structured by the varied repetition of numbers. III.56, an All God hymn, is of this type. This 8-verse hymn contains numbers, especially "three" in every verse except 1 and 4, as in the obscure verse 2:

> III.56.2 Six burdens does the One, unmoving, bear. The cows have approached the highest truth.
>
> Three great females stand below, as steeds: two were deposited in hiding; one has become visible.

As so often in the Ṛgveda, numbers and riddles go together; an even more impenetrable example is X.114, which treats the mystery of the sacrifice.

Questions

Questions provide another type of structure, where variation in the question word provides novelty within the larger pattern. IV.23 is an Indra hymn, whose first six verses (of 10) contain questions, often more than one per verse, as in

> IV.23.3 How does Indra hear the call being called? How, hearing it, does he know the place for his unhitching?
> What are his many distributions of goods? How do they call him a provider for the singer?

The question words in the six verses include "how?" "who?" "whose?" "when?" "what?" but the interrogative structure remains constant.

Ring composition and the omphalos

A different kind of repetition is found in the well-known and often discussed phenomenon of ring composition. In ring composition the beginning and end of a poem or of a unified section therein is marked by repeating at the end, either verbatim or, more usually in the Ṛgveda, a variation on material found at the beginning. In the Ṛgveda this generally involves the reappearance of lexical items or derivational variants of them, or phrases with partial agreement. For example, in the Agni hymn I.59, verse 1 contains the phrase *víśve amṛ́tāḥ* "all the immortals" ("In you do all the immortals bring themselves to euphoria") while the last verse (7) describes Agni with the possessive compound *viśvákṛṣṭiḥ* "belonging to all (human) communities" ("Vaiśvānara, belonging to all communities by his greatness, worthy of the sacrifice among the Bharadvājas, far-radiant"). The repetition of *víśva* "all" provides the ring, and the contrastive nouns it modifies (immortals, [human] communities) express Agni's role as mediator between gods and men. The word *víśva* is not otherwise found in the hymn, *except* in the derivative *vaiśvānará*, an epithet of Agni meaning "belonging to all men," a form of which occurs in every verse. The ring thus reinforces the message implicit in the epithet.

Ring composition frequently demarcates smaller segments in a larger hymn, and paying attention to these clues often allows us to make structural sense of apparently sprawling hymns. For example (though the hymn in question is hardly "sprawling"), in I.167, an 11-verse hymn to the Maruts, the middle section, verses 3–6ab, is a mythological account of their relationship to Rodasī, their consort. This subsection is marked off by two derivationally related words, *vidathyà* "appropriate to the ceremony, ceremonial" in 3d and *vidátha* "ceremony" in 6b, inviting this three-and-a-half verse segment of the hymn to be perceived as a unity, even though it connects well thematically with the more general expressions of praise for the Maruts on both sides of it.

The term "ring composition" focuses attention on the beginning and end of the section demarcated, but a particularly elaborate form of ring composition instead defines and focuses on the center of the section. We call this the "omphalos" (navel) structure (see Jamison 2004 as well as 2007: 80–89). In its most developed form, a series of concentric outer and inner rings isolate the middle verse or verses, which contain the mystery or the message of the hymn and are often phrased in mystical and complex fashion. Good examples of omphalos hymns include the famous cosmogonic hymn X.129 (see Brereton 1999), enigmatic compositions like I.105 and X.28, dramatic presentations like the Vasiṣṭha-Varuṇa hymn VII.86, and hymns like VII.76 whose content is relatively conventional but which nonetheless shows formal omphalos structure. To present just one example, X.28 contains a dialogue between a sacrificer and the god Indra. The first verse expresses concern that Indra has not come to the sacrificer's sacrifice, and in the next two verses, with the arrival of Indra, the sacrificer and Indra engage in dialogue about successful and unsuccessful sacrifices. The last two verses (11–12) echo this dialogue thematically with more general reflections on successful and unsuccessful sacrifices. This is the outer ring. An inner ring, consisting of verses 4–5 and 9–10, presents some of Indra's instruction to the sacrificer, in the form of animal allegories, a genre otherwise completely absent from the Ṛgveda. These allusions to animal fables are intriguing and mostly impenetrable, as in 9 "The hare swallowed the razor coming towards it." The omphalos itself, verses 6–8 and especially 6–7, nestled within these two rings, shows Indra in full epiphany and engaged in self-praise (*ātmastuti*) and self-description. This brief scene is reminiscent of the extended and overwhelming self-revelation of Kṛṣṇa in the Bhagavadgītā, though of course it is a very miniature version of that divine epiphany. In it Indra, responding to the sacrificer's request for enlightment, vaunts his power and describes his own great deeds. The two omphalos verses proper, 6–7, are verbally responsive, as often in omphalos hymns, with the openings of the two verses identical: *evá hí mā́m tavásam* "For thus me, the strong one . . . ," with the first-person phrase the object of different verbs. Once Indra has displayed himself in this way, the hymn transitions back to the fables that form the inner ring and thence to the outer ring. Omphalos structure is also prominent in the Old Avestan Gāthās and has been more discussed there (though not by that term) than the corresponding phenomenon in the Ṛgveda (see Jamison 2007: 86–89 with references).

Initial and final verses

Initial and final verses are especially privileged sites in the architecture of a hymn, though they are not "structuring devices" per se. The first verse often poses a problem or sets the theme that the rest of the hymn will seek to work out. Probably the most famous Indra hymn, I.32, begins "Now I shall proclaim the heroic deeds of Indra," after which the poet does just that—though it must be admitted that he only relates one of them, the Vṛtra battle. A number of other hymns use the same or similar locutions in their initial verses, e.g., I.154.1 "Now shall I proclaim the heroic deeds of Viṣṇu," with the minimal substitution of one divine name for another, or, with more variation, VI.8.1 "Now I proclaim the might, proclaim the rites of Jātavedas." Journey and invitation hymns often begin with an exhortation to the god to come to the sacrifice, as in the briskly efficient opening of V.40, addressed to Indra: "Drive here; drink the soma pressed by stones, o lord of soma." Agni hymns often begin with his birth (/kindling) or installation as Hotar priest, as in II.5.1 "As Hotar he has just been born," or with exhortations to the priests to kindle or praise him, as in V.14.1 "Agni—awaken him with a praise song, kindling the immortal one." Dawn hymns often begin with the sighting of first light, as in VII.78.1 "Her first beacons have been seen opposite." The initial verse can also set the puzzle that will be explored for the rest of the hymn; the most famous example of this is surely the (anti-)cosmogony of X.129, which begins with the radical paradox "The non-existent did not exist, nor did the existent exist at that time."

Final verses can be of two types, integral to the hymn or extra-hymnic. The latter include the clan refrains discussed earlier, which repeat across a spectrum of hymns and have no intrinsic connection to the foregoing content. A different type of extra-hymnic verse is what we might call the meta-summary. The poet often ends his hymn with an announcement of what he has just done, often expressed in the aorist of the immediate past and breaking the mood of immersion in the divine world. For example, the final verse (16) of the exquisitely crafted Indra hymn I.61, which is full of praise for Indra's deeds and attributes, begins with the brisk hemistich "Thus have the Gotamas [=the poet's poetic clan] made you sacred formulations for the 'fallow-bay-yoking' libation, o Indra." The sacrifice is complete, their job is done, and they point out their achievement to the god to spur his benevolence as they return to the mundane world. Final verses that are integral to the body of the hymn often subtly break patterns established earlier in the hymn to bring the composition to a climax. Such for example is the final verse (10) of VIII.29, a hymn mentioned several times earlier. In that All God hymn the first nine verses each identify, in riddling fashion, a particular god or gods, introduced by the numbers "one" (*ékaḥ*) or "two" (*dvā́*). The last verse returns to the number "one," but in the plural *éke* "ones," that is, "some." Many scholars have attempted (and failed) to identify the gods referred to by this "some," but close attention to the content and wording of the verse makes it clear that the referents are not gods, but mortals—priests involved in praising the gods mentioned earlier. Thus the last verse in this hymn both maintains the pattern set previously and breaks it, by switching from divine to human reference. It also implicitly equates the human subjects of the last verse with the divine subjects of the other nine, because they all conform to the same rhetorical pattern. Other examples of final verses are discussed in Jamison 2007: 79–80 and passim.

Poetic repair

One last technique to be mentioned, "poetic repair" (Jamison 2006), is not a structuring device but a method for producing forward momentum. The poet sets a problem—lexical, syntactic, or thematic—earlier in the hymn and then "repairs" this problem later in the hymn by substituting the expected word, syntactic construction, or thematic element for the problematic one. The audience is thus first put off-balance by a disturbance in the poetry and then rebalanced when the superficial solecism is fixed. Audiences used to this type of repair will build expectations that propel them through the poem. A simple example of such repair is provided by the Marut hymn V.52, the first hymn in the magnificent Marut cycle composed by Śyāvāśva. It begins with the poet's self-addresses (V.52.1) "Śyāvāśva, chant forth [*prá . . . árcā*] boldly along with the Maruts possessing chants." Since the hymn is dedicated to the Maruts, it seems strange that the poet exhorts himself to chant "along with" the Maruts, in the instrumental case, rather than "to" them, in the dative: they should be receiving his praise, not chiming in with it. But in verse 5 we find the expected alternative, using the same verb (*prá . . . arcā*) and the dative of the Maruts: "chant forth *to* the Maruts." The tension produced in the audience by the off-balance opening has been resolved. But, as often with cases of poetic repair, the "wrong" expression can also yield an intelligible interpretation, for the Maruts are also known as praise singers, who direct their praises to Indra. That Śyāvāśva could be singing along with them is perfectly possible; by first giving us an unexpected alternative to a banal and predictable expression, the poet seems to want us to dig deeper for the meaning.

Riddles and lists

So far we have been discussing various structures and techniques found in the bread-and-butter of the R̥gvedic repertoire, the praise hymn. But there are other, less widespread genres represented in the text as well. One type combines the list structure discussed above with that prime intellectual preoccupation of the Vedic period, the riddle, also discussed before (IX.D). As we noted previously, a major task of the poet is to discern the covert connections between the visible world and the divine world. They often embed that knowledge in hymns that are stylistically tight and elliptical, expressively oblique, and lexically resonant and that pose an implicit question or questions to which the audience is invited to supply the answer, often a divine name or the name of a cosmic or ritual element—in other words, riddles. Such hymns are purposefully composed to cloak their subjects or to withhold them until late in the verse or hymn. These riddle hymns challenged the interpretive ability of their hearers and demonstrated the cleverness of their poets. Many of them are structured as lists, as we noted, with each verse posing a different question and either leaving it hanging in the air or supplying the answer at the very end of the verse, and the riddling descriptions are often intended to mislead, inviting the wrong answer. Since many of the riddles treat the attributes and actions of gods, the riddle lists are often technically classified as All God hymns.

But gods are not the only targets of riddles. One particularly appealing example is the so-called "weapon hymn" (VI.75), whose verses each describe the appearance and action of a particular weapon of war, often in anthropomorphic and indeed paradoxically feminine terms, with the verse also containing the solution to the riddle. A taste of this hymn can be found in the following verse, whose solution is found in italics:

> VI.75.3 Just like a woman about to speak, she keeps going up to his ear, while embracing her dear partner.
>
> Like a maiden (with her anklets?), she jangles when stretched out on the bow: this *bowstring* here which makes the arrow cross over into the melee as if to a [festive] gathering.

More seriously, the sacrifice and its constituent parts are often treated as mysteries and their hidden connections to cosmic phenomena and elements explored. The most famous riddle hymn in the Ṛgveda is I.164, whose second verse was quoted earlier. It is also technically an All God hymn and a very long poem (at 52 verses, one of the longest hymns in the Ṛgveda) that moves in different directions as it unfolds. The hymn makes both implicit and explicit reference to Vedic ritual, including rites other than the soma ritual. In referring to these rites, the hymn suggests hidden links between ritual objects and acts, realities and processes of the natural world, and constituents and functions of the human body. These hidden connections continue to be hidden, for while we can see the general pattern of the hymn, the interpretation of its specific elements often remains difficult and many competing solutions have been offered.

Some specialized types of hymns

Cosmic speculation and poetic self-reflection

The meditation on ritual and cosmic questions that lies behind the riddle genre also finds expression in a number of generally late hymns that are often characterized as "philosophical" or "speculative" and that reflect on the nature of the world and its inhabitants, on the performance of the ritual, and on the functions of poets and priests. They often treat the origins of things—e.g., of the cosmos (X.129, the opening of which was quoted earlier) or of humankind (X.90, discussed under "Social organization" in chapter 5). These "philosophical" hymns have sometimes been faulted for being inconsistent or insufficiently worked out, but this misses the point. Such hymns represent speculative explorations, "what-if?" scenarios: starting with a conceptual premise, they work out the implications inherent in that premise. Each such exercise displays the creativity and intellectual boldness of the poet. A sober and consistent "theory of everything" is not the aim, and there is no reason to expect the sum total of these hymns to present a uniform picture of the cosmos, its parts, its history, and its functioning. These speculative hymns are the best-known R̥gvedic compositions, familiar to many outside the narrow circle of Vedicists, and overrepresented in selective anthologies. Their fame is certainly deserved: X.129 on the origin of the cosmos is one of the best crafted and profoundly conceived hymns in the collection (see detailed analysis in Brereton 1999). But concentrating on such hymns gives a very distorted view of the text as a whole. Unlike most of the rest of the R̥gveda, they were not composed as liturgical texts for the performance of Vedic rituals and therefore do not represent the principal nature and role of R̥gvedic hymns. Rather, they anticipate post-R̥gvedic brāhmaṇa and āraṇyaka literature, for like these post-R̥gvedic texts, hymns such as I.164, X.90, and X.129 not only explore the nature of things but also interpret Vedic rituals or elements of those rituals. Because they do so, they provide insight into how the ritual was understood, at least during the late Ṛgvedic period, and they represent one clear connection between the Ṛgveda and the later Vedic literature.

What we might consider a subtype of speculative hymns is the genre of poetic self-reflection, in which the poet ponders his poetic training and the tradition he inherited and learned from his father(s), worries about his own skills in comparison with those who preceded him (or are currently competing with him), and finally, triumphantly comes into his own as a fully fledged professional of the word. Particularly well-developed examples of this genre are IV.5 and VI.9, which are both technically dedicated to Agni Vaiśvānara. In the latter the poet begins by confessing his uncertainty about his poetic gifts, expressed in the common metaphor for poetic composition, weaving:

> VI.9.2 I do not know the thread, nor know how to weave, nor (know) what the wanderers [=fingers? threads? shuttles?] weave at their meeting.
> Whose son will be able to speak what is to be said here, as someone higher than his father, who is below?

As the hymn continues, the poet realizes that his inspiration and skill will come from Agni, to whom the hymn is dedicated, and at the end the poet feels the breadth of vision that will guide his composition:

> VI.9.6 My two ears fly widely, widely my sight, widely this light which was deposited in my heart.
> Widely goes my mind, my intentions at a distance. What shall I say, and what now shall I think?

A particularly intricate example is V.44 to the All Gods, sometimes called "the hardest hymn in the Ṛgveda," in which the development of a poet's craft is combined with a hymn-length buried pun on the two ritual substances/deities Agni and Soma, thus showing that the poet's craft has indeed developed quite nicely. It is difficult in brief citations to make this hymn intelligible to the reader, but a hint of the poet's self-discovery and his realization, like that of the poet of VI.9, that Agni is the source of his skill is found in this snippet: "He [=poet] pursues the older sonority of the seers by means of you [=Agni/Soma]" (V.44.8ab).

Dialogues and monologues

Another (relatively) famous genre is the *ākhyāna* or dialogue hymn, also a phenomenon primarily of the late Ṛgveda. In these a pair (or sometimes a trio) of speakers, generally divine or semi-divine, trade verses with each other, often in a fraught or agonistic fashion. There is no scene setting—at least none that has been preserved; the audience is simply plunged into the midst of the dialogue and must intuit the circumstances that led to it. Generally one of the speakers is a female, and sexual tension is on display—as in the dialogue between the legendary seer Agastya and his wife Lopāmudrā (I.179, translated in full later), with Lopāmudrā urging her husband to stop work and have sex with her. She begins her remarks (and the hymn) quite forthrightly:

> I.179.1 For many autumns have I been laboring, evening and morning, through the aging dawns.
> Old age diminishes the beauty of bodies. Bullish men should now come to their wives.

Agastya at first verbally resists in favor of joint ascetic practice but gives in to his growing lust shortly after.

There is a similar argument between the twins and first mortals, the male Yama and his twin sister Yamī (X.10), with Yamī urging her brother to have incestuous sex with her and people the world, while he cites moral objections. A brief snatch of dialogue will give the flavor of this testy exchange:

X.10.11 [Yamī:] What will "brother" mean when there will be no refuge. And what will "sister," if Dissolution will come down?

Driven by desire many times I murmur this: mingle your body with my body.

12. [Yama:] Verily, I must not mingle my body with your body. They call him evil who will go down on his sister.

With another than me arrange your pleasures. Your brother does not want this, well-portioned one.

The dialogue ends in a stalemate, with Yamī in frustration calling him a *bata*—a word found only here whose meaning we don't know (but "jerk" seems a reasonable equivalent)—and Yama sticking by his adamant refusals. But we know from elsewhere that he too ultimately yielded.

Other such dialogue hymns include X.95, the final marital quarrel of the Apsaras (nymph) Urvaśī and her human husband Purūravas, when she curtly dismisses him and her tedious married life to go off and join her sister Apsarases, and the three-way discussion among Indra, his wife Indrāṇī, and a monkey (the Vṛṣākapi hymn, X.86), with the monkey making crude sexual advances to the goddess and she responding partly in kind.

However, not all dialogue hymns involve gendered pairs or racy content: in I.165 Indra and the Maruts argue over who deserves the sacrifice of the seer Agastya, who makes an appearance at the end; in X.28, already discussed, Indra makes a late appearance at the sacrifice of Vasukra and instructs him by means of truncated animal fables (Vasukra's wife appears briefly at the beginning but is not part of the dialogue proper). As noted above, the dialogues all begin in medias res; no speakers are identified (except insofar as they address each other by name), and what the issue is that prompted the exchange only emerges in the course of the conversation. The appearance of these remarkable proto-dramas in the otherwise predominantly liturgical Ṛgveda may seem surprising, but ritual applications or connections to sacrificial concerns can usually be discerned. For example, the argument between Indra and the Maruts in I.165 seems connected to a ritual innovation, the incorporation of the Maruts as recipients of the Midday Soma Pressing, as was discussed. The Vṛṣākapi dialogue is a parodic representation of the Aśvamedha or Horse Sacrifice. The Yama/Yamī dialogue opens the collection of Yama hymns that contain the funeral hymns; since Yama and Yamī were the first mortals, he was the first to die and therefore reigns as king of the dead.

In addition to these dialogues, there are several remarkable monologues. In X.34, known as the Gambler's Lament, the first-person speaker recounts his intoxicated addiction to gambling, the subsequent loss of all he held dear, and his ultimate renunciation of the practice. His description of his own plight is colored with pathos (or bathos), as in this verse:

> X.34.4 Others fondle the wife of a man whose possessions the die with eyes on the prize has hungered for.
>
> Father, mother, brothers say about him, "We do not know him; lead him away bound."

Since gambling remained a cultural touchstone throughout Vedic and Classical Indian literature—particularly associated with kings, and in fact a ritualized part of the Rājasūya, the royal consecration—the inclusion of this hymn in the Ṛgveda is not as odd as it would be in, say, a modern Christian prayer book.

Two separate hymns (X.145 and X.159, the latter translated in full later) are in the voice of a wife, performing a spell against a co-wife and proclaiming her conquest over her, in a victory paean that would not be out of place on a battlefield, as in this verse:

> X.159.4 Without co-wives, smiting co-wives, conquering, overcoming—
>
> I have ripped off the luster of the other women, like the gifts of the feckless.

It is not only humans who take the first-person role: X.125 is a hymn to—and by—the goddess Speech, in which the goddess's name is never mentioned. She indulges in extravagant self-praise, like that of Indra in X.28 discussed previously, a genre known as *ātmastuti*. In the following verse she boasts about her ability to make or break careers:

X.125.5 Just I myself say this, savored by gods and men:
"Whom I love, just him I make formidable, him a formulator, him a seer, him of good wisdom."

Frogs: sui generis

Another hymn with an apparently secular surface but covert religious content is the remarkable Frog Hymn (VII.103, translated in full later), which depicts the frenzy of frogs at the beginning of the rainy season, but also presents models both of early Indian pedagogy and of the ritual called the Pravargya. Thanks to the poet's skill, the hymn is both recognizably "froggy" and true to the ritual details, as in this comparison between the nocturnal croaking of frogs at a pond and priests performing a particular nighttime ritual: VII.103.7 "Like brahmins at an 'Overnight' soma ritual, speaking around a soma vessel full like a pond."

Hymns for domestic rituals; spells

The ritual association of the Frog Hymn reminds us that, though the Soma Sacrifice is the overwhelmingly dominant ritual in the Ṛgveda, other types of rituals find a place in the text. These include the rituals that will later be known as *gṛhya* or "domestic," life-cycle rituals celebrated within the family; these hymns are found primarily in the Xth Maṇḍala. We have just mentioned the funeral hymns in the Yama cycle. These five hymns (X.14–18) describe the delights of the world of the dead, the journey there, the cremation fire, and the funeral service proper, including the return of the mourners to everyday life, among other topics. (See Chapter 8 above.) The sequence ends with a touching appeal to the Earth not to weigh too heavily on the dead man:

> X.18.11 Arch up, Earth; do not press down. Become easy to approach for him, easy to curl up in.
> Like a mother her son with her hem, cover him, Earth.

One very long hymn, X.85 with 47 verses, treats the wedding. It is clearly made up of separate pieces somewhat haphazardly joined together, ending with benign wishes for the long life and happiness of the married couple:

> X.85.42 Stay just here, you two; don't go apart. Attain your entire lifespan,
> playing with your sons and grandsons, rejoicing in your own house.

Both the funeral hymns and the wedding hymn have parallel versions in the Atharvaveda, and their verses are employed in the marriage and funeral rituals preserved from later.

Like the co-wife hymns noted earlier, a number of short hymns in the late Xth Maṇḍala consist of private spells against potential threats or for the successful accomplishment of pending actions—e.g., a spell against miscarriage (X.162) or for successful conception (X.183, 184). A verse from the former shows the dangers envisioned that might beset the embryo and also provides a minimal sketch of the sequence of events involved in conception and gestation:

> X.162.3 Who smites your embryo as it flies, when it is emplanted, as it squirms,
> who intends to smite your embryo when it is just born, that one we banish from here.

These spells resemble the great mass of spells in the Atharvaveda, and they usually have parallel versions in that text. Although most such hymns are found in the late Xth Maṇḍala, we should note the final hymn of the first Maṇḍala, I.191, against stinging and poisonous insects, which is delightfully full of low-register words and word-formations and which also captures the universal experience of being beset by tiny pests:

> I.191.7 The ones on my shoulders, the ones on my limbs, the little needle bugs with their stingers out—
> you no-see-ums, there is nothing at all for you here. All of you, get worn down at once!

Praise of the gift

We might also mention again a genre that is not a hymn *type*, but a hymn section: the *dānastuti* "praise of the gift" (a word that is in general usage in Vedic studies, but that is not actually attested in Vedic), discussed in part previously. At the end of some hymns, particularly commonly in the VIIIth Maṇḍala, the poet turns from his praise of the gods and their gifts and directly faces his patron, generally a king—to praise the gifts the patron has bestowed on him—or, more likely, hopefully will bestow on him—in return for his skillfully turned hymn. As we saw, the listed gifts are often quite extravagant in number and variety—cows, horses, gold, women, all in profusion—another reason to assume that there's some element of wishful thinking and would-be encouragement in this praise. Although some dānastutis play it safe, conforming to the standard style of the rest of the praise hymn, the verbal form of many dānastutis contrasts strongly with that of the rest of the hymn. They are often couched in a lower linguistic register than the high style of the divine praise, using slangy words (which we often cannot decode, since this register is so little used in the rest of the text) and teasing turns of phrase. They often also contain sexual innuendo, especially when women form part of the gift. Even when the patron is actually praised, this praise can be cleverly oblique, and sometimes the poet, feeling bilked of his deserved fee, produces not praise but deflating and satirical censure, sometimes sarcastically listing the disappointing and inadequate gifts, as we saw previously.

Before leaving the subject of hymn types, we should emphasize once again that, though the minor types most recently discussed have attracted disproportionate attention in treatments of the R̥gveda, they are far, far outnumbered by the standard praise hymns. This has had the further unfortunate effect that the sophisticated structure, bold imagery, and daring verbal pyrotechnics found in the praise hymns barely rate a mention in general or popular treatments of the text, in contrast to the compositional outliers.

Imagery, metaphors, similes

Let us now turn to style. The R̥gveda is rich in imagery: the procedures of sacrifice, the exploits of the gods, the activities of men, and the elements and functioning of the cosmos are constantly presented in images of *something else*, images based on similarity and parallelism—the semantic linkages discussed earlier that led to the *bandhu*s of the later Vedic period. On the formal level by far the most common way of expressing these images is in a simile—the most common poetic device in the R̥gveda, as it is in Classical Sanskrit poetry. Although to Indologists the dominance of the simile may seem too predictable to be worth noting, in fact this is one of the features of R̥gvedic style that looks forward to the Classical era, and seems to represent something of a break from the stylistic parameters of the poetic tradition from which R̥gvedic practice emerged. The Avesta contains very few similes—none, for example, in the Old Avestan Gāthās to which the R̥gveda is otherwise so akin—and the so-called Homeric simile of ancient Greek epic, with its elaborately imagined world expressed in verb phrases, is structurally very different from the Sanskrit simile.

In both Vedic and Classical Sanskrit poetry the simile is essentially nominal: that is, in a syntactic structure nominal elements are compared with each other, while the verb is held constant. An English example would be "Indra attacked the enemy, like a lion a sheep," where the verb "attack" serves for both frame and simile, while Indra=lion and enemy=sheep provide the comparisons. In a case language like Sanskrit both "Indra" and "lion" will be coded as nominative case (that is, as grammatical subject), and "enemy" and "sheep" as accusative (that is, as grammatical direct object). Neither Vedic nor Classical Sanskrit regularly has similes of the type "Indra attacked the enemy, as a lion devours a sheep," with two different clauses constituting the comparison and a difference in verb as well as in the nouns connected to it. The "like" of the English example has overt expression in Sanskrit as well: by *iva* or *ná* in the Ṛgveda. For more on the structure of the simile and the ways that Ṛgvedic poets exploit it see Jamison 1982.

Although the simile, with its explicit comparisons, is ubiquitous in the Ṛgveda, it is not the only vehicle of imagery in the text. *Implicit* identifications of disparate elements are another inescapable stylistic feature, and, as was discussed, regularly recurring identifications (*bandhus*)—the fire as sun, the chariot as sacrifice, etc.—provide the conceptual structure of the Vedic cosmos. Thus, poetic style coincides here with the shared notions of the world that shape "the Vedic mind." However, in making comparison and identifications the poets do not confine themselves to these shared and stable associations, but often make bold and superficially puzzling equations, as when the goddess Dawn is compared in a single verse (I.124.4) to "the breast of a preening waterfowl," "a female elephant revealing her intimate parts," and "a fly [literally 'one sitting on food'] waking a sleeper." Decoding the shared features that allow such equations to be made is one of the intellectual challenges that the poets posed to their own audience and that engages us, and often eludes us, to this day.

Although the poetic foundation on which the R̥gveda rests was an ancient one, the imagery of its poems comes from the immediate world of its poets. As already remarked, the R̥gveda is fundamentally a collection of hymns for the soma rite, in which Indra is the principal deity. Indra is a warrior, and therefore images of battle, war, contest, and conflict provide the background for a great many R̥gvedic hymns. In the IXth Maṇḍala, for example, the ritual process of creating soma can represent a war campaign by king Soma. The dripping of soma as it is pressed is the beginning of Soma's attack or raid. The flow of soma over the woolen filter and into the soma vessels is the destruction of Soma's enemies. With the mixing of soma with milk, Soma wins cows and distributes them to his subjects, who are the sacrificers. A good example is IX.90, which is couched in martial imagery. In the first verse Soma "has driven forth like a chariot, striving to win the prize, sharpening his weapons." This martial stance is emphasized even more in verse 3:

> IX.90.3 Having a horde of champions, having hale heroes, purify
> yourself as victorious conqueror and winner of stakes,
> with your sharp weapons and snapping bows invincible
> in combats, vanquishing your rivals in battles.

In the rest of the hymn Soma's ability to win peaceful lands and booty is praised, and the whole campaign is summed up in the last verse with (IX.90.6) "In this way, like a king full of resolve, ever smiting all obstacles to progress with your onslaught, purify yourself."

Other items associated with war and periods of mobilization also loom large in the poems, perhaps none more than the chariot. The chariot was one of the most visible cultural symbols of the Āryas, for it was likely unique to them among the peoples of ancient South Asia, and it was critical to their success in battle and their mobility.

As has been noted, in Ṛgvedic poetry the chariot becomes the hymn that travels to the gods or the sacrifice that brings the gods (II.18.1). When they perform the ritual or compose the hymns, priests and poets become the fashioners of the chariot (I.61.4, V.2.11). Indeed, poets repeatedly compare themselves to chariot-makers, as in V.2.11 cited earlier. Just as a chariot brings booty from war or a winning chariot the prize of a race, the sacrifice carries goods from the gods to humans (X.53.7). In I.129.1 Indra is asked to lead a chariot that is both an actual, racing chariot and a metaphorical chariot, the sacrifice. The chariot is also the vehicle of the gods, by which they come to the sacrifice. Distinctive animals pull the chariots of different gods: the two fallow bay horses of Indra, the dappled mares of the Maruts, the mares of the Sun, the ruddy cattle of Dawn, the goats of Pūṣan, the birds (as well as horses) of the Aśvins, and these animals can often generate their own webs of association—e.g., very commonly, Dawn's ruddy cows as rays of light.

More abstractly, the imagery of war is also implicit in the frequent symbols of expansion and confinement. This imagery is most evident in the principal Indra stories. Vṛtra, whose very name means "obstacle," as we have seen, represents what hinders and blocks, and when Indra kills Vṛtra, he shows himself to be the power that can destroy any other obstacles to life and prosperity. The Vala cave enclosed and entrapped the cattle, and Indra must break open Vala to free the cows, the dawns, and the light. One of the most common word for distress in the Ṛgveda is *áṃhas*, which literally means "narrowness, constraint" and which is cognate with English "angst" (and its German source). The wish is frequently expressed that some god or other will "make broad space from narrowness." Finding open and well-watered pasturelands was essential for the Āryas, since their cattle, horses, and other livestock depended on them. The second half of IX.113 is a poetic vision of heaven, where there are "inexhaustible light" (verse 7) and "youthfully exuberant waters" (verse 8), where one moves "following one's desire" (verse 9), and where there is "independence and satisfaction" (verse 10).

It is the heavenly vision of a pastoral people, longing for a place of freedom and abundance. The place of the afterlife depicted in the funeral hymn X.14 is similar: "well-watered" (verse 9) "pastureland" (verse 2).

Pastoral imagery dominates R̥gvedic poetry at many turns. As was discussed, cows are everywhere; here we might mention a bovine aspect not treated earlier: cows as the symbols and substance of wealth. The attention of the gods, which will bring rewards to humans, is a cow (II.32.3), and rain is milk from heaven (V.63.5). In II.34.8 the Maruts are compared to a cow, since they "swell" with rain, the way cows swell with milk. In VI.45.7 Indra, as the god who inspires poetic formulations, is a cow whose milk is the hymns. Or again, in VIII.1.10 Indra is both the milker of the cow and the cow whose milk is refreshment for sacrificers. Speech is a cow that gives the forms of speech as her milk in VIII.110.10, and in X.64.12 the insight that the gods have given the poet should swell like a cow with milk. VI.48.11–13 combines several images of the cow, beginning with an actual cow, whose milk is the milk that is mixed with soma, but including also the cow that represents poetic inspiration and prosperity. In X.133.7 prosperity brought by the gods is a cow giving her milk "in a thousand streams." The connection of the dawns with cows was discussed previously, but we should remember that this link goes through the dakṣiṇā, the sacrificial reward, and the distribution of riches more generally.

As an aside, this preoccupation with the sacrality and symbolism of the cow of course endures to this day in Hindu India, but it should be noted that killing and eating cows are found throughout the Vedic period, starting in the R̥gveda. Although the cow is sometimes called *ághnyā* "she who is not to be killed," bovines are certainly slaughtered for ritual and for food. In X.86.14 Indra boasts, "They kill fifteen, twenty oxen at a time for me, and I eat only the fat meat"; in later Vedic guest reception rituals, especially honored guests are always offered a cow to eat, and they can choose whether to have it slaughtered for the meal or not. (See Jamison 1996: 157–59, 169–74.)

While the poets have particular fondness for cows, male animals too figure significantly in the hymns. Bulls and buffaloes embody strength and virility, and therefore they represent mighty gods, potent sacrifice, and strong men. Agni is a bull with a strong neck (V.2.12), horns (V.1.8), and a powerful bellow (X.8.1). In V.40.1–4 the bull-like pressing stone and bull-like soma are prepared so that the bull Indra will join together with his bulls, the Maruts. Indra is "the bull overcoming the powerful, the tempestuous king, smasher of Vṛtra, soma-drinker" (verse 4). Parjanya, the Thunderstorm, roars like a bull (V.83.1), has the powers of a bull (verse 2), and pours his fertilizing streams as a "bullish stallion" (verse 6). Indeed, anything associated with their ideal of masculinity is likely to be bull-like for the Ṛgvedic poets.

The cultural role of horses—racehorses and warhorses—was obviously central to the Āryas and, as a result, so was their poetic role. Agni receives the same praise as a steed (III.22.1), for he is a horse that brings rewards (I.27.1). When he is kindled, he is a hungry horse who breaks free of his enclosure (VII.3.2). Soma is a racehorse groomed by the fingers of the priests and running over the woolen filter (IX.6.3, 5, cf. 13.6). The waters too are like racehorses that should run forever (IV.3.12). A sacrificer harnesses himself to the sacrifice like a horse (V.46.1), and the sacrifice is brought to success like a horse (IV.10.1). The significance of the horse is perhaps most obvious in the Dadhikrāvan hymns, IV.38–40. Dadhikrāvan was likely the actual horse of King Trasadasyu, but Dadhikrāvan also represents the rule of the Pūrus, the tribe to whom Trasadasyu belonged, and the sun, which can represent the king. The three hymns dedicated to him include both a very formal encomium (IV.39), utilizing the same poetic tropes that would be used for divinities and in similar high-register language, and two (IV.38, 40) that exuberantly capture the horse-iness of the horse and stretch the boundaries of poetic language, as in this snatch of description: "greedy with his hooves like a champion seeking his meal, outstripping chariots, swooping like the wind" (IV.38.3). In X.178 Tārkṣya is a protective deity of chariot drivers and perhaps a deified racehorse himself. Of the two hymns devoted to the Horse Sacrifice (Aśvamedha), I.162 and 163, the first is a detailed account of the procedure of the sacrifice, but the second lyrically evokes the sacrificed horse's miraculous birth and mythic history, its cosmic connections and divine identifications.

Domestic animals beyond livestock are relatively uncommon in the R̥gveda, but mention should be made of the female dog Saramā, who is the loyal and indeed incorruptable companion of Indra: when the Paṇis attempt to bribe her when she serves as Indra's messenger and scout on the edge of the world, she indignantly rebuffs them (X.108, translated in full later). Of the smaller animals that hang around humans, mice make a memorable appearance in a simile in which worries afflicting the speaker are compared to mice eating their tails (I.105.8=X.33.3), and a poet, with charming self-deprecation, refers to himself as Vamraka "little ant," creeping up to Indra on his (multiple) feet (X.99.12). We have also already mentioned the biting stinging insects against which I.191 is directed.

Although the poets are focused on pastoral life and the herd animals they know best, wild animals also occasionally appear in R̥gvedic hymns (see Jamison 2009a). Birds are frequently mentioned (e.g., I.164.21, X.80.5, 123.6) and often figure in similes (e.g., I.166.10). Unlike other birds, the falcon is not only fast but can be trained, and it is significant mythologically, since it brought the soma from heaven to Manu (IX.48.4, IV.26-27). The wolf is a recurring symbol of lurking danger (e.g., I.42.2, 105.11, 18, 120.7, II.28.10), particularly because it straddles the boundary between wild and domestic. The most dangerous creature of all is Vr̥tra, constantly referred to as a snake, probably a gigantic cobra (I.32). More benignly, the inseparable Aśvins are compared to a pair of cakravāka ducks (II.39.3), and in I.64 the Maruts are not only bulls and buffaloes, but they also roar like lions and devour trees like elephants. Perhaps the broadest array of animals appears in X.28, which is built around various animal fables, as was discussed earlier (see Jamison 2009a).

Various human pursuits play significant roles in poetic imagery. The poets frequently mention weaving (e.g., I.115.4), which is compared to the intricate patterns of hymn composition and sacrifice (e.g., VI.9.2–3, X.101.2, 130). This is an inherited Indo-European trope. Given the pastoral symbolism elsewhere, it is not surprising that cattle tending is a major source of poetic imagery. Indra is like a herdsman who separates his flocks from those of others (V.31.1; cf. VI.19.3). The poet too can be a herdsman driving his praise to Indra (VI.49.12). Or we have the reverse image: in VII.18.10 enemies run helter-skelter like cows without a herdsman. Milking is an especially important part of livestock tending, and the production of many intangible things—like the composition of poetry—is homologized to milking, while precious essences are likened to milk—especially soma (X.94.9, etc. etc.), but also rain (milked out by Varuṇa in V.85.4), semen (III.31.10 "milking out the milk of the age-old semen," with the semen here probably standing metaphorically for yet another substance), fame (VI.48.12 "who will milk out undying fame [*śrávó 'mṛtyu*] for the self-radiant troop of Maruts"), and goods of all kinds, as when Indra "will milk out for us (wealth) in horses, in cows, in grain, like (a cow) yielding a broad stream" (VIII.93.3). Even birth can be conceived of as milking: the mighty Maruts were milked out of their mother (VI.66.4). Curiously, given the ritual importance of ghee (*ghṛtá*, clarified butter), butter churning is absent from the text, which is especially surprising because one of the enduring myths of the later period is the churning of the ocean of milk. Judging from the compound *ghṛtadúh*, "milking out ghee" (IX.89.5), and passages like I.134.6 "all the milk-cows have milked out the ghee and the milk-mixture for you" (also VI.70.2, VII.41.7, etc.), ghee was considered a product of the milking process, and the intermediate step received no recognition.

In addition to animal husbandry, as we have seen, the Āryas also raised crops, such as barley, but agricultural imagery does not figure much in R̥gvedic poetry, with the exception the sowing of seeds, an image that is occasionally encountered. In such passages the seed (*bī́ja*, a resonant word in later Sanskrit) is "scattered" (√*vap*), as in this image "like grain-producers scattering seed" (X.94.13), and the ploughing (√*kr̥ṣ*) of grain or grainfields also provides images such as "as if plowing a grain(field) with oxen" (I.23.15). A word derived from the "plough" word, *kr̥ṣṭí*, which must have originally meant "ploughing" and then "furrow," is a common designation for communities, defined by their boundaries. There is one late and popular hymn devoted to agricultural divinities, appended at the end of Maṇḍala IV (IV.57); it is notable that the word *sī́tā* "furrow," later the name of Rāma's noble wife, is first met in the R̥gveda (IV.57.6–7) in this hymn. The curiously formed and probably non-Indo-Aryan word *lā́ṅgala* "plough," widespread later, is first found in this hymn (IV.57.4). Gathering fruit by shaking a tree with a crook provides a simile in III.45.4, though the fruit tree was probably wild. The reason for the comparative lack of attention to agriculture may be the connection of the soma rite to Indra and to the period of mobilization (*yóga*). In the period of settlement (*kṣéma*), agriculture would have had a larger role.

Language

Grammar

The style of the R̥gveda—the unfolding of its thought and the organization of its poetic embellishments—cannot be separated from the language in which it is expressed: Vedic Sanskrit. Since the structure of this language is very different from that of English, some background about the way the language works will be useful. Sanskrit is an inflectional language with an especially rich morphology [=word-level grammar], and most of the grammatical information that is carried in English by word order and by separate elements such as prepositions and auxiliary verbs is coded in Sanskrit on the word itself. Ṛgvedic poets glory in their grammar and are skillful in exploiting not only the many distinctions it provides but also grammatical ambiguities and neutralizations of those grammatical distinctions. Moreover, since basic information, such as the identity of the grammatical subject and object, is coded on the word, the poet is free to use word order for rhetorical purposes, placing particularly significant words in emphatic positions such as initial in the verse line, as we have already seen. In addition, since their formal grammatical shape signals which words belong together syntactically (what are known as constituents, such as adjective + noun, verb + object, etc.), they do not have to be adjacent to each other and isolated into distinct units, but can be sprinkled through the sentence at will. (There are certainly some constraints—"free" word order is a myth—but far fewer than in languages like English.) Thus an English sentence like "The lofty gods give splendid gifts to pious mortals" could appear in Vedic as, for example, "The gifts lofty pious give mortals gods splendid" perfectly intelligibly because the grammatical form would sort the words that belong together into separate piles, as it were, and their syntactic roles would also be marked by that form (no "to" is needed, for example, because "pious mortals" would be in the dative case appropriate to indirect objects).

Although this is not the place for a sketch grammar of Vedic, a few particularly prominent facts merit mention here. The Sanskrit noun has eight grammatical cases, expressing most of the syntactic relations pertaining in a sentence, including subject (nominative case), direct object (accusative case), possessor (genitive case), etc. The noun also has three numbers: singular, dual (for both naturally occurring pairs and two entities that happen to be associated), and plural (three or more). The combination of three numbers and eight cases means that in principle every Sanskrit noun (/adjective / pronoun) has twenty-four separate forms, but in fact some of these distinctions are collapsed, with a single form representing several different case/number pairings. For example, the dual has only three separate forms for the eight cases. Thus, despite the elaborate grammatical system, ambiguities abound, and poets are quick to exploit them, often reading the same form in several different ways in the same sentence. The noun also has three grammatical genders, masculine, feminine, and neuter, which only loosely coincide with "natural" gender. Most males are grammatically masculine, most females are grammatically feminine, but the grammatical genders of the rest of the universe of beings and things are essentially arbitrary or determined by linguistic, rather than real-world considerations.

The verb is even more complex than the noun. Its basic unit is a nine-member grid of three persons (1st [I/we], 2nd [you], 3rd [he, she, it, they]) and three numbers (matching those of the noun) of the subject of the verb form.

I	we two	we (all)
you (sg.) ["thou"]	you two	you (all)
he, she, it	they two	they (all)

This basic unit is deployed in a plethora of tenses, moods, and voices, including at least four ways to express the past tense (the imperfect, aorist, and perfect tenses, plus the use of an adjectival form [the past passive participle] in lieu of a verb). Of these three tenses, the aorist is often used to express the immediate past (in English, "has [just] done" versus "did") and is therefore frequently encountered in ritual situations, in which the poet announces a sacrificial act as just completed (like the kindling of the fire) or a poem just composed. But the differences among the past tenses are often difficult to assess, and varying interpretations of these formal markers can lead to very different interpretations of the meaning of a passage. The verbal system also has a special category called the injunctive, which has no formal marking for tense or mood and therefore can be employed in a variety of functions, including, often, past tense—another ambiguity that the poets often exploit.

Register

Another important parameter cross-linguistically is language *use* and particularly the feature known as "register"—formality or informality, archaism versus neologism, and other stylistic choices made among the range of possibilities within the capacious grammar of what we think of as a single, unified language. We should first remark that most of the language we encounter in the Ṛgveda was not the standard everyday idiom of the poets themselves. Instead, they composed in a deliberately archaic and deliberately elevated register appropriate to the poetic tradition they were a part of and the solemn nature of the high sacred purpose of their hymns. Such reaching for the archaic and the elevated is common across religious traditions; one need only glance at modern prayer books and liturgies, even those supposedly updated to reflect contemporary language, to encounter the same phenomenon. The problem (for us) with regard to the Ṛgveda is, of course, that we possess no control sample of the "standard everyday" language of the poets, though occasional forays into a lower register, as well as phonological and morphological forms embedded in the text that show developments characteristic of later forms of Sanskrit and Middle Indo-Aryan, give us some hints of what everyday language might have looked like, and the language of the only slightly later text, the Atharvaveda, may be closer (though certainly not identical) to what the poets spoke "at home."

Although most of the Ṛgveda is couched in very high-register language, the poets sometimes—sometimes quite abruptly—slip into what appears to be a colloquial, even slangy, register—a switch that almost always has a dramatic purpose. As we have already noted, these passages are especially found in dānastutis, which are often filled with puns, often obscene, and obscure terms, and characterized by "popular" phonological and morphological forms. An extended example is found in the last three verses of IV.32, where the poet celebrates his patron's gift to him of "two brown ones," also described as "two tiny little girls on a post," using diminutives and words otherwise unknown—in other words, using low-register morphology and lexicon.

> IV.32.22 I solemnly proclaim the two brown ones of yours, o far-gazing grandson of the Goṣan.
> But with the gift of these two, don't slack off on the giving of cows!
> 23 Like two little baby-dolls on a post—the two new little ones, undressed—
> the two brown ones go in beauty on their travels.
> 24. Ready for me when I travel at dawn, ready for me when I don't,
> the two brown ones don't falter on their travels.

There has been much speculation about what these two might be. But we think it very likely that this is a reference to the breasts of a woman given to the poet in payment for his hymn; women often form part of the "gift" along with livestock and gold. Befitting the general style of dānastutis, the tone is light, playful, and a bit bawdy, though it begins with mock solemnity "I solemnly proclaim" (*prá . . . śáṃsāmi*).

When women's speech is represented in the text, it also appears to belong to a lower register and also makes use of diminutive morphology (the equivalent of "itty-bitty") and rare or otherwise unattested words. The following is presented in the hymn as if it were the advice on demure behavior given by a mother to her little daughter (though it's actually an insult directed at a man, claiming he's turned into a woman). Note the "little" on two body parts and the apparent coy reference to female genitalia.

VIII.33.19 Keep your eyes to yourself: look below, not above.
Bring your two little feet closer together.
Don't let them see your two little "lips" (?).

(For further discussion of women's language in the Ṛgveda and for these passages in particular, see Jamison 2008, 2009b, and 2011.)

In addition, the technical terms of Vedic pastimes like dicing and horse-racing and occupations like stockbreeding and agriculture introduce us to lexical levels and turns of phrase different from the high style of praise poetry and again presumably closer to ordinary language. Not surprisingly, it is harder to determine the meaning and reference of the words in these low-register passages than those in the elevated discourse that generally prevails in the Ṛgveda. For example, the word "dog-killing" (*śvaghnín*) has no literal reference to either dogs or killing; it refers to the winner in a game of dice. A little reflection on the part of modern readers will suggest numerous slangy or idiomatic terms in English that would be completely opaque to people outside our culture who attempted to interpret them literally.

Lexicon

This brings up the topic of the lexicon. The vocabulary that Ṛgvedic poets use is simply enormous relative to the size of the text: Grassmann's lexicon of the Ṛgveda (1872–1875, but still the standard today) is a very fat volume, with 1685 pages of lemmata—a giant word-hoard, full of rarities and hapax legomena, slang and colloquialisms. Determining the meaning and reference of Ṛgvedic words has always been one of the greatest challenges in Vedic studies, going all the way back to the indigenous lexicographer Yāska in the first millennium BCE (discussed later). Even words that are continued into later Sanskrit often have radically different values in the R̥gveda from their later representatives. (Especially cogent examples are the resonant terms *dhárma(n)* and *bráhman*, which cannot be read with their later meanings.) But many R̥gvedic words simply do not appear in later Sanskrit or in Middle-Indo-Aryan. Much help is given by cognates in other Indo-European languages, especially closely related Avestan, and by Indo-Iranian and Indo-European root etymologies. But of course cognates and root etymologies are not always a reliable guide to synchronic semantics, as meaning changes over time and space. Moreover, some words are simply isolated, attested only once (the technical term for this is hapax, or more fully hapax legomenon) or only a few times in non-diagnostic contexts. The poets clearly revel in their lexical riches, employing what seem like dozens of synonyms and near synonyms for key concepts (like "shine" or "sing") and seeking out rarities and archaisms.

Syntax, grammar, and the pursuit of obscure style

The poets' manipulation of language was not limited to change of register or the employment of arcane lexical items. The most significant and salient feature of the poets' relationship to language is their deliberate pursuit of obscurity and complexity. The strong privileging of obscurity is found in all aspects of R̥gvedic poetry, some of which have been mentioned previously, such as the scrambling of narrative in mythological passages and of the steps in the progress of the ritual, as well as the fondness for riddles and conundrums. And so it is also with their use of language. The poets push their syntax to the limits of intelligibility (and, at least for us, sometimes beyond) by permutations of word order, radically breaking up constituents and scattering their words through a verse, omitting key constituents (like the direct object or even the verb), and violating expected case frames and other grammatical conventions. They delight in confecting variant morphological forms and in deforming words.

They also exploit grammatical ambiguity. As noted, grammatical differences (like case and number) are sometimes neutralized in particular paradigms—such that, for example, the same form of a noun can sometimes be genitive singular, ablative singular, or accusative plural, and it is not uncommon for such a form to stand for one of those grammatical identities in one syntactic construction in a sentence and another in another construction, even though it is found only once in the passage. Often the poet will position this Janus-faced word directly between the two elements with which it could be construed. IV.1.9 provides a simple example: the form *mánuṣaḥ* belongs to the stem *mánus*, which means both "Manu" (the name of the first man and first sacrificer) and "man." The form can also be either genitive singular ("of Manu/man") or accusative plural ("men" as grammatical object). In IV.1.9 it is positioned between a transitive verb *cetayat* "he [=Agni] instructs" and a compound *yajñábandhuḥ* "tie to the sacrifice." At least in our view, *mánuṣaḥ* here is *both* accusative plural, as object of the preceding verb, and genitive singular, dependent on the following compound: *sá cetayan mánuṣo yajñábandhuḥ*, yielding a translation "He instructs **men** as their tie to the sacrifice of **Manu**."

The poets also exploit another feature of the language that we have not yet discussed: sandhi. In all forms of Sanskrit, words have different shapes depending on what words precede or follow them. This phenomenon is similar to what produces informal English gotcha (from got + you) and gonna (from going + to), but unlike in English, this process is applied to every word sequence in the language in all registers. Sometimes the application of sandhi rules produces ambiguities; e.g., word-final *-as* and *-e* both end up as -*a* under certain circumstances, and the poets will sometimes enable a pun that involves two distinct underlying forms of the same word, say *devás* and *devé* nominative sg. and locative singular of "god" respectively, each of which could be at home in the sentence. IV.1.9 just treated provides an example of such phonological ambiguity: the sequence reads in the Saṃhitā text *cetayan mánuṣo yajñábandhuḥ*. The middle word *mánuṣo* can be unambiguously restored to the underlying form *mánuṣaḥ* discussed earlier—its grammatical multivalence is independent of its form—but *cetayan* in the text could stand either for *cetayan* or *cetayat*; in this case, the latter is correct.

Another way to exploit grammatical ambiguity is through the modulation from one type of construction to another via a word that has neutralized a crucial grammatical parameter. Especially common is the switch from a second- to third-person subject ("you" to "he/she/it") or the reverse, by way of a verb that can be read either way. This is very like musical modulation whereby a chord that is structural in two different keys is used to switch from one to the other. A famous example in the R̥gveda is found in I.32, the great Indra-Vr̥tra hymn, in which the first three verses contain three examples of the verb *áhan*, which the other grammatical forms in those verses establish as a third-person "he smashed"—followed immediately by another form of *áhan* in verse 4, which must be instead second-person "you smashed" as shown by other words in the verse, such as the immediately preceding vocative "o (you) Indra"—with a further *áhan* in verse 5, a modulation back to "he smashed," as the audience only discovers later in the verse.

The just-mentioned examples are grammatical puns, but the poets also frequently employ lexical puns as well. One of the less elaborate examples in found in I.27.1, a hymn to Agni, in which Agni is extolled as *vā́ravantam* and compared to a horse. *vā́ra-vant-* means possessing *vā́ra; vā́ra* means both "choice thing(s)" and "tailhair." Here the first is appropriate to Agni, who (we hope) has and bestows on us choice things. But in the comparison to a horse, "having tailhair" is a reasonable descriptor, and in fact this secondary meaning brings out another aspect of Agni the fire god: his flames can be thought of as tailhairs waving wildly in his mad rush.

Punning often goes beyond the single-word pun of whatever type, to what we might call the thematic pun. By failing to use the names or uniquely identifiable epithets, the poet can construct expressions that apply to two different entities at one time because all the descriptors and indications of action are applicable to both. This type of dual application can be quite lengthy and elaborate. For example, as was discussed, V.44 is an almost impenetrable 15-verse hymn that has dual reference throughout to the ritual substances Agni (the ritual fire) and Soma (the ritual drink).

Another boundary-pushing use of language involves alternate analyses of the same sequence of syllables, a type of poetic play enabled by the fact that there are no distinct word boundaries in the Saṃhitā (continuous, literally "put-together") form of the recited text. A particularly striking example involves the beginning of the first verse of X.29.1, a hymn attributed to the very wily poet Vasukra Aindra, in which the first six syllables, *vánenávāyóní*, can be interpreted in six different ways (see Jamison 2015). This kind of layered reading is known in later Sanskrit art poetry (*kāvya*) as *śleṣa*, where it reaches almost absurd extremes, with, for example, the same text simultaneously narrating both great Sanskrit epics, the Mahābhārata and the Rāmāyaṇa. For an illuminating discussion of this device in later texts see Bronner (2010), but it is already present in sophisticated form in the Ṛgveda, along with many other tricks of Classical Sanskrit kāvya poets.

Poets frequently also indulge in etymological figures, deploying derivatives of the same root in a single clause or construction (of the type English "do a deed," "fight the good fight"), as in I.62.1 *árcāma arkám* "we chant a chant." Figures in which the etymological connections are obscured by phonological developments are especially noteworthy. Thus, in I.55.8 the noun phrase *áṣāḷhaṃ sáhaḥ* "undominatable dominance" consists of a noun "dominance" (*sáhas*) and its negated adjective "undominated, undominatable" (*áṣāḷha*), both belonging to the verbal root √*sah* "dominate, overpower," but because of regular phonological processes, the root syllable of the negated adjective, *ṣāḷh*, shares no surface phonemes with the noun. The opposite—false etymological figures, where phonological similarity masks etymological divergence—are also found, like VI.6.3 *vánā vananti* "they conquer the woods," in which the two phonologically matching words, verb and direct object, are etymologically distinct.

Less elaborate poetic effects also abound in R̥gvedic verse. Phonological play is the bread-and-butter of the R̥gvedic poet, with alliteration and assonance very common effects. Due perhaps to the complex but regular phonological relationships produced by morphophonemic changes in grammatical paradigms, the poet will not limit these effects to repetition of the exact same sound, but will play on phonetically related sounds, such as the three sibilants (*ś*, *ṣ*, and *s*), e.g., IV.21.7 *síṣakti śúṣma stuvaté*, which contains examples of all three sibilants, and the voiceless, voiced, and aspirated dentals (*t, th, d, dh*). Rhyme, by contrast, is quite rare and probably for the most part inadvertent; because, for example, case forms of nouns and adjectives that belong together often have the same ending, rhyme would have been too easy and a byproduct of constituent construction and so would have been no test of the poet's skill—better to find ways to *avoid* rhyme in such constructions. Phonological patterns can be quite intricate, involving reversal, chiasmus, scrambling, and so on, in addition to straight repetition. Some examples include VIII.4.20 *nírmajām aje nír*, which would in recitation come out as *nírmajāmajenír*, with apparent repetition *majVmajV* flanked by *nír*; VIII.7.28 *pŕ̥ṣatī ráthe / práṣṭir . . . róhitaḥ* (with a nice scrambling of *th* → *h* . . . *t* in *ráthe . . . róhitaḥ*); VIII.14.10 with mirror image *ajirā / arāji*, and so on: examples abound. Patterns can also be deployed "vertically"—with the repeated elements taking the same position in a series of verse lines, as we saw above.

Meter

Technical description

The mention of verse lines brings us to one of the most salient aspects of Ṛgvedic style, namely meter. The hymns are composed in a variety of meters, but all of the meters are *syllable-counting* and *quantitative*. That is, they consist of lines containing a fixed number of syllables, arranged in patterns of "heavy" and "light" syllables (the "quantity" referred to by the term "quantitative"). Heavy syllables contain a long vowel (a class that includes *e* and *o*) or diphthong or a short vowel followed by two consonants (which need not belong to the same word) and are symbolized in Western analysis by a macron (¯). Light syllables contain a short vowel followed by, at most, a single consonant and are symbolized by a breve (˘). (Aspirated consonants—those written in transliteration with two roman letters, the second of which is *h*, e.g., *th*—count as single consonants.) The final syllable of a line is metrically indifferent and symbolized by x. The distinction between heavy and light metrical syllables simply formally enshrines patterns inherent in the language itself, where various linguistic processes are sensitive to distinction in syllable weight and the difference between short and long vowels is lexically and morphologically crucial.

This type of metrical structure was inherited from the Indo-European poetic tradition, most clearly evident in ancient Greek meter, especially the Aeolic meters utilized by the lyric poets Sappho and Alcaeus, which are also syllable-counting and quantitative; these Aeolic meters have long been considered cognate to Vedic meter. The meter of the Old Avestan Gāthās is also closely akin: although the quantitative aspect has been lost, Gāthic lines have a fixed number of syllables.

Ṛgvedic meter is also identical in its structural principles to most of the meters encountered in Epic and Classical Sanskrit (with the exception of the ārya and related types, in which a heavy syllable can be the equivalent of two light syllables). The major difference between Vedic meter and Classical syllable-counting meter has to do with the regulation of quantities. In the earlier parts of the line R̥gvedic meter has relatively unfixed quantities; it is only toward the end of a line (the cadence) that the quantity of each syllable is fixed (especially in trimeter meter, see later). By contrast, most Classical literary meters regulate the quantity of each syllable in the line; in other words, the relative flexibility of R̥gvedic meter has become frozen. The exception is the eight-syllable epic anuṣṭubh, or so-called *śloka* meter—the overwhelmingly predominant meter in the two great epics and the workhorse meter of nonliterary Classical verse texts such as Manu's lawcode—whose quantities are precisely fixed only in the second half of each line.

R̥gvedic meters are generally divided into "dimeter" and "trimeter" types. The former consists of eight-syllable lines, which can be conveniently considered to consist of two equal segments, with the second half tending more toward fixed quantities, generally in an iambic pattern. However, it is important to keep in mind that there is no fixed caesura (word-break) in dimeter meter, and even the four cadential syllables are not rigidly fixed in quantity. Trimeter meter is more complex. It generally consists of lines of either 11 or 12 syllables (triṣṭubh or jagatī respectively), characterized not only by a fixed cadential sequence of 4 (triṣṭubh) or 5 (jagatī) syllables but by a strong caesura after the first 4 or 5 syllables in the line. The caesura and the cadence thus effectively divide the line into three parts—the opening (the first 4–5 syllables before the caesura), the "break" (the 2–3 syllables following the caesura), and the cadence.

Examples of the three most common types of lines, dimeter, trimeter (triṣṭubh), and trimeter (jagatī) follow, with heavy and light syllable scansion given below the text. We have provided two examples each for the trimeter lines, one with 4-syllable opening and 3-syllable break, one with 5-syllable opening and 2-syllable break.

Dimeter:

8-syllable dimeter

I.1.1a *agním īḷe puróhitam*

– ˘ – – ˘ – ˘ x

Note the iambic rhythm of the last 4 syllables.

Trimeter

Trimeter cadences:

trisṭubh – ˘ – x

jagatī: – ˘ – ˘ x

Note that 12-syllable jagatī can be seen as a 1-syllable extension of triṣṭubh, with an extra light syllable inserted right before the end, resulting in a 5-syllable cadence. The structure of the rest of the line is the same.

11-syllable trimeter: triṣṭubh—opening of 4

I.32.1a *índrasya nú vīríyāṇi prá vocam*

– – ˘ ˘ | – ˘ – – ˘ – x

The obligatory caesura (word break) after the opening is marked by a slash; the break is three syllables (– ˘ –) and is *not* followed by a caesura, while the cadence is the proper triṣṭubh one (– ˘ – x).

11-syllable trimeter: triṣṭubh—opening of 5

I.32.1b *yā́ni cakā́ra prathamā́ni vajrī́*

– ˘ ˘ – – | ˘ ˘ – ˘ – x

Note that the rhythms of the openings of the two triṣṭubh lines are quite distinct. Here the break is two syllables (˘ ˘), and the cadence the same as the previous line.

12-syllable trimeter: jagatī—opening of 4

II.1.16b *ágne rātím upasr̥jánti sūráyaḥ*

– – – ˘ | ˘ ˘ ˘ – ˘ – ˘ x

The opening is different from either of the triṣṭubh openings above; the break is three shorts (˘ ˘ ˘), unlike the short/long/short (– ˘ –) three-syllable break of the quoted triṣṭubh line. The cadence is the standard jagatī 5-syllable one (– ˘ – ˘ x).

12-syllable trimeter: jagatī—opening of 5

II.1.16c *asmā́ñ ca tā́ṃś ca prá hí néṣi vásya ā́*

– – ˘ – – | ˘ ˘ – ˘ – ˘ x

Yet another opening pattern. The two-syllable (˘ ˘) break is identical to that of the triṣṭubh with opening of 5, as shorter breaks have fewer possible patterns. The cadence is the standard jagatī cadence. Note that though there happens to be a word break between break and cadence in this line, it is not an obligatory one, and in fact none of the other three trimeter lines quoted shows a word break at this position.

The *lines* just described are called *pāda*s. A R̥gvedic *verse* (*r̥c*) consists of a group of pādas, generally three or four, though meters with fewer than three pādas or more than four are also found. There is another significant division within the verse: the hemistich or half-verse. In four-pāda verses this consists of two two-pāda units; in three-pāda verse, the first two pādas are considered the hemistich, with a single pāda following.

The most common dimeter meter is *gāyatrī*; a gāyatrī verse consists of three 8-syllable pādas. Approximately one-quarter of the R̥gveda is composed in this meter. The other common dimeter meter is anuṣṭubh, which contains four such 8-syllable lines and is the ancestor of the Epic and Classical śloka mentioned previously. The most common trimeter meter, in fact the most common meter in the R̥gveda, is triṣṭubh, which accounts for approximately 40 percent of the text. It normally consists of four 11-syllable pādas, while jagatī likewise consists of four pādas, though of 12 syllables each. *Jagatī* is the third most common meter, after triṣṭubh and gāyatrī. Besides these mono-type meters, some hymns are composed in what are referred to in general as "mixed-lyric meters," whose verses consist of combinations of 8- and 12-syllable pādas. There are a number of different combinations, each with a different name.

Relevance of meter for the general reader

The details just given are relevant not only to professional metricians but also to the general reader, for the rhetoric and semantic structure of the Ṛgveda are strongly driven and shaped by meter. Syntactic constituents often occupy single pādas, for example, and metrical boundaries (the beginning and end of the line, as well as the position immediately after the caesura) are favored sites for positioning emphatic elements. The hemistich is a particularly salient unit, dividing the verse into syntactic and semantic halves. It is almost always possible, and generally desirable, to render the hemistich division in English—that is, to translate the first half and the second half of the verse as separate units. It is remarkable how faithful it is possible to be to the Sanskrit hemistichs without significantly compromising the English. (The hemistich division is less important and more often syntactically breached in gāyatrī, since the division results in uneven parts: two pādas followed by one, but even in gāyatrī the third pāda is often independent of the first two.)

The verse is the most significant unit in a Ṛgvedic hymn—hence the name Ṛg-veda, or Veda of verses (*ṛc*). It is almost always a self-contained syntactic construction, and even when that construction is not entirely independent syntactically (e.g., when it is a relative clause, dependent on a main clause in a verse following or preceding), it will be internally unified. There are almost no examples of syntactic enjambment between verses. This focus on the internal unity and syntactic independence of the verse is continued in later Sanskrit poetry, where it reaches its defining limit in so-called muktaka verses or single-verse poems.

Nonetheless, some hymns are structured into larger groupings of two to three verses, which are sometimes referred to as "strophes." The *tṛca*, or "triplet," is the most common such grouping, consisting of three verses, generally in gāyatrī, though other meters are also found. Sometimes the tṛca unit is strongly defined by shared lexicon or a shared refrain, or by parallel syntactic structures, or by a common theme; other tṛcas have only the faintest signs of unity in rhetoric or content. Quite long hymns can be built from these three-verse units, which are especially common in Maṇḍala VIII and were the special province of the Udgātar (singer) priest, as noted earlier. Many of these strophes were borrowed into the Sāmaveda, whose principal priest in classical śrauta ritual was the Udgātar and one of whose major textual sources is R̥gveda VIII. The other major strophic type is the *pragātha*, consisting of two verses in two different types of "mixed lyric" meters. The usual combination is *br̥hatī* (8 8, 12 8) and *satobr̥hatī* (12 8, 12 8). Again, pragāthas are especially common in the VIIIth Maṇḍala and frequently taken over into the Sāmaveda. Thus, the standard types of multiverse groupings tended to provide the lyric or sung portion of the ritual, as against the recited portions associated with the Hotar priest.

10

Canonical Status and the Reception of the Ṛgveda

The Ṛgveda in the śrauta tradition

The Ṛgveda was created to be a canon, a defining and authoritative collection. Those who assembled and organized the hymns intended to create a composite text that would unify the ritual and poetic traditions of the disparate clans and tribes of the Ṛgvedic period and therefore contribute to the unification of those clans and tribes themselves. This enterprise was likely carried out in stages. Developing the work of Oldenberg and Bergaigne, Witzel has plausibly suggested that the first multi-clan collection of Ṛgvedic hymns occurred within the Ṛgvedic period itself to reinforce the union of the two dominant Ṛgvedic tribes, the Pūru and Bharata (Witzel 1995a: 337–38). The core of this early collection was Ṛgveda II–VII, the Family Books of six clans of Ṛgvedic poets. Later, other collections were attached to this old core eventually to form the entire 10 maṇḍala Ṛgveda. The first and last hymns of the final collection marked the boundaries and completion of the text. The Ṛgveda's first hymn is dedicated to Agni; indeed, the Ṛgveda's first word is *agní* "fire." In this way the god of fire and fire itself begin the Ṛgveda as they do the Vedic ritual. The last hymn of the Ṛgveda echoes the first by again invoking Agni in verse 1, and then the verses that follow state the common purpose of all the priest poets of the Ṛgveda. Again, in order to represent the perfection and completion of the text, the creators

The Rigveda. Joel P. Brereton and Stephanie W. Jamison, Oxford University Press (2020). © Oxford University Press.
DOI: 10.1093/oso/9780190633363.001.0001

of the R̥gveda collected 191 hymns in the last maṇḍala to balance the 191 hymns of the first maṇḍala. When exactly the final work of consolidation and organization occurred and who carried it out are not entirely certain. But again, following Witzel's lead, we could place the "when" around 1000 BCE and identify the "who" as the Kuru rulers, who consolidated the R̥gveda as they created the first Indian state.

Following the collection of the R̥gveda, the next stage in the development of Vedic religion was the shaping of unified śrauta rites, the elaborate public rituals based on the Veda. This śrauta system consisted of three types of rituals distinguished by their principal offerings: *iṣṭi* offerings of grain cakes and butter, *paśu* or animal sacrifices, and Soma Sacrifices. These rituals enfold one another since animal sacrifices included iṣṭi rites, and Soma Sacrifices included both iṣṭi rites and animal sacrifices. As we noted above, in the period of the composition of the R̥gvedic hymns, each priestly clan practiced rites that were analogous but not identical to those of other clans, and their rites likely evolved over the generations. The creators of the śrauta rituals fused these clan rites into a system that was largely but not completely uniform (Bergaigne 1889: 7–8). With regard to its poetic recitations, the emerging śrauta tradition differed substantially from R̥gvedic rituals. As we previously observed, the liturgical recitations of the śrauta rites were not the new creations of individual poets but rather compilations of the work of several past poets. In the R̥gveda itself there are already compilations of the poetry of individual clans. So, for example, R̥gveda IX.97, a hymn to the "Self-Purifying" Soma, consists of verses from various poets of the Vasiṣṭha clan. Similarly, III.27 is a composite of the Viśvāmitras, V.28 of the Atris, and VI.16 of the Bharadvājas. The next step was the creation of hymns that combined the work of poets of different clans, and again, such compilations also appear in the R̥gveda. As mentioned earlier, IX.67, for example, consists of verses attributed to seven or eight poets of various clans and is an early attempt to create an ecumenical liturgy that united the different clan traditions (on these developments, see Proferes 2003: 8–10).

Comparable ecumenical compilations, called *śastra*s, became the norm in the śrauta tradition. These śastras are recited by the Hotar priest or by the *hotraka*s, priests associated with the Hotar. In the Agniṣṭoma, a one-day soma ritual, which in the classical Vedic tradition represents the basic form of the soma ritual, there are altogether 12 śastras distributed among the rite's three soma pressings in the morning, at midday, and in the evening. An example illustrating how the creators of the śrauta rites reconfigured Ṛgvedic verses into recitations is the first of these śastras, the Prātaranuvāka, the "Morning litany." The Kauṣītaki Brāhmaṇa, one of the two early commentarial texts of the Ṛgvedic tradition, allows different numbers of Ṛgvedic verses to be recited in the Prātaranuvāka. According to Kauṣītaki Brāhmaṇa XI.7, it may have 100 or 120 or 360 or 720 or even 1,000 verses. Following a later Kauṣītaki *prayoga* or ritual manual, Caland and Henry (1906–1907 I: 132) list the verses of the 360-verse Prātaranuvāka. In 1975 Frits Staal documented a performance of an Atirātra or Overnight ritual that continues the Agniṣṭoma to the following morning. The priests, who were followers of the Kauṣītaki tradition, recited this litany in the 360-verse form described by Caland and Henry (Staal 1983 I: 600). All the maṇḍalas of the Ṛgveda are represented in this Prātaranuvāka, except Maṇḍala IX, whose hymns were composed for a different ritual moment. But the hymns of two maṇḍalas dominate the recitation: there are 102 verses from Maṇḍala I and 71 from Maṇḍala VII. Maṇḍala I contains the work of later poets and VII, the Vasiṣṭha maṇḍala, is among the later clan collections. The selection therefore leaned toward more recent compositions and more recent poets and perhaps reflects the influence of the Vasiṣṭha clan in the formation of the Vedic ritual in the post-Ṛgvedic period. In the recitation there is an introductory verse, repeated three times, to the Waters. Then there are 155 verses to Agni, whose kindling marks the beginning of the sacrificial day, followed by 72 verses to Uṣas, the goddess Dawn, and finally by 130 verses (including the last verse, which, like the first, is repeated three times) to the Aśvins, who characteristically arrive at the rite in the early morning. Thematically, therefore, the verses chosen for this recitation are appropriate to the ritual moment, the early morning, and represent the śrauta replacement for individual hymns to Agni, Dawn, and the Aśvins in the rituals of the R̥gvedic period.

Metrical considerations also governed the selection of verses. Each of the three sections of the Prātaranuvāka recitation has verses in all of the principal meters of R̥gvedic hymns, and each section repeats the same sequence of meters. The meters are in order: gāyatrī, anuṣṭubh, triṣṭubh, br̥hatī/satobr̥hatī, uṣṇiḥ (these last being mixed-lyric meters), jagatī, and paṅkti (Śāṅkhāyana Śrautasūtra VI.4–6). The sequence of the meters thus begins with a meter of three eight-syllable lines (gāyatrī), followed by one of four eight-syllable lines (anuṣṭubh), and it ends with a meter of five eight-syllable lines. The verses in paṅkti, which conclude each section, are all from the same maṇḍala, Maṇḍala V (V.6.1–10, V.79.1–10, V.75.1–9), and all have a refrain (see Caland 1953 on Śāṅkhāyana Śrautasūtra VI.3.11). In its content the recitation does not have the thematic unity of a R̥gvedic hymn, but its repeated metrical sequence and formal organization provide coherence to the whole recitation.

Finally, among the verses of the Prātaranuvāka, there are complete R̥gvedic hymns. Each of the three deities of the Prātaranuvāka has at least two hymns of nine verses or more: R̥gveda IV.2, VIII.23, and V.6 to Agni, I.48 and V.79 to Dawn, and VIII.8, V.74, I.116, I.34, and V.75 to the Aśvins. The remaining verses, over half the total number, represent shorter selections, most commonly sets of three verses extracted from various hymns. In this we can see a shift away from the hymn as the unit of composition to individual verses and assemblages of verses.

Thus the form of the Prātaranuvāka shows the principles that shaped the ritual recitations. These included consideration of the poets and maṇḍalas from which the verses were taken, the ritual context of the recitation, the gods appropriately invoked in that context, and the meter of the verses chosen. One major difference between Ṛgvedic hymns and this recitation is that, according to Śāṅkhāyana Śrautasūtra VI.3.9, the verses are to be recited in a single tone, rather than with the carefully preserved tonal accents of the Ṛgveda itself.

Such śrauta recitations as the Prātaranuvāka also illustrate the great difference between the Ṛgveda and the other two Vedas of the śrauta tradition, the Sāmaveda and Yajurveda. The order of mantras and liturgical formulae in the Yajurveda reflects the sequence of Vedic rites, and one of the parts of the Sāmaveda gives the texts to be chanted according to the order of the liturgy. On the other hand, while the Ṛgveda is the principal source from which recitations are drawn, the organization of the text is unconnected with the sequence of śrauta rites. This situation led some early scholars to posit the existence of a ritual Ṛgveda that paralleled the other two Vedas. If there ever was such a text, it has disappeared without a trace. More likely, the retention of the Ṛgveda in an order that does not conform to its use in the śrauta rites implies that the recitation of the Ṛgveda with tonal accents, apart from its use in śrauta rites, was a valued practice from very early on. It certainly became so after the Ṛgvedic period and remains so in the present.

A story in the Mahābhārata (I.64) illustrates the place of the Ṛgveda in the early post-Vedic world. While on a hunt, a king comes upon a brahmin hermitage, an *āśrama*, a place of religious study and practice. There he encounters a very different world, a world, the text says, like that of the god Brahmā. There "the tiger among men heard *ṛc*-verses being recited word-by-word and step-by-step by foremost Ṛgvedins, while here sacrifices were stretched out" (Mbh I.64.31). The hermitage shines "with those who know the sacrifices and its ancillary disciplines" (vs. 32) and it has "experts in the Atharvaveda" (vs. 33). There are still others who are skilled both in recitation and interpretation, those who understand the dharma that governs life in the world, those who know the final goal of religious release, and those who grasp the absolute truth of things (I.64.34–37). Thus the hermitage is a place where the R̥gveda is recited and where sacrifices are carried out, and both recitation of the R̥gveda and ritual contribute to the sanctity of the place. The passage also implies the precedence of the R̥gveda. The recitation of the R̥gveda occurs first in the description of the hermitage, and the R̥gveda is the only one of the three Vedas connected with the śrauta tradition that is mentioned by name. The hermitage is not only a place belonging to those who know how to recite or how to perform sacrifices, but also a place of scholars who understand the interpretation of texts and ultimate religious goals. Even though the tradition developed various methods for the precise preservation of the R̥gveda and emphasized the exact oral performance of the Veda, these were not the only concerns of the brahmins of the hermitage. The meaning of the texts was also central to their religious effort. This is a point to which we will return, since such concern with the meaning of texts becomes part of the R̥gvedic tradition throughout its history.

R̥gvedic Schools

In the post-R̥gvedic period, the preservation, interpretation, and transmission of the R̥gveda became the responsibility of priestly schools, called *śākhā*s or "branches," which specialized in the different Vedas. These Vedic schools are defined by the set of texts that they produced or preserved and that they utilized in ritual performance. The core of this set is śruti texts, texts of "hearing," composed and originally transmitted orally, which comprise the Veda. The principal texts for each of these schools were the saṃhitās, the collections of verses, chants, and ritual formulae, arranged for continuous recitation, that provided the spoken parts of the Vedic rituals. Attached to these central collections are brāhmaṇa texts, commentaries describing the application of saṃhitā texts in ritual and other matters of ritual performance, the āraṇyakas "forest books," which teach the esoteric meaning of rites, and the upaniṣads, texts that explore the nature of things and interpret the intersections of the person, the world, and the ritual. In addition to these śruti texts, the schools produced smr̥ti or texts of "remembering." These included works outlining both the śrauta rituals and the domestic or gr̥hya rites of the Vedic tradition and other texts on grammar, phonetics, and the like deemed essential for the preservation and use of the ritual texts.

While some of these schools shared common texts, śākhā divisions normally began with different saṃhitā recensions. In the case of the Yajurveda, these were very different recensions. In this respect, the R̥gveda stands apart, since there were relatively few differences among the saṃhitās of the R̥gvedic śākhās. Among the early texts describing Vedic śākhās is the Caraṇavyūha, a work that belongs to the Yajurvedic tradition but that describes Vedic schools from other traditions as well. According to the list in two recensions of the Caraṇavyūha (see Siegling 1906: 14), there were five śākhās of the R̥gveda: the Śākala, Bāṣkala, Āśvalāyana, Śāṅkhāyana, and Māṇḍūkāyana (elsewhere called the Māṇḍūkeya or Māṇḍukeya). The list of R̥gvedic śākhās increases in other old sources. The Atharvaveda Pariśiṣṭa 49.1.6 says there are seven R̥gvedic śākhās, and Mahābhāṣya I, p. 9, l. 22 and Mahābharata XII.330.32 both claim there are 21 śākhās. Still later, the purāṇas, texts dating largely from middle of the first millennium CE to the middle of the second, mention various numbers of śākhās: 18 (a sacred number that represents completeness), 21, and 24 (Renou 1947: §15). We cannot be sure, therefore, just how many R̥gvedic śākhās there actually were in either ancient or medieval India.

There are two recensions of the R̥gveda that survived from an early period and alongside one another for an extended time and whose differing contents are described in later literature. These two recensions are linked to two of the śākhās mentioned by the

Caraṇavyūha. One is the Śākala Saṃhitā, or the Śākala Ṛgveda, the recension that is most widely known, recited, and studied. The second is the Bāṣkala Saṃhitā, for which manuscripts or oral recitations are either no longer extant or not yet discovered. Although the purāṇas date from a much later period, two of the older purāṇas, the Viṣṇu- and Vāyupurāṇas, provide a history of the transmission of the Ṛgveda through a succession of teachers. According to Viṣṇupurāṇa III 4.16–21, a teacher named Paila, having received the Ṛgveda from Vyāsa, the sage who arranged the Vedas, "divided the tree of the Ṛgveda." He gave saṃhitās to his students Indrapramati and Bāṣkala. Bāṣkala gave his collection to four of his disciples, and Indramati gave his to his son, Māṇḍūkeya, from whom it was eventually passed down to three students, including Śākalya, who in turn passed it on to five of his students. Because other purānas give other lineages (Chaubey 2009 I: 4–6), we cannot say that this is the history of the Ṛgveda, but only that this is the kind of transmission that likely occurred and that led to differences, albeit minimal ones, among Ṛgvedic recensions.

The Śākala Saṃhitā is attributed to Śākalya, one of the teachers named in the passage from the Viṣṇupurāṇa and mentioned already by Pāṇini in the mid-fourth century as a grammarian. According to the Anuvākānukramaṇī, one of the indices to the Ṛgveda, the Śākala Saṃhitā comprises 1,017 hymns. That number does not include 11 hymns that form a supplement to the Śākala text called the Vālakhilya hymns. While these Vālakhilya hymns are included in editions and translations of the Śākala Ṛgveda, normally as Ṛgveda VIII 49–59, literature on the Ṛgveda continued to recognize them as appendices to the main collection. According to Mahīdāsa, a commentator on the Caraṇavyūha, for example, the Vālakhilya hymns originally were not part of the Śākala Ṛgveda but rather belonged to the Bāṣkala tradition. Neither of the two complete Sanskrit commentaries on the Śākala Ṛgveda discusses these hymns, and they are not included in seven of the nine manuscripts used by Macdonell in his edition of the Sarvānukramaṇī. In addition to the Vālakhilya hymns, there are other collections of supplementary hymns, called khila or "appendix" hymns. Although they originated outside of the Śākala tradition, they were sometimes incorporated in it even though they were still distinguished from the core collection. For example, a Śākala Ṛgveda manuscript from Kashmir, now located in the Bhandarkar Oriental Research Institute in Pune, includes a large collection of khila hymns. That collection of khila hymns was originally edited by Scheftelowitz (1906), and with the addition of new material, it was re-edited by Kashikar and included as an adjunct to the Śākala recension of the Ṛgveda published by the Vaidika Samshodhana Mandala in Pune (Sontakke 1933–1951).

Even though we do not have manuscripts of the Bāṣkala Saṃhitā, other sources describe its contents. According to the commentary of Mahīdāsa on the Caraṇavyūha, the Bāṣkala Saṃhitā had 1,025 hymns, eight more than the core Śākala recension. These included the first seven Vālakhilya hymns, although in a different arrangement from that in the Śākala recension, and a final hymn added to the end of the collection. In addition, according to the Anuvākānukramaṇī, the Bāṣkala Saṃhitā placed the hymns of Kutsa, a poet of the first maṇḍala, in a slightly later position than where they appear in the Śākala recension. That is to say, the differences are minor and involve only the youngest parts of the Ṛgveda. Otherwise, the two core saṃhitā collections were identical.

From other sources, we can also infer the contents of another early Ṛgvedic saṃhitā, the Śaiśirīya Saṃhitā. This is the principal recension of the Ṛgvedaprātiśākhya, a late Vedic or early post-Vedic text that discusses matters concerning Ṛgvedic recitation, and the Anuvākānukramaṇī says that it also deals with the Śaiśirīya recension. On the basis of these two texts, Bronkhorst (1982) concludes that the Śaiśirīya recension did not contain the Vālakhilya hymns but did include other khila hymns, and that it may have had 15 additional verses not in the Śākala Ṛgveda. Once again, therefore, the differences between this recension and the Śākala recension were slight. The similarity of these two saṃhitās—and of all the other early saṃhitās—enabled the leveling of the R̥gvedic tradition and the general adoption of the Śākala Saṃhitā as the single R̥gveda saṃhitā.

Vedic schools were differentiated from one another not only by their core texts but also by the subsidiary texts they produced. Within the Vedic corpus, the texts second oldest to the R̥gveda, Atharvaveda, Yajurvedic recitations, and Sāmaveda are the brāhmaṇa texts, which comment on the ritual. For the R̥gveda the two extant brāhmaṇa texts are the Kauṣītaki Brāhmaṇa and the Aitareya Brāhmaṇa. It was probably the Bāṣkala śākhā that produced the Kauṣītaki Brāhmaṇa, and this śākhā may have been connected in some fashion to the Aitareya Brāhmaṇa as well. Gradually, however, despite a trail of post-R̥gvedic texts, traditions once connected to the Bāṣkala Saṃhitā adopted the Śākala Saṃhitā.

Later in the post-R̥gvedic period, there emerged two other R̥gvedic śākhās that continued to exist into the present era. These are the Āśvalāyana śākhā and the Śāṅkhāyana śākhā. The division between the two appears most clearly at the level of their śrauta and gr̥hya sūtras, the texts that lay out the ideal forms of public and domestic ritual practice. Recently, editions of an Āśvalāyana Saṃhitā (Chaubey 2009) and a Śāṅkhāyana Saṃhitā (Gautama 2012–2013) have been published. The two saṃhitās largely follow the text and order of the Śākala recension but supplement it with khila hymns and additional verses, which they have included in their core collections. The Āśvalāyana Saṃhitā, for example, accepts 212 verses that are not part of the Śākala R̥gveda or its Vālakhilya collection. Of these, 172 verses are in 15 supplementary hymns and 40 verses are attached to hymns shared with the Śākala recension. It also omits three verses from Śākala R̥gveda Maṇḍala VIII. Neither the additional hymns nor the additional verses of the Āśvalāyana and Śāṅkhāyana Saṃhitās were composed within the R̥gvedic period. Some of them are relatively old, since they occur in other Vedic or other early texts, but others reflect a religious context quite distant from the early Veda. So, for example, the Āśvalāyana Saṃhitā includes a hymn to Mahālakṣmī (V.89), the "Great Goddess Lakṣmī," which reveres Lakṣmī as the wife of the Viṣṇu. The worship of Lakṣmī and Viṣṇu developed after the Vedic period and well into the Common Era. This Saṃhitā also contains the Śrī Sūkta, which invokes the goddess Śrī as the giver of wealth. This hymn also occurs in Ṛgveda khila collections and became a very popular hymn in the post-Vedic period. On the other hand, the last hymn of the Āśvalāyana Saṃhitā includes the Mahānāmnī verses, a set of nine verses in praise of Indra, which occur in other Vedic texts. They show archaic diction and meter, but they were likely constructed in the post-Ṛgvedic period. These two saṃhitās, therefore, may represent the recitational custom of certain followers of the Āśvalāyana and Śāṅkhāyana śākhās with the addition of hymns that continued forms of Ṛgvedic composition and reflected changing religious circumstances.

This history of Ṛgvedic recensions shows that the boundaries of even a text as fundamental and as carefully preserved as the Ṛgveda can yet be soft, as the canonical boundaries of the Veda as a whole are softer still. The core of the text was stable, but around the edges late hymns appeared and disappeared. Even more importantly, the differences among these recensions establish that the Śākala Ṛgveda is substantively the Ṛgveda compiled at the beginning of the Vedic period. To be sure, the Śākala Saṃhitā shows post-Ṛgvedic innovations in phonetics and in the regularization of the sound changes that occur at the boundaries of words, but these innovations did not alter the essential content of the Ṛgveda. With the exception of some Vālakhilya hymns and a very few other verses, the Śākala collection is the core of all Ṛgvedic collections and was not subject to alteration of content or substantial addition after its collection. Finally, while the end of the Ṛgvedic period marked a shift away from the creation of new hymns for recitation in the Vedic rites, it did not mark the end of Vedic poetry. Although they may differ in language, register, and metrics from those of the Ṛgveda, late hymns in recensions of the Ṛgveda and in khila collections as well as Atharvavedic hymns are direct descendants of the practices of Ṛgvedic poetry. In addition, as we have remarked before, literary features of Ṛgvedic poetry continued in other genres of classical literature.

Transmission

We owe the preservation of the Śākala Ṛgveda to a tradition of oral transmission that insisted on absolute fidelity. This oral transmission continued even after writing gained widespread use, probably around the third century BCE. This oral transmission evolved from earlier traditions in which training Ṛgvedic poets required them to learn the earlier poetry of their own clans and perhaps also the poetry of other clans. In this way younger poets could find models in other poems, master their rhetorical turns, adopt and reconfigure their phrasing, and even respond to them. At the end of the Ṛgvedic period, however, the focus shifted from memorization in order to learn the art of poetic creation to memorization in order to preserve the poetic legacy of the past.

Throughout the ancient and medieval periods of Hindu history we find repeated assertions that the Veda should not be written. The Mahābhārata sternly declares that "they who write down the Vedas go to hell" (XIII.24.70). In the eleventh century the Muslim traveler Al-Bīrūnī reports that Hindus "do not allow the Veda to be committed to writing," and in the fourteenth century the great commentator on the Veda, Sāyaṇa, says in his introduction to the Ṛgveda that "the text of the Veda is to be learned by the method of learning from the lips of the teacher and not from a manuscript." This persistent condemnation of a written Veda likely means that there were those who did produce Vedic manuscripts, even from an early period. And at some point, there was a loosening of strictures against writing and greater acceptance of a written Ṛgveda. Note too that Sāyaṇa's comment on writing the Veda is a rejection not of Vedic manuscripts per se but of using manuscripts in teaching the Veda. Even the opposition to using manuscripts in teaching was not and is not without exception. Al-Bīrūnī also reports that "recently" a teacher named Vasukra from Kashmir had written down and explained the Veda, and later writers permitted manuscripts as a teaching aid (Scharfe 2002: 9).

Why was there such resistance to writing down the Ṛgveda? Various scholars have suggested various possibilities: it might have been to keep the Veda, whose very sounds carried power, out of the mouths of non-brahminical castes and of unworthy students, or it might have been to remain loyal to a tradition firmly in place before writing developed in India. But also, at least according to the most exacting standard, the written Ṛgveda is not really the Ṛgveda at all, just as the Qur'ān in translation is not really the Qur'ān. The true Qur'ān exists only in Arabic; the true Ṛgveda exists only in recitation. The Ṛgveda consists not only of words but also of sound, accent, and intonation, and these are neither fully represented nor communicated in writing. Another important motivation for memorizing the Ṛgveda or other Vedas was the traditional connection between a man's status as a brahmin and Vedic learning. According to the Laws of Manu, Vedic memorization is obligatory for a brahmin if he is truly a brahmin at all: Manu II.157 "Like an elephant made of wood, like a deer made of leather, is a Brahmin without Vedic learning: these three only bear the name" (Olivelle tr.).

According to the dharma tradition, initiation into Vedic learning is obligatory not just for brahmins but for all three upper classes or *varṇas*—brahmins, kṣatriyas, and vaiśyas—and this initiation makes these men *dvija* "twice-born," born once from their parents and a second time from the Veda. But for non-brahmin classes this initiation was not nearly so significant as it was for brahmins. In actual use, the term *dvija* usually referred to brahmins, even if in theory the other two upper varṇas were dvija as well. The rite of initiation into Vedic study, *upanayana*, developed during the Vedic period. In that rite the beginning of Vedic learning was marked by memorizing the Sāvitrī or Gāyatrī verse, R̥gveda III.62.10. The recitation of this verse should then become part of every initiate's daily ritual throughout his life. For many, especially for non-brahmins, Vedic learning might advance no further than learning this verse, but for others this initiation would begin many years of study, in which students might learn not only one Vedic saṃhitā but also variant forms of recitation, other Vedic texts connected to the saṃhitā, or even more than one Veda.

The methods of teaching the Vedas were established early in the tradition and were likely inherited from the training regimen of poets during the R̥gvedic period. The R̥gvedaprātiśākhya is an old work, much of it dating to the late Vedic period. In R̥gvedaprātiśākhya 15 there is a vivid description of the method of teaching the R̥gveda. Sitting on the teacher's right and first touching the teacher's feet, the student or students invite him to teach, saying, "Recite, sir!" The teacher responds with the sacred syllable *oṁ*, which, the text says, should always begin the recitation. The teacher then recites a word or several words of a verse and these are repeated by the students. In this way, the students learn a set of three verses—or only two if the verses are composed in a longer meter. They are then instructed to repeat the set of verses without a break while keeping the words slightly separate or inserting the word *iti* "thus" after certain short verbal particles, which might otherwise become lost. Sixty of these sets of verses make up one *adhyāya* or "lesson," which therefore consists of at least 120 and as many as 180 verses. Two thousand years later, based on his visits to Vedic schools in various parts of India, Parameswara Aithal (1993: 11–12) described similar instruction among Vedic reciters. He reported that young students sit in front of the teacher and the teaching begins with the mantra *hariḥ oṁ*, thus adding an invocation to the god Viṣṇu to the syllable *oṁ*. The teacher first recites a verse first pāda by pāda, that is, line by line. The students repeat each pāda three times after the teacher, and the teacher repeats this pāda-by-pāda recitation 12 times. The teacher follows the same method in reciting the verse half-verse by half-verse, and finally as a complete verse. In this way, students repeat a verse of three pādas altogether 108 times, which itself is a sacred number.

In learning the Ṛgveda, students might not study just one form of recitation but one or more others. The most familiar form of the text of the Ṛgveda is the *saṃhitā* or "continuous" form, the expected word-by-word connected reading. In this form, as they would be in speech, the endings of words are altered depending on the initial sounds of their following words (the sandhi discussed previously). The Śākala tradition holds that their first teacher Śākalya developed both the *saṃhitāpāṭha*, the "continuous recitation," and also the *padapāṭha*, the "word recitation." In this latter method, the reciter also speaks the words in sequence, as in the saṃhitā recitation, but pronounces them individually without altering the endings. In another form of recitation, the *kramapāṭha* or "stepwise recitation," the reciter divides words into pairs, repeating the second word in one pair as the first word in the next. That is, if we use letters to designate words, the recitation took the form a-b, b-c, c-d, d-e, and so forth. A still more advanced form of recitation was the *jaṭāpāṭha* "the matted-hair recitation," which wove words back and forth: a-b, b-a, a-b, b-c, c-b, b-c, etc. And even more intricate is the *ghanapāṭha* the "dense recitation," which further extends the word reversals: a-b, b-a, a-b-c, c-b-a, a-b-c. This recitation of the first three words of a verse is then followed by a recitation of the second, third, and fourth words following the same pattern: b-c, c-b, b-c-d, d-c-b, b-c-d, and so forth. And there are other even more intricate forms of recitation. The formation and reformation of the words in these methods of recitation guaranteed the accuracy of transmission, and the reciter who could learn difficult forms of recitation earned great prestige.

The mastery of even one of these forms of recitation requires years of dedicated practice. According to Staal (1961: 40), students in the Ṛgvedin Nambudiri tradition of Kerala begin around eight years old and take up to six years to memorize the Ṛgveda Saṃhitā. Traditionally, students should then learn another or other forms of advanced recitation. Paraswara Aithal (1993: 12) reported "Where there is a regular and complete recitation of the Veda, with the modified forms of *pada, krama*, etc., the course extends to more than eight years, with ten to twelve hours of learning each day." (For further illustrations of contemporary Vedic training, see Knipe 2015, especially chapters 2 and 4.) And beyond the core text of their traditions, students should also memorize other ancillary texts of their śākhā, including brāhmaṇa texts. In the ancient period, students likely spent even more years in study than they may now, since unlike contemporary forms of Vedic learning, in the ancient period instruction was seasonal, not year-round. In the early periods of Vedic transmission, this instruction was typically given at home, from father to son. This is a tradition that goes back to the Ṛgveda itself. Ṛgveda VII.103 describes frogs as they emerge with the coming of the rainy season and compares the sounds that frogs make to the recitations of priests: VII.103.3 "When it has rained on them, who are yearning and thirsting, when the rainy season has come, saying *akhkhala* like a son to a father, one goes up close to the other who is speaking." The poet here puns *akhkhala,* the sound of a frog, on the word *akṣara* "syllable," referring to the syllables that a father recites to his son and his son recites back to his father (Thieme 1954).

This tradition of learning the Vedic texts at home has not been lost even now (Knipe 1997: 312), but from early in the Vedic tradition, training in the Veda also took place outside the home. Early texts describe how students would come to the houses of Vedic teachers to live with them, to serve them, and to learn the Veda from them, and this mode of teaching at the place of the teacher too has continued into the modern period. Various kinds of religious institutions carried on Vedic instruction. As we saw in the Mahābhārata, there were āśramas, communities of brahmins that performed Vedic recitation and ritual. From the beginning of the Common Era, we hear of royal support for *agrahāra*s, brahmin settlements or brahmin areas within larger settlements. Individual teachers within these communities earned royal donations by transmitting the Vedic tradition. Kings and wealthy temples might also establish Vedic colleges, which provided tuition, room, and board for students of the Veda. Scharfe (2002: 180–181) cites two eleventh-century inscriptions from South India that illustrate the size and scope that these colleges might have. One inscription records the endowment of a Vedic college at Eṇṇāyiram, south of Chennai in Tamilnadu. This endowment supported 240 students and 15 teachers. There were to be 75 students and three teachers of the Ṛgveda, 75 students of the Black Yajurveda and 20 students of the White Yajurveda, 40 students of the Sāmaveda (20 for each of the two branches taught there), 10 students of the Atharvaveda, 10 students of the Baudhāyana sūtras, which laid out the rituals for the Black Yajurveda tradition, and there were other seats for students of ancillary Vedic disciplines. The second inscription describes a smaller college established at the Veṅkateś Perumāḷ, a Viṣṇu temple also in Tamilnadu. The temple supported 60 students with 10 seats for those studying the Ṛgveda, 10 seats for the Yajurveda, 20 for grammar, 10 for the Vaiṣṇava Pāñcarātra ritual and theological system, three for Śaiva Āgama texts, and seven seats for ascetics. The latter college was both much smaller and also broader in scope, encompassing both Vedic study and study of religious traditions that developed after the Vedic period. The prominence of the Ṛgveda, especially in this geographic area in which the Taittirīya śākhā of the Black Yajurveda was dominant, illustrates its continued prestige among the Vedas. Government funding and the support of wealthy temples have allowed such Vedic schools also to survive into the present.

Recitation of verses from the Ṛgveda is an essential part of the śrauta sacrificial tradition, but the recitation of the Ṛgveda itself can also be a ritual performance. This may be a private ritual, such as the practice of *svādhyāya*, literally "self-study" but meaning an individual's private recitation. Manu calls such recitation a form of *tapas* or "ascetic toil": Manu II.167 "When a twice-born, even while wearing a garland, performs his Vedic recitation every day according to his ability, he is surely practising the fiercest ascetic toil down to the very tips of his nails" (Olivelle tr.; cf. also Taittirīya Āraṇyaka II.14.2 and Śatapatha Brāhmaṇa XI.5.7.4). An ascetic would not be indulging himself by "wearing a garland," but a householder might, and therefore this passage guarantees that the devoted householder can earn the same religious reward through his Vedic recitation as an ascetic can through his fierce austerities. Not only is Vedic recitation a form of ritual performance, but it can even replace the elaborate rituals of the śrauta tradition: Śatapatha Brāhmaṇa XI.5.7.3 "Now, whatever portion of Vedic poetry [*chándas*] he recites as his self-study [*svādhyāyá*], by just that as his sacrificial rite, he makes a sacrificial offering—he who, knowing thus, recites his self-study." And likewise, the Āśvalāyana Gr̥hyasūtra I.1.5 first quotes R̥gveda VI.16.47 "Here to you, Agni, we bring with a verse an oblation fashioned by our heart: let the oxen, bulls, and mated cows be yours," and then interprets the verse to mean that recitations are like offerings of "oxen, bulls, and mated cows." The text goes on to say that the verses recited in svādhyāya are likewise equivalent to sacrificial offerings to the gods. This tradition of understanding recitation of the Veda to be a ritual in and of itself and even to be a replacement for śrauta rites was thus already well-established at an early period.

In addition to private forms, R̥gvedic recitation and the recitation of other Vedas have been part of public rituals as well. In South India, temples support brahmins' recitations of their Vedas both as part of the daily temple ritual and on special religious occasions (Knipe 1997: 319). Such temple-sponsored recitation is not a recent innovation. A fourteenth-century inscription from Siṃhāchalam temple in Andhra Pradesh records payment from the temple treasury for the recitation of the Puruṣa Sūkta, R̥gveda X.90, in the temple (Reddy 1991: 83). Likewise, in his survey of Vedic study and recitation, Raghavan (1962: 22) says that "even the institution of chanting of Vedas behind the processional deities taken out during festivals goes back to ancient times," citing an eleventh-century inscription of Rājādhirāja I, a ruler of the Chola Empire. Raghavan (p. 23) goes on to say that in North India "the practice is getting wide-spread of setting Vedic hymns to modern Hindustani tunes and getting them sung by girls as prayer-songs at the opening of public functions." Not one to take kindly to such unorthodox innovation, Raghavan comments that this development "is undesirable from every point of view." Whether Raghavan's dissatisfaction with such innovation is justified or not, such reapplication of Vedic hymns does attest to an ongoing interest in public Vedic recitation.

Interpretation

While the Hindu tradition has evolved during the three millennia since the close of the Ṛgvedic period, the tradition of Vedic recitation and ritual practice has continued, even though it has weakened in the modern era. The Vedic schools and the Mīmāṃsā tradition, which provides the most influential interpretation and explanation of Vedic ritual, placed primary importance on the meticulously correct recitation of the text. Accordingly, Paraswara Aithal (1993: 11) comments that in the tradition the "mere recitation of the Vedic hymns in the proper way is believed to produce a spiritual effect irrespective of understanding the meaning of the texts recited." But from the Vedic period onward, there has also been a tradition of Ṛgvedic exegesis that was concerned with the meaning of the text. We have mentioned the Ṛgveda Padapāṭha as a form of Ṛgvedic recitation, but the Padapāṭha was also an early commentary on the text, for in separating words and constituents of compounds, it provided an implicit grammatical analysis of the text. The Ṛgvedic brāhmaṇas, which attach to the saṃhitā, discuss the ritual use of

Ṛgvedic texts, often drawing the justification for the ritual application of the verses from the verses themselves and elaborating on the verses through narratives (*ākhyānas*) that tell how they came to be. In the manner of later commentaries, they will occasionally explain the meaning of mantras, phrase by phrase (Chaubey 1983: 87). While the need for accurate transmission of the Ṛgveda gave rise to ancillary disciplines such as phonetics, grammar, and metrics, alongside these there were texts pointedly devoted to the study of the meaning of the Ṛgveda. These are represented first by a number of texts that generally date from the latter part of the first millennium BCE. An early work on the lexicon of the Ṛgveda is the Nighaṇṭu. Its first three chapters contain groups of synonyms, the fourth a study of difficult words, and the last a glossary of Vedic deities. Utilizing the Nighaṇṭu, around the third century BCE Yāska composed the Nirukta, a treatise on Vedic words and their etymologies.

These works show that already before the Common Era the archaic language of the Ṛgveda was no longer fully understood. But they also demonstrate that there were scholarly efforts to reconstruct and thereby preserve the meaning of the Ṛgveda. These efforts had been going on for some time before Yāska, who refers to other schools of interpretation and other authorities on etymology. The excellent intentions of Yāska's work were not always matched by its results. Yāska trusted that etymology could explain more than it can, utilized some implausible principles of etymological analysis, and offered some impossible etymologies. Over-reliant on etymology though Yāska was, it is also true that in both traditional and contemporary scholarship, etymological analysis remains an important means for interpreting Ṛgvedic words and deities. A different interpretative approach is represented by another early work, the Bṛhaddevatā, roughly "The Enlarged (Index) of Divinity," which builds on the *anukramaṇī* or indexical literature. This work develops narrative references in Ṛgvedic verses and provides the stories behind the hymns. Its narratives are not a direct inheritance from the Ṛgvedic period, however, but rather draw on later sources. The Bṛhaddevatā therefore represents a remolding of the Ṛgvedic narrative tradition.

Although they approximate commentaries, these texts do not systematically explain Ṛgvedic verses and hymns. Dating to the seventh century CE, the earliest known full commentary is the Ṛgarthāgamasaṃhṛti, approximately "The Consolidation of the Traditions of the Meanings of the Ṛk-verses," a title implying that it stands within a tradition of Vedic interpretation. Only parts of the work are extant, most of which are by a scholar named Skandasvāmin. The surviving parts of his work are the commentary on almost all of the first maṇḍala (I.1–56.1, I.62–121), on five hymns from fifth maṇḍala (V.57–61), and on the last two-thirds of the sixth maṇḍala (VI.29–75.6). In his commentary Skandasvāmin gives an interpretation of every hymn and moves through the text explaining it verse by verse and word by word. A later commentator, Veṅkatamādhava, says that Skandasvāmin wrote the commentary in collaboration with two other scholars, Udgītha and Nārāyaṇa. Nothing of the latter's work survives, but we have part of Udgītha's commentary on Maṇḍala X and references to a commentary by him on Maṇḍala VIII. Only two complete premodern Sanskrit commentaries on the Ṛgveda are extant: one by this same Veṅkatamādhava (twelfth century) and the other by Sāyaṇa (fourteenth century). The latter became far and away the most influential and authoritative commentary in the traditional interpretation of the Ṛgveda. Influenced by the Mīmāṁsā, Sāyaṇa discusses the ritual application of the Ṛgveda and gives central place to the exegesis of verses by means of the ritual. Sāyaṇa also comments on issues of grammar and accent, cites Yāska's discussions of etymology, and further extends the Bṛhaddevatā's narrative explanations. That is to say, Sāyaṇa's commentary, while an original and focused work, draws on the long tradition of exegesis that preceded it.

In addition to Sanskrit commentaries anchored in the Vedic or Mīmāṁsā tradition, there are also commentarial appropriations of the Ṛgveda, often for sectarian purposes. They do not tell us much about the Ṛgveda itself, but they do attest to the prestige of the Ṛgveda and to the continued interest in what the Ṛgvedic verses could mean or could be made to mean. So, for example, a work of the seventeenth century by the scholar Nīlakaṇṭha Caturdhara interprets 47 Vedic verses as a *mahātmya* or "glorification" of Banaras and asserts that the whole of the Ṛgveda is actually in praise of the city (Minkowski 2002). Along similar lines, Nīlakaṇṭha also wrote two works called the Mantrarāmāyaṇa, "The Rāmāyaṇa in the (Ṛgvedic) Mantras," and the Mantrabhāgavata, "The Story of the Bhāgavata Purāṇa in the (Ṛgvedic) Mantras." In the first he comments on 157 Ṛgvedic verses, primarily from Maṇḍalas IX and X, to show that they refer to the epic story of Rāma, and in the second he reads 109 verses, mainly from Maṇḍalas I and III, to reveal the story of Kṛṣṇa (Minkowski n.d.). The basic principle behind Nīlakaṇṭha's interpretations, a principle that he shares with other interpreters of the Ṛgveda, is that Vedic verses have multiple meanings on various levels. They can refer to the Vedic ritual or gods, as Sāyaṇa understands them, but simultaneously they can also refer to the sacred traditions explicitly revealed in the later epic and purāṇic texts. This principle of the multiplicity of meaning in the Ṛgveda goes back at least as far as Yāska, who interpreted verses as praising both gods and the self and who based his different readings on multiple interpretations of the same Ṛgvedic word.

Also reaching back to Yāska's time was a theory that the mantras of the Ṛgveda are without meaning, *anarthaka*. In this view, their value rests only in their recitation and in the effects that recitation and ritual could bring about. Yāska rejects this view, and after him, in the introduction to his Ṛgvedic commentary, Sāyaṇa offers a vigorous and extended defense of the meaningfulness of the mantras. It is not clear how influential were the ideas that Yāska and Sāyaṇa rejected, but what is clear is that the mainstream of Vedic interpretation did find the mantras meaningful and did expend considerable effort in discovering their meanings. Learning to recite the Ṛgveda properly was the first step and for many the only step in its traditional Vedic study, but the ideal was to understand the meaning of the texts. At one point in the Mahābhārata Kuntī criticizes her son King Yudhiṣṭhira for sticking to a rigid course of action and for failing to see the complex possibilities of the present situation. She compares him to a Vedic scholar who only knows how to recite the text and nothing more: Mbh V.300.6 "O king, your understanding, crushed by rote repetition, like that of a simple-minded, uninspired Vedic scholar, sees only a single rule [*dharma*]." A true leader and a true scholar, she believes, should be better than that and should know more that the rote recitation of texts.

Reception

The reception of the Ṛgveda was not confined to the continuing traditions of Vedic śrauta ritual and Vedic recitation, as the recitation of the Ṛgveda in temple rituals already illustrates. In particular, the Gāyatrī, or Sāvitrī, verse, Ṛgveda III.62.10, taught during the rite of initiation into the study of the Veda, has achieved outsized significance in the daily rituals of many brahmins. It is recited multiple times in the *saṃdhyā* or "junction" rite, which, according to its earliest descriptions (e.g., in Ṣaḍviṃśa Brāhmaṇa IV.5 and Taittirīya Āraṇyaka II.2), marked the morning and evening twilight. Also, while a brahmin should recite different verses each day, recitation of the Gāyatrī could meet the minimal requirement for the practice of svādhyāya "self-study" of the Veda. For these reasons the Gāyatrī has become the most familiar verse of the Ṛgveda. The original Gāyatrī is *tát savitúr váreṇ(i)yam, bhárgo devásya dhīmahi / dhíyo yó naḥ pracodáyāt*, which in the Ṛgvedic period meant "Might we make our own that desirable effulgence of god Savitar, who will spur on our insights." Later tradition, however, reinterpreted the verb *dhīmahi* "might we make our own" as "we contemplate" or "we meditate on," reflecting the increasing presence of contemplative practices within the Hindu tradition and the loss of the verbal category to which the form originally belonged. But the Gāyatrī was adapted to the changing religious context not only through reinterpretation but also through re-composition. In these variant forms the Gāyatrī verse was directed toward different deities and divine powers. For example, in Maitrāyaṇī Saṃhitā II.9.1 (119:7–120:15) there are 11 variations on the Gāyatrī, which are dedicated to the gods Rudra, Gaurī, Skanda, Gaṇeśa, Brahmā, Viṣṇu, Bhānu (the Sun), Candra (the Moon), Agni, Dhyāna (Thought), and Sṛṣṭi (Creation). As an example, the Gāyatrī for Rudra is *tác púruṣāya vidmahe, mahādevā́ya dhīmahi / tán no rudráḥ pracodáyāt* "We know this [mantra, dedicated] to the cosmic Man, we contemplate it to the Great God: Rudra will spur this on for us." This verse has become a popular mantra for Śiva, who is identified with the Vedic god Rudra. The same structure we find in this variant is repeated in all 11 mantras and elsewhere as well, as for example in Taittirīya Āraṇyaka X.1, which has a Gāyatrī for the elephant-headed god Gaṇeśa: *tát púruṣāya vidmahe, vakrátuṇḍāya dhīmahi / tán no dántiḥ pracodáyāt* "We know this [mantra, dedicated] to the cosmic Man, we contemplate it to him with the curved trunk: the tusked one will spur this on for us." We should mention that the first lines of both the Rudra and Gaṇeśa mantras are normally interpreted somewhat differently from the translations given here, closer to "We know the Man, we contemplate the Great God . . . " and "We know the Man, we contemplate the one with curved trunk . . . " Madhav Deshpande (pers. comm.) suggested that these later Gāyatrīs take the basic elements of the Ṛgvedic Gāyatrī—*tát . . . dhīmahi . . . naḥ pracodáyāt*—and insert divine epithets and names within this frame. As such, these mantras may not be grammatical or translatable in the normal way. Such versions of the Gāyatrī are late additions to Vedic texts, but their presence in these texts at all speaks again to the effort to embed later devotional worship within the Veda and to connect it to the Ṛgvedic tradition.

In other ways the Gāyatrī provided a means to embed later traditions in the Veda. For example, the Sanskrit Rāmāyaṇa of Vālmīki tells the story of the god-king Rāma, whom his later worshippers regarded as an incarnation of Viṣṇu. Although Viṣṇu appears in the Ṛgveda, albeit marginally, Rāma does not. But the Gāyatrī, here diffused rather than remolded, offered a way of conjoining the story of Rāma to the Ṛgveda by means of a text called the Gāyatrī Rāmāyaṇa. This Gāyatrī Rāmāyaṇa comprises 24 verses extracted from the Rāmāyaṇa of Vālmīki that follow the order of the Rāmāyaṇa narrative. The first syllable of each of the 24 verses corresponds to the beginning of each of the 24 syllables of the Gāyatrī. The verses of the Gāyatrī Rāmāyaṇa extend from the first verse of the Rāmāyaṇa, which introduces the poet Vālmīki, to a verse from the last book—Rāmāyaṇa VII.58.1 in the critical edition—which speaks of the birth of the Rāma's two sons. All the books of the Rāmāyaṇa are represented in the verses of the Gāyatrī Rāmāyaṇa, which trace the story of the Rāmāyaṇa. A tradition comparable to the Gāyatrī Rāmāyaṇa holds that the first syllable of every one-thousandth verse of the Rāmāyaṇa is a syllable of the Gāyatrī, and since there are supposed to be 24,000 verses in the Rāmāyaṇa and there are 24 syllables in the Gāyatrī, the Gāyatrī comprehends the whole of the Rāmāyaṇa. Linking the Gāyatrī and the Rāmāyaṇa in these ways envisions both the Gāyatrī as the seed of the Rāmāyaṇa and Gāyatrī recitation as the recitation of the essence of the Rāmāyaṇa. The Gāyatrī thus functions to recreate the Rāmāyaṇa as a Vedic text.

Other Ṛgvedic verses have not been reworked in the manner of the late Gāyatrīs but have been reinterpreted or readapted. For example, the first verse in a Ṛgvedic hymn to the god Bṛhaspati is II 23.1 "We call upon you, the troop-lord of troops, the most famous poet of poets." The word *gaṇápati* "troop-lord" is another name for Gaṇeśa, in the later tradition and therefore, unsurprisingly, the verse has been repurposed as an invocation to Gaṇeśa. It is especially appropriate for this god because one of

Gaṇeśa's characteristics is his cleverness, and the end of the verse praises "Gaṇapati" as a poet and sage. Another readapted verse is VII.59.12 "We sacrifice to Tryambaka the fragrant, increaser of prosperity. Like a cucumber from its stem, might I be freed from death, not from deathlessness." This is a verse to Rudra, who bears the epithet Tryambaka, and therefore to Śiva. It was likely composed for use in the Sākamedha rite, a Vedic seasonal ritual celebrated in the autumn, but it has become the Mr̥tyuñjaya mantra, the mantra in honor of Śiva as the god "conquering death." In thus extracting R̥gvedic verses, the later tradition continues to root itself in the R̥gveda.

In the Gāyatrīs to Gaṇeśa and to Rudra Śiva, these gods are revered as the *púruṣa*, the "Man." The reference to the "Man" goes back to another R̥gvedic hymn, X.90, which honors the primal or cosmic "Man," whose parts became the four varṇas; from whom were born the Sun, the Moon, Indra, Agni, and Vāyu the Wind; and out of whom came heaven, the midspace, and the earth, the elements of the sacrifice, and sacrificial animals. That is, the Man is the being that gave rise to the world. Implied in the R̥gvedic hymn is that the Man is the Vedic sacrifice. Therefore this hymn interprets the Vedic sacrifice to be the ultimate creative power, an interpretation developed especially in Śatapatha Brāhmaṇa X in connection with the Agnicayana rite, a Soma Sacrifice that features the construction of a brick altar forming the body of the sacrifice. The entire hymn to Puruṣa was recomposed in various versions, sometimes with verses in a different order, sometimes with verses added, and in these various versions it appears in all four Vedas. In the post-Vedic period, the hymn spawned widely accepted cosmological concepts that inscribed the form of the world onto the body of a person. Before rehearsing such a philosophic discussion of the *puruṣa* as the ultimate principle, the Mahābhārata states the special role of this hymn: "This Hymn of the Puruṣa is in all the Vedas, o descendant of Pr̥thu; it is known as the truth and the real, reflected upon by the lion of sages" (Mbh XII.338.5).

Like the Gāyatrī, the Puruṣa hymn also became part of the devotional tradition. One point of entry was its putative author. The Anukramaṇī identifies Nārāyaṇa as the poet of the hymn, and Śātapatha Brāhmaṇa XIII.6.2.12 refers to Ṛgveda X.90 as the Puruṣa Nārāyaṇa hymn. Since Nārāyaṇa became a name of the god Viṣṇu, therefore the hymn became a part of the worship of Viṣṇu, both as the poet and as the subject of the hymn. The Ṛgvidhāna, much of which concerns the use of Ṛgvedic mantras in domestic rituals for individual, personal ends, also lays out the ritual for the worship of Viṣṇu in III.149–85. The recitation of X.90 is one of the offerings to Viṣṇu, and in reciting it the worshipper reveres everything that has come from Viṣṇu, who is the Puruṣa: Ṛgvidhāna III.153 "Who would offer flowers or water together with the Puruṣa Hymn, by him is revered this whole world, both moving and unmoving." Later, the Ṛgvidhāna opens a section on the practices of meditation and yoga with another reference to the Ṛgveda X 90: III.186 "The Hymn of the Puruṣa, of Hari, leading to heaven, leading to wealth, creating fame—this is the merit-winning knowledge of the self, this is the highest knowledge of yoga." That is, the hymn reveals not only the nature of the world but also the nature of the self. Ṛgveda X.90 is not the only example of a Ṛgvedic hymn that continued to be cited in philosophic, meditative, and devotional literature—Ṛgveda X.129 is another—but more decisively than any other hymn, it demonstrates the Ṛgveda's continuing religious role beyond its ritual recitation.

Publication

For much of its history, the text of the Ṛgveda was preserved within brahminical communities. When the West encountered Sanskrit literature beginning in the late eighteenth century, the Ṛgveda was not among the first works to attract European attention. It was not until almost the middle of the nineteenth century that manuscripts of the Ṛgveda began to arrive in Europe, particularly in London and Paris. A German Indologist, Friedrich Rosen, began an edition of the Ṛgveda, but his first and only publication was the first aṣṭaka of the Ṛgveda, Ṛgveda I.1–121, which appeared in 1838. The name most associated with the Western publication of the Ṛgveda is that of F. Max Müller, who set out to publish not only the text of the Ṛgveda in *devanāgarī*, the dominant script of northern India, but also to accompany it with Sāyaṇa's commentary. It was a massive undertaking, which was sponsored by the East India Company as a public relations effort. The six volumes of Müller's Ṛgveda appeared over the course of 25 years, from 1849 to 1874. And by the time it was complete, Müller's edition was not the first European publication of the Ṛgveda. Theodor Aufrecht, who also worked on Müller's edition, published his first edition of the Ṛgveda in 1861–1863 and a second, revised edition in 1877. But Aufrecht's edition was romanized and without Sāyaṇa's commentary, and while it gained significant attention in Europe, it did not in India. Müller's edition, on the other hand, created a sensation in India. There had been resistance from orthodox brahmins to the dissemination of manuscripts of the Ṛgveda to Europe and then to the printing of the Ṛgveda, and Müller's edition encountered efforts to ban it. There were claims that Müller's Ṛgveda was the product of fraud and pollution, written by a *mleccha*, a despised foreigner, in cow's blood (Alsdorf 1962: 306). But to others the printed edition, which would make the Ṛgveda more widely accessible, known, and appreciated, was reason for celebration. Within such circles, Max Müller received the Sanskritized name Mokṣa Mūla "Root of Salvation" for the blessing constituted by his work.

One result of Müller's edition of the Ṛgveda was that the Ṛgveda played a role in Indian religious and social reform movements of the nineteenth century. At that time the contemporary culture and religion of India had been subject to harsh criticism by some British writers, who characterized India and Hinduism as decadent. They claimed that the religion was infested with superstition, that it fostered weakness, and that it propped up a hopelessly fragmented society. Why else, the argument went, would Hindu India have fallen to Muslim invaders, who, having achieved their own decadence, had now given way to British rulers? Of course, when deployed by British imperial interests, such criticism was entirely self-serving. To be sure—not differently from every other nineteenth-century society—India in the nineteenth century no doubt needed reform. The combination of British rhetoric and Indian reality encouraged various movements within India to address the situation. One such movement was represented by the Arya Samaj, a society to bring about a reformed Hinduism, which was founded by Dayanand Sarasvati in 1876. Dayanand accepted that Hinduism did need to be reformed and that it had fallen away from its roots. And where were its roots? In the Vedas, he said, and more especially in the R̥gveda. Dayanand aspired to return to the R̥gveda to recover India's lost tradition and thereby to make India great once more. The completion of Müller's R̥gveda shortly before the founding of the Arya Samaj and the access it gave to the R̥gveda contributed to Dayanand's call for people to return to the R̥gveda for their religious and social inspiration.

Meanwhile, the R̥gveda entered the Western intellectual tradition in the wake of Müller's publication of the text. The discovery that Sanskrit belonged to the same language family as ancient Greek and Latin meant that the R̥gveda, as the oldest work in Sanskrit, might also reflect the ancient roots of the European peoples as well as of the Indic peoples. Müller himself saw the origins of religion in primitive awe before the beauty and power of nature, an awe that he believed was reflected in the hymns of the R̥gveda. This view of the R̥gveda seemed to find confirmation in the Indic tradition itself, since later literature rationalized the pantheon of the R̥gveda by assigning its gods to different aspects and forces of nature. This understanding of the R̥gveda was misbegotten from the beginning. There is nothing naïve in the R̥gveda, nothing in the R̥gveda that suggests the birth of religion or poetry. The darker side of the belief in the Ṛgveda as revelatory of ancient Indo-European religion was its appropriation within Nazi ideology, which promoted the twisted fantasy that the people of the Ṛgveda, the Āryas, constituted a "pure" race and that the Ṛgveda represented a "pure" strand of religion.

Text and Translation

Ṛgvedic scholarship in North America, Europe, and both South and East Asia has significantly advanced since the mid-nineteenth century. While much remains to be done, this scholarship has reached an appreciation for the complexity of Ṛgvedic poetry, ritual, religion, history, and society. The foundation of this research remains the text of the Ṛgveda since there is no other direct evidence for the period of the Ṛgveda. In the twentieth century the Ṛgveda and Sāyaṇa's commentary were published again under the editorship of N. S. Sontakke (1933–1951), together with the Padapāṭha, an edition that has superseded Müller's Ṛgveda. More recent is publication of a metrically restored version of the Ṛgveda text by Barend A. van Nooten and Gary B. Holland (1994). The Śākala recension applied post-Ṛgvedic phonetic rules in its Ṛgvedic recitations and in the writing conventions of its Ṛgvedic manuscripts. In doing so, it no longer represented the meter in which Ṛgvedic hymns were composed. The van Nooten and Holland edition attempts to present the text of the Ṛgveda in the metrical form that reflects its original composition.

The uniformity and reliability of the text of the Ṛgveda cannot be said of its translations, which vary considerably. For much of the last century the standard scholarly translation was that of Karl Friedrich Geldner into German. This translation was published in full only in 1951 but was complete in the 1920s and partially published then. Louis Renou (1955–1969) was able to finish most of a French translation of the Ṛgveda, in a series of thematic publications under the general title *Études védiques et pāṇinéennes*, organized by the divinity addressed rather than the order of the Ṛgvedic text. But he left undone substantial parts, notably the Indra and Aśvin hymns, and the later publications are rather sketchy. T. Ya. Elizarenkova (1989–1999) completed a Russian translation of the text. Currently in preparation is a new German translation of the Ṛgveda under the direction of Michael Witzel and Toshifumi Gotō. The first two volumes of the Witzel-Gotō translation have appeared: the first (2007) covering Maṇḍalas I and II, and the second (2013) Maṇḍalas III–V.

English has not been as well served as these other European languages. This circumstance is deeply regrettable, since it has hindered access to Ṛgveda for the English-speaking world, including English-speaking readers from South Asia. Aside from anthologies, the English version that was long in general use was R. T. H. Griffith's translation, which was first published in four volumes between 1889 and 1892, then in a revised edition in 1896, and then yet again in another revised edition, this time by J. L. Shastri, in 1973. Griffith's translation has been reprinted several times since 1973 and is available online (http://www.sacred-texts.com/hin/rigveda/index.htm). Sadly, this translation really does not deserve as many rebirths as it has had. Its philology was already dated when it was first published, and the English style of the translation is cloying and almost unreadable. There were several efforts in the twentieth century to supersede Griffith's translation. From the late 1940s until the early 1960s, H. D. Velankar steadily published English translations of the Ṛgveda, which were a decided improvement over Griffith's work. These were published as independent volumes dedicated to Maṇḍalas II, V, VII, and VIII of the Ṛgveda and as collections of hymns to different deities published in the *Journal of the University of Bombay*. Partly because these translations are scattered, incomplete, and difficult of access, they have received less attention than they deserve. Also, several anthologies of Ṛgvedic hymns have appeared. In English, the most notable are those of Doniger [O'Flaherty] (1981) and Maurer (1986). In the twenty-first century, there is now a complete English translation by Stephanie Jamison and Joel Brereton (2014), also the authors of this guide. All translations from the Ṛgveda in this book are drawn from this translation.

APPENDIX

Selection of Ṛgvedic Hymns

In order to give readers a better sense of the Ṛgveda, we have included a small selection of one dozen hymns. At the beginning of this book, we mentioned that one of the problems with existing anthologies of Ṛgvedic hymns is that they under-represent the liturgical hymns that form the bulk of the text and over-represent later hymns, dialogue hymns, and hymns that have become influential and famous in the later tradition. There is a good reason that they do so: those latter hymns are more engaging for a general readership and more rewarding for those interested in post-Ṛgvedic religion and literature. Despite our admonitions about such anthologies, our selection will reflect a similar imbalance for the same reasons. Of the 12 hymns, eight come from Maṇḍalas I and X, the later books of the Ṛgveda. We have tried to present the range of hymn types within the text: there are hymns closely tied to the ritual (e.g., I.1 to Agni, I.124 to Dawn, IX.93 to Soma), dialogue hymns (X.108, 179), "speculative" or "philosophical" hymns (X.90, 129), and a hymn illustrating ritual concerns beyond the soma rite (X.159). There are two hymns describing the two greatest deeds of Indra, the foremost god of the Ṛgveda (I.32, X.108), and hymns to other prominent Ṛgvedic deities, such as the Maruts (V.58) and Varuṇa (VII.86). But our primary aim was to choose hymns that would catch the eye and interest of the reader.

We introduce each hymn by giving the name of poet to whom the Anukramaṇī attributes the hymn. As noted, the Anukramaṇī's attributions are fairly reliable, at least regarding the poetic lineage of the composer. But these hymns also illustrate the limits of that reliability. In the dialogue hymns, the Anukramaṇī attributes the composition of the individual verses to the deities or other figures meant to be speaking them and therefore gives us no information concerning the actual poet. Also, especially in Maṇḍala X, the Anukramaṇī occasionally attributes hymns to unlikely composers. For example, it attributes Ṛgveda X.76 and X.94 to snakes and as one possibility VIII.67 to fish caught in a net. In this selection, perhaps to emphasize the particular significance of these hymns, it names the deities Nārāyaṇa and Prajāpati as the poets of X.90 and X.129 respectively.

In the headnote, we also give the meter of the hymn. Most hymns are composed in a single meter, but not rarely, a verse or verses, especially an opening or concluding verse, may break the metrical pattern of the rest of the hymn. Ṛgveda VII.103, I.179, and X.90 below provide examples.

The hymns we have selected are the following:

I.1 Agni
I.124 Dawn
I.32 Indra
X.108 Saramā and the Paṇis
V.58 Maruts
IX.93 Soma
VII.86 Vasiṣṭha/Varuṇa
VII.103 Frogs
I.179 Agastya and Lopāmudrā
X.159 Against co-wives
X.90 Puruṣa
X.129 Creation

I.1 Agni

Madhuchandas Vaiśvāmitra
gāyatrī meter

The first verse of this hymn was apparently the first verse of the Ṛgveda already at the time of the composition of Ṛgveda X.20–26, a collection that also begins with the same words as does this hymn: *agním īḷe* "Agni do I invoke." The two hymns that follow, I.2–3, together name the principal deities of the three soma pressings in a day-long soma rite. This hymn to Agni, the sacrificial fire, thus forms an appropriate opening for them and for the Ṛgveda as a whole, since the sacrifice is instituted first by the kindling of fire and by invocation to the gods. Agni here, however, is not just the divine Fire of the soma rite, since in verse 7 the poet speaks of revering the fire every day. Agni includes all the ritual fires, from those of the elaborate soma rites to the fire in the home that receives the daily offerings.

Agni is present in heaven and on earth and therefore moves between the divine and human realms. Agni is a god, and yet he is also the visible fire, accessible to humans. As both god and visible fire, Agni is "placed to the fore" (vs. 1) because the principal fire of the sacrifice is placed in the east of the sacrificial area—east, toward the rising sun, is the "forward" direction—and because the god Agni leads the appearances of the other gods of the rite. As mentioned above in (pp. 54–55), Agni is a divine priest, who carries the offerings and praises of the human priests to the gods (vss. 1, 4), and he is a divine guest, who brings the other gods to the sacrifice (vss. 2, 5). Verse 3, a kind of omphalos in the middle of these opening verses (see pp. 151–53 on "ring composition and the omphalos"), proclaims the prosperity Agni brings to the one who performs sacrifice.

These opening five verses also form a unit because they create what Saussure describes as a "versified paradigm of Agni." As detailed on pp. 145–46 on "repetition," the hymn mentions the god's name in various grammatical cases as the first word in the first pāda of each of these first five verses. Displaying one of the verbal tricks R̥gvedic poets delight in, this pattern is broken by modification at the beginning of verse 6, which opens *yád aṅgá* "when truly," the latter word being a scrambling of the god's name, and ends with an epithet of Agni in the vocative, *aṅgiraḥ*, likewise a phonological play on his name. The vocative *agne* "o Agni" also occurs in three of the last four verses. Verse 8 is the exception, but notice that unlike the other verses of the hymn, this verse is not grammatically independent but a continuation of verse 7. Thus in verses 7–8 there is protracted statement across two verses before the final summing up in verse 9. This structure not only displays the artfulness of the poet but also suggests the various forms or shapes of the sacrificial Fire that are analogous to the many grammatical forms of the word, *agni*, "fire."

1. Agni do I invoke—the one placed to the fore, god and priest of the sacrifice,
   the Hotar, most richly conferring treasure.
2. Agni, to be invoked by ancient sages and by the present ones—
   he will carry the gods here to this place.
3. By Agni one will obtain wealth and prosperity every day,
   glorious and richest in heroes.
4. O Agni, the sacrifice and rite that you surround on every side—
   it alone goes among the gods.
5. Agni, the Hotar with a poet's purpose, the real one possessing the brightest fame,
   will come as a god with the gods.
6. When truly you will do good for the pious man, o Agni,
   just that of yours is real, o Aṅgiras.
7. We approach you, o Agni, illuminator in the evening, every day with our insight,
   bringing homage—
8. You, ruling over the rites, the shining herdsman of the truth,
   growing strong in your own home.
9. Like a father for a son, be of easy approach for us, o Agni,
   Accompany us for our well-being.

I.124 Dawn

Kakṣīvant Dairghatamasa
triṣṭubh meter
One of the loveliest of the Dawn hymns and a fitting showcase for one of the most virtuosic poets in the R̥gveda, Kakṣīvant. Here the poet takes the usual

generic themes, especially Dawn as a beautiful woman, and creates highly specific images, especially in verses 7–8, which provide a series of almost sociological portraits of ancient Indian female figures. In verse 7 we first (pāda a) meet a brotherless girl boldly approaching men; since the brother was important in finding and arranging suitable matches, a brotherless girl was at a disadvantage in the marriage market and needed to take initiative on her own. (See Schmidt 1987: 30–75.) The next image is a pun (pāda b), with one harmless generic image and one shockingly specific one. In the harmless reading a (presumably male) figure mounts a chariot to seek prizes; in the other a woman, presumably a prostitute, shows herself off on a platform for money. The third image (pādas cd) is of the legitimate wife adorned for her husband, but even there the image shades into that of a loose woman showing her breast. The next verse (8) treats the common theme of the sisters Dawn and Night, but again Dawn is presented in a particular female role. In the second pāda, the "girl to be gazed upon" may well refer to the display motif of the ancient Indian "self-choice" marriage (*svayaṃvara*) (see Jamison 2001), while the "maidens with a choice" may refer to the same phenomena, girls making their choice of bridegroom at a specially called assembly (see Jamison 2003).

Even more striking perhaps is verse 4, where Dawn is compared to three different animals or their parts: she is glossy like the breast of a waterbird who preens; she reveals herself like an elephant kneeling to drink; and she wakens the sleeping like a fly, buzzing around again and again. (We owe these interpretations to Thieme 1965 [=Kl. Sch. 214–227].)

Nothing in the rest of the hymn is quite so quirky, but the standard tropes are well handled. The hymn begins (vs. 1) with the daily coincidence of the kindling of the ritual fire, the advent of the dawn, and the rising of the sun. The common counterpoint between individual Dawn and the multitude of identical dawns that have preceded and will follow today's dawn is found in verses 2–3, 6, and 9. Another common theme, the diversity of beings that Dawns awakens, appears in verses 1, 6, and 12. The final verses of the hymn raise the hope of gifts and rewards that will come with the dawn.

1. Dawn as she dawns when the fire is being kindled; the sun as it rises—each has propped up its own light widely.
God Savitar here and now has impelled forth our two-footed, forth our four-footed each to go to its task.

2. Not belittling the divine commandments, but diminishing human life-spans,
the last of those who, one by one, have gone, the first of those who come hither—Dawn has flashed forth.

3. This Daughter of Heaven has appeared opposite, dressed in light, in the same way (as the others), from the east.

She follows along the path of truth, straight to the goal. Like one who knows the way, she does not confound the directions.

4. She has appeared like the breast of a preening waterbird. Like a female elephant she has revealed her intimate parts.

Wakening the sleeping like a fly, she has come as the latest of those who, one by one, have come here again and again.

5. In the eastern half of the dusky realm that cannot be flown to, the begetter of cows has put forth her beacon.

She spreads out further, more widely, filling both laps of her two parents [=Heaven and Earth].

6. Just thus is she, the latest of many, to be seen. Neither the non-kin does she avoid, nor the kin.

Exulting in her spotless body, neither from the small does she retreat, nor from the great, as she shines forth.

7. Like a brotherless girl she goes right up to men—like one mounting a chariot seat to win prizes [/display-platform to gain property].

Like an eager wife, richly dressed, for her husband, Dawn, like a wanton, lets her breast spill over.

8. The one sister has left the natal place to her older sister. She goes away from her, like a girl to be gazed upon.

Dawning forth with the rays of the sun, she smears unguent on herself, like maidens with a choice going to assemblies.

9. Day after day the latest of those earlier sisters advances from behind towards the earlier one.

Let the newer ones now dawn richly for us as of old—the day-bright dawns.

10. Awaken those who grant, bounteous Dawn; unawakening let the niggards sleep.

Richly dawn for the bounteous ones, o bounteous one, richly for the praiser, o liberal-spirited one, as you rouse them.

11. This young woman has whitened down from the east. She yokes the forefront of the ruddy cows.

She will dawn forth now; her beacon will stand out. Agni will reverently come to house after house.

12. The birds have also flown up from their dwelling and the men who partake of food, at your first flush.

To the one who is at home you convey much of value, goddess Dawn, and to the pious mortal.

13. You have been praised, praiseworthy ones, by my sacred formulation. You, eager for it, have been strengthened, o Dawns.

Goddesses, with your help may we win spoils in hundreds and thousands.

I.32 Indra

Hiraṇyastūpa Āṅgirasa
triṣṭubh meter

This justly famous hymn tells of Indra's most significant victory, his triumph over Vṛtra and the release of the waters, in perhaps the clearest treatment of this myth in the Ṛgveda. Vṛtra was a gigantic cobra who lay coiled around a mountain within which all the waters were entrapped. In his battle with Indra, Vṛtra spread his "shoulders," his cobra's hood, and struck at Indra with his fangs, but Indra finally killed Vṛtra with his vajra, his mace, broke open the mountain, and let the waters pour out. These waters then flowed to Manu (vs. 8), the first sacrificer, and by implication to his descendants. Vṛtra's name means "obstacle," and this victory over "Obstacle" is therefore paradigmatic for Indra's victory over all obstacles. Thus, when the poet in the first words of the hymn declares the "heroic deeds of Indra," he both calls upon Indra to perform these deeds once again and by means of his recitation makes real in the present the truths of the primal past.

The hymn repeatedly contrasts Indra, who embodies virility and life, and Vṛtra, who represents sterility and death. A bull (vss. 3, 7), Indra drinks the invigorating soma (vs. 3), while Vṛtra is a steer, a castrate (vs. 7), and fights like a drunkard (vs. 6). Indra is a "great hero" (vs. 6) and the "generous one" (vs. 13), while Vṛtra is a "non-warrior" (vs. 6). Indra releases the life-giving waters (vss. 1, 2, 11, 12), while Vṛtra kept them hemmed in (vs. 1) and stagnant (vs. 11). In his battle with Indra Vṛtra hurls lightning, thunder, mist, and hail (vs. 13), but significantly not rain. The only thing with which Vṛtra soaks the earth is finally his own blood (vs. 5). Vṛtra was the "husband" of the waters (vs. 11), but he never lets them give life. In death he lies beneath his mother (vs. 9) in an intimation of incest and of a reversed sexual position, once again suggesting his sterility and perversity. As a final act of disgust with their former husband, the waters trample Vṛtra's "private parts"—the expression in Sanskrit is equally oblique—as they flow away from him (vs. 10).

Despite the relative clarity of the treatment of Indra's battle with Vṛtra, the hymn has a curious structure, obsessively circling around and alternately focusing in on and drawing back from the moment of dramatic confrontation between the adversaries. After the initial verses of summary and the preliminaries to the battle (vss. 1-4), the next three verses (5–7) depict the battle, and it is portrayed as extremely one-sided, with the overconfident Vṛtra overmatched from the beginning and decisively smashed by Indra. (The signature verb of the first section of the hymn is √*han* "smash, smite.") Defeated and dismembered, Vṛtra lies dead, and the released waters flow over him (8–11). After this interlude the hymn returns to a new description of the battle (12–13), which in this reprise is depicted as far more of an even match. Vṛtra strikes at Indra with his fangs and deploys various natural forces against his adversary.

This more equal battle is encapsulated in the perfectly balanced construction *índraś ca yád yuyudhā́te áhiś ca* "when both Indra and the serpent fought with each other . . . " (13c). It is unclear why the first triumphalist account has been revised to the more ambiguous, less glorious version—though both, of course, end with Vr̥tra's defeat.

The most mysterious part of this hymn is the conclusion. Vr̥tra is destroyed, and even his mother Dānu has been killed, so there is no possibility of a new Vr̥tra. And yet Indra apparently becomes terrified and flies across the rivers "like a frightened falcon" (vs. 14). Perhaps this puzzling ending is related to the second version of the battle, in which Indra does not have quite the unchallenged heroic role that he plays in the first version. Or perhaps in addition to freeing the waters, which bring life, Indra ironically also brought death by killing Vr̥tra. The poet does not explain. This is not a note on which to conclude, however, and therefore in the last verse the poet simply returns to a praise of Indra as victor and king.

1. Now I shall proclaim the heroic deeds of Indra, those foremost deeds that the mace-wielder performed:

He smashed the serpent. He bored out the waters. He split the bellies of the mountains.

2. He smashed the serpent resting on the mountain—for him Tvaṣṭar had fashioned the resounding [/sunlike] mace.

Like bellowing milk cows, streaming out, the waters went straight down to the sea.

3. Acting the bull, he chose for his own the soma. He drank of the pressed soma among the Trikadrukas [=soma cups? the Maruts?].

The generous one took up his missile, the mace. He smashed him, the first-born of serpents.

4. When you, Indra, smashed the first-born of serpents and after that wiped out the wiles of the wily, after that giving birth to the sun, the heaven, and the dawn, you surely never found a rival since.

5. He smashed Vr̥tra ["Obstacle"], the very great obstacle, whose shoulders were spread apart—Indra with his mace, his great murderous weapon.

Like logs hewn apart by an axe, the serpent would lie, soaking the earth with blood.

6. Because he challenged the great, hard-pressing hero, whose is the silvery drink [=soma], like a drunken non-hero.

he did not withstand the clash of his weapons. His mouth destroyed by the shattering blow, he whose rival was Indra was completely crushed.

7. Handless and footless, he gave battle to Indra. Indra smashed his mace upon his back.

A steer trying to be the measure of a bull, Vr̥tra lay there, flung apart in many pieces.

8. Delivering themselves to belong to Manu, the waters go over him, lying like a split reed.

Those very ones whom Vr̥tra in his greatness once surrounded, at *their* feet the serpent came to lie.

9. The strength of Vr̥tra's mother ebbed: Indra bore his weapon down upon her.

The mother was above; the son below: Dānu lies there like a milk-cow with her calf.

10. In the midst of the race markers of the never-standing, never-resting waters, his body sank down.

The waters move everywhere over the private parts of Vr̥tra. He whose rival was Indra lay there in the long darkness of death.

11. The waters stood still—their husband was the Dāsa, their herdsman the serpent—hemmed in like the cows by the Paṇi.

What was the hidden opening for the waters—that Indra uncovered after he smashed Vr̥tra.

12. You, Indra, then became the tail of a horse when he struck his fangs at you—you, the god alone.

You conquered the cows and you conquered the soma, o champion. You set loose the seven rivers to flow.

13. Neither the lightning nor the thunder, neither the mist nor the hail that he scattered repelled Indra for him.

When both Indra and the serpent fought with each other, the generous one achieved victory also for all later times.

14. Whom did you see, Indra, as the avenger of the serpent when fear came into your heart after you had smashed him

and when you crossed the ninety-nine flowing rivers, like a frightened falcon through the airy realms?

15. With his mace in his arms, Indra is the king of the one hitching up and the one settled, of the horned and the hornless.

As just he alone as king rules over the different peoples: like a rim the spokes of a wheel, he encompasses these all.

X.108 Saramā and the Paṇis

Saramā and Paṇis

triṣṭubh meter

In the interpretation of this delightful dialogue hymn we follow the compelling study by H.-P. Schmidt (1968: 185–189). Like I.32 this hymn provides a narrative of one of Indra's great deeds, here the opening of the Vala cave and the release of the cattle (see pp. 70–71 on Indra). Unlike I.32, however, this hymn does not tell the whole story, but treats a single episode in the form of a dialogue. The setting for the dialogue is as follows: a tribe or people called the Paṇis have entrapped cattle in a cave. Indra and the ancient Vedic seers wish to free these cattle from the Paṇis, and therefore, Indra sends his dog Saramā to track down the Paṇis and to demand the cattle. She crosses the Rasā, the river at the border of the world that separates heaven and earth, and finds the Paṇis. The hymn tells of Saramā's encounter with the Paṇis and of their refusal to surrender the cattle.

The hymn begins with the Paṇis asking Saramā what has brought her here and how she was able to come on such a long and dangerous journey (vss. 1–2), and she tells them her mission is to take their cattle to Indra (2). The Paṇis first try to convince her that they will make some sort of bargain with Indra (3), but she will have none of the Paṇis' trickery: if there is any deceiving to be done, she says, it will be Indra who does it (4). Then the Paṇis tell Saramā that they are good warriors, that their defenses are strong, and that they will not give up the cattle without a fight (5, 7), but Saramā again rejects their bluster and boasting (6). Finally, the Paṇis make one last attempt, this time to enlist Saramā: they offer to make her their "sister" and to give her a share of the cattle (9), but Saramā remains loyal to Indra (10).

At the end, beyond the narrative scope of the hymn, Indra and the seers—the Aṅgirases and Navagvas—themselves will come to the place where the Paṇis have hidden the cattle and they will break open the cave. But they will do so through the power of the hymns they compose and recite, not by Indra's mace or by other weapons. This climax is already intimated in verse 6, in which Saramā declares that the Paṇis are weak, for they only have false words, while Indra and the ancient seers hold the power of the truth. Because Indra's weapon in this story is the truth embodied in the hymns, Indra is here called Bṛhaspati, "Lord of the Sacred Formulation."

The story also tells of the coming of the dawns, since the power of Indra's and the seer's words rests in the secret truth that the cattle are the dawns (see p. 70). At the end, the poet uses the power of this truth to his own ends: through the truth of his hymn and because of its elegant formulation in this hymn, he also should acquire cattle. These cattle may be actual cattle that the poet seeks or has lost, or they may also be the dawns, or they may be both.

Despite the seriousness of the theme, it is hard to believe that the audience did not relish the depiction of a talking dog, especially one as saucy and forthright as the faithful Saramā, who resists the offered blandishments of the Paṇis to remain loyal to her master Indra.

1. [Paṇi:] Seeking what has Saramā arrived here, for the road is far, swallowing up the traveler in the distance?

What is your mission to us? What was the crucial turn bringing you here? How did you cross the waters of the Rasā?

2. [Saramā:] Sent as the messenger of Indra I travel, seeking your great hidden treasuries, Paṇis.

With fear of leaping across—that helped me!—in that way I crossed the waters of the Rasā.

3. [Paṇi:] Of what sort is Indra, Saramā? What is his appearance?—he as whose messenger you raced here from afar?

If he will come here, we will make an alliance with him, and then he will become the cattle-master of our cattle.

4. [Saramā:] I know him not as one who can be deceived. *He* will deceive!—he as whose messenger I raced here from afar.

Deep flowing rivers do not keep him hidden. Smashed by Indra, Paṇis, you will lie still.

5. [Paṇi:] Here are the cattle that you sought, Saramā, as you were flying around the ends of heaven, o well-favored one.

Who will release these to you without a fight? And our battle weapons are sharp!

6. [Saramā:] Your words have no weapons, Paṇis! Let your evil bodies be impervious to arrows;

let the path to you be one no one dares to follow—either way, Bṛhaspati will have no mercy on you!

7. [Paṇi:] This treasury with its a foundation of rock is overflowing with cows, horses, and goods, Saramā.

The Paṇis, who are good cowherds, guard it. In vain have you come along an empty track.

8. [Saramā:] The seers, sharpened by soma, will come here to this place: Ayāsya ["the Unbridled One"=Indra], the Aṅgirases, and the Navagvas.

These will divide among themselves this pen of cattle. Then will the Paṇis vomit this speech of theirs!

9. [Paṇi:] Even though you have come in this way, Saramā, compelled by divine force,

I shall make you my sister. Do not go back. We will give away a portion of the cows to you, o well-favored one.

10. [Saramā:] I know no brotherhood and no sisterhood between us. Indra and the terrifying Aṅgirases, they know these things.

They seemed desirous of cattle when I came. Go away from here, Paṇis, a very long way!

11. [Narrator:] Go far from here, Paṇis, a very long way! Let the cows, exchanging with the truth, come up,

the cows that Bṛhaspati found hidden—he and the soma, the pressing stones, and the inspired seers.

V.58 Maruts

Śyāvāśva Ātreya

triṣṭubh meter

This pleasing Marut hymn contains a typical mixture of storm imagery (see especially vss. 6–7) and portrayal of a wild but beneficial Männerbund. The sheer power and energy of the group is well conveyed in the first few verses. In verse 4 the Maruts are seen as creators of similarly energetic and successful human men, their earthly counterparts. Another common theme, the lack of distinction among the various members of the band, is also mentioned (vs. 5). In verse 7 the virility of the band is captured in the striking image of their sexual relationship with the Earth herself.

1. Now will I praise this flock full of power, their Marutian flock of newer hymns [=thunderclaps],

those possessing swift horses who drive themselves impetuously and who as self-rulers are masters of the immortal —

2. the turbulent, powerful flock with bangles on their hands, of boisterous commandment, masters of artifice, granting wishes,

who are joy itself, immeasurable in their greatness. O poet, extol the powerfully generous men.

3. Let the water-conveyors come here to you today, all the Maruts who speed the rain.

This fire which is kindled here, o Maruts, enjoy it, you sage poets, youths.

4. You beget for the people a take-charge king, fashioned for distinction, you who deserve the sacrifice.

From you comes the fist-fighter, quick with his arms, from you the one of trusty horses and good heroes, o Maruts.

5. Just like wheel spokes, there is no last one; like the days they keep arising, not stingy with their mighty powers.

The sons of Pr̥śni, highest, wildest—the Maruts have equipped themselves with their own poetic thought.

6. When you have driven forth with your dappled mares, your horses, with your chariots with their firm wheel rims, o Maruts,

the waters surge; the trees dissolve; let the ruddy bull, the Heaven, roar down.

7. Even the Earth has spread herself at their journey. Like a husband an embryo, they have implanted their own strength in the earth.

Certainly they have yoked the winds as horses to their yoke pole; they have made their own sweat into rain—the Rudras.

8. Hail, Maruts, superior men! Be merciful to us—o you of great bounty, immortal, knowing the immanent truth,

hearing the realized truth [=poetic formulations], sage poets, youths, belonging to the lofty mountains, loftily growing.

IX.93 Soma Pavamāna

Nodhas Gautama

triṣṭubh meter

This is a typical Soma hymn, chosen from among the 114 in the IXth Maṇḍala, and displays some of the recurrent themes in that collection and also the intertwining of images that so characterizes the soma hymns. The first three verses concern the journey of the soma to the vessels and the mixing with water and with milk. The last two (4–5) are requests for bounties. In verse 1 we first meet "the ten sisters," the standard trope for the 10 fingers of the priest who prepares the soma. These "sisters" groom the soma, which, as so often, is likened to a horse running around a racecourse—the filter that removes impurities from the soma juice. After the filtering, the juice is poured into a cup, as at the end of verse 1. The mixing of soma first with water and then with milk is treated in verse 2, in which the soma is pictured as a calf, a bull, and a virile young man in the course of three pādas. By the end of verse 2 the soma has been mixed with the milk, depicted strikingly as a sexual tryst in pāda c. A different view of the mixture with milk is provided in verse 3. The last two verses (4–5) ask for wealth and an extended lifespan.

1. The ten sisters, grown strong all together, the insightful thoughts of the insightful one, the runners, groomed him.

The tawny offspring of the sun dashed around the filter. He reached the wooden cup like a prizewinning steed.

2. Like a calf bellowing along with the mothers, the bull of many favors [/tailhairs] has run together with the waters.

Like a young blood going to a maiden at the trysting place, he comes together with the ruddy cows in the tub.

3. And the udder of the inviolable cow has swelled forth; the drop of good wisdom is accompanied by streams.

The cows prepare his head with their milk in the cups, as if with freshly washed goods.

4. O self-purifying drop, along with the gods excavate wealth in horses for us as you bellow.

Let Plenitude come eagerly on her chariot in our direction, for the giving of goods.

5. Now, as you are being purified, mete out to us all-glittering wealth, abounding in superior men, befriended by the wind [/whose friendship is sought].

The lifetime of the extoller has been extended, o drop.—Early in the morning—soon—he should come, bringing goods through his insight.

VII.86 Varuṇa

Vasiṣṭha

triṣṭubh meter

This hymn and the three hymns that follow it (VII 87–89) are justly famous because they strike an unusually intimate tone and because the poet Vasiṣṭha as a literary creation of the poem emerges as a distinct personality. Jamison (2007: 91–118) offers a detailed study of the hymns in this group and of the creation of the poet's personality. Like the other hymns in this small collection, this poem centers on just two figures, the poet—Vasiṣṭha according to tradition—and the god Varuṇa, and Vasiṣṭha speaks personally, even confessionally with Varuṇa. Apparently Vasiṣṭha has been suffering from some kind of affliction, which, he has been told, is the punishment of King Varuṇa for an offense. He begs Varuṇa to accept his offerings and repentance, to forgive his transgressions, which he says were not intentional (vs. 6), and to restore him to prosperity and health.

The relationship between Vasiṣṭha and Varuṇa constantly shifts as the hymn unfolds. The literary strategy of the poem appears in its use of pronouns and other markers of person. Use of the third person "he" distances the speaker and the object, while addressing another in the second person as "you" is a token of closeness and presence to one another. The first-person "I" signals the presence of the speaker; the third person, "he, him," the absence of the one addressed but the vocative "o Varuṇa" his presence. The poet deploys these pronouns and forms first to distance Vasiṣṭha and Varuṇa, then to bring them close, and finally to separate them once again. Thus, at the beginning of the poem, the relationship between Vasiṣṭha and Varuṇa is completely broken. In verse 1 Vasiṣṭha is absent because there is no reference to the speaker, and Varuṇa is distanced by the third-person pronoun *asya* "of him." In verse 2 Vasiṣṭha is present (first person in each of the four lines), and Varuṇa remains distanced. In verse 3 Vasiṣṭha is present once again (first person) and Varuṇa is partly present: he is addressed in the vocative but he is also mentioned in the third person. In verse 4 both Vasiṣṭha (first person) and Varuṇa (second person) are present. Then there begins a retreat from their full presence to one another. In verse 5 Vasiṣṭha is less present (the first-person plural "we" generalizes rather than personalizes the speaker) and Varuṇa is present (through the vocative address and second-person imperative). In verse 6 Vasiṣṭha is distanced (note especially *svá* "one's own," not "my own"), and Varuṇa is present (through the vocative address), although perhaps less so than in the previous verse. In verse 7 Vasiṣṭha is present (first person), but Varuṇa is distanced (third person). The last verse, verse 8, is a concluding, extra-hymnic verse, a coda that stands outside the main structure of the hymn.

This analysis also shows the omphalos structure of the hymn (see pp. 151–53 on ring composition and the omphalos). The central verse, not including the extra-hymnic coda, is verse 4. It is the thematic fulcrum of the hymn because it is in this verse that the poet and the god are both present and present to one another. It also signifies the determination of Vasiṣṭha, who looks forward to the resolution of his conflict with Varuṇa. Varuṇa will—perhaps even must—proclaim what Vasiṣṭha has done, and Vasiṣṭha promises to humble himself before the god to receive the god's forgiveness. Although the latter part of the hymn moves away from this encounter between Vasiṣṭha and Varuṇa, the last verse suggests that the problem has been resolved. Varuṇa has returned to the distance, but Vasiṣṭha and he now mutually support one another. Varuṇa has enlightened Vasiṣṭha, and Vasiṣṭha ritually serves the god to his greater "wealth," his power and glory (vs. 7).

In verse 2 the meaning of *váruṇe* "within Varuṇa" may play on the possible etymological relation of *váruṇa* and *vratá* "commandment." That is, "within Varuṇa" has the sense of "under, or in conformity with, the commandment of Varuṇa." The very last pāda, "Protect us always with your blessings," is the signature line of the Vasiṣṭha hymns, which trademarks the hymn, so speak, as belonging to this poetic circle.

1. Insightful are the races of gods and mortals through the greatness of him who propped apart the two wide world-halves.
He pushed forth the vault of heaven to be high and lofty, also the star [=the sun] once again, and he spread out the earth.

2. And together with my own self, I speak this: "When shall I be within Varuṇa?
Might he take pleasure in my offering, becoming free of anger? When shall I, with good thoughts, look upon his mercy?"

3. I ask myself about this guilt, Varuṇa, wanting to see; I approach those who understand in order to inquire.
Even the sage-poets say the very same thing to me: "Varuṇa now is angry with you."

4. Was the offense so very great, Varuṇa, that you wish to smash a praise singer and companion?
You will declare this to me, o you hard to deceive, o you of independent will! With reverence I would swiftly bow down before you to be freed of guilt.

5. Release from us ancestral deceits and those which we ourselves have committed.

O King, like a cattle-stealing thief, like a calf, release Vasiṣṭha from his bond.

6. This was not one's own devising nor was it deception, Varuṇa, but rather liquor, frenzy, dice, thoughtlessness.

The elder exists within the misdeed of the younger. Not even sleep wards off untruth.

7. Like a servant, I will give satisfaction to the generous master; freed from offense, I will give satisfaction to the ardent one.

The civilizing god [=Varuṇa] made those without understanding to understand; the better poet-sage [=Vasiṣṭha] speeds his clever patron [=Varuṇa] to riches.

8. This praise song is for you, Varuṇa, you of independent will: let it be set within your heart.

Let there be good fortune in peaceful settlement for us and let there be good fortune in war for us. —Protect us always with your blessings.

VII.103 Frogs

Vasiṣṭha

triṣṭubh meter, except anuṣṭubh 1

As noted in p. 163, there is nothing else quite like this hymn in the R̥gveda. It is a rain charm, which cleverly matches accurate description of frogs noisily emerging from estivation and mating at the beginning of the rainy season with the behavior of priests at a particular ritual, the Pravargya (see esp. vss. 7–9). Although there has been much debate about whether this hymn satirizes priests by comparing them to frogs, or instead is to be taken with deadly seriousness, the truth no doubt lies somewhere in between. The poet obviously took great delight in his skill at matching frog behavior with ritual behavior and is unlikely to have been unaware of the potentially comic aspects of the comparison; however, the explosive fertility of the frogs provides a model for similar increase in the human sphere, and therefore the comparison has a serious purpose.

Attention to modern studies of animal behavior allows us to see just how much careful observation of frogs lies behind the depiction of the frogs here, and understanding anuran mating habits deepens our understanding of the poem. (See Jamison 1991–1992.) For example, the frog lying "like a dried-out leather bag" (vs. 2) is a counter-intuitively accurate representation of a frog in estivation: some really do go dormant and dry up during the dry season, and "just adding water" plumps them up and revives them. Once revived, the chorus of frogs begins, the purpose of which is to draw female frogs to the males who are vocalizing, for mating. This antiphonal chorus is described in verses 2–6. Since the calls of different species are quite distinctive (as sketched in vs. 6), the different cries serve to attract conspecific females to the appropriate male. The actual mating posture of frogs is described in verse 4: it involves the male approaching the female from behind and grasping her firmly for as long as it takes—which for some species can be quite a while (days or weeks).

Another important aspect of the hymn is its comparison of the frog chorus to a pedagogical situation (see especially vss. 3, 5), in which the father/teacher speaks and the pupils exactly repeat his utterance. This is the clearest and earliest depiction of pedagogy in ancient India and is an example of how our knowledge of everyday life at that time must be obliquely won. The most famous word in this hymn is found in verse 3, the phonologically aberrant *akhkhala* (underlying the so-called cvi-formation *akhkhalī-[kṛ́tya]*). On the one hand, it would take a very austere interpreter, and a killjoy, not to recognize this as an onomatopoetic imitation of a froggy sound; on the other hand, in the inspired analysis of Paul Thieme (1954), this is, in Middle Indic guise, a representation of the word *akṣara* "syllable." What the frog pupils are doing is "making syllables," that is, repeating the utterance of the teacher verbatim, as sound, not meaning. This is a pedagogical technique that endures to this day in traditional Vedic learning (see above p. 204). It is also telling that the word *akhkhala* is in a Middle Indic linguistic form, as the everyday language of the Ṛgvedic poets, and especially of their wives and children, had most likely already undergone many of the phonological and morphological changes characteristic of Middle Indic, but only found in preserved texts from a much later period. Instruction of the young, as well as most ordinary conversation, was no doubt carried out in this language rather than in the high Vedic Sanskrit of the hymns.

As for the ritual application, the Pravargya rite occurs after a year-long consecration, like that referred to in verse 1 and brought to an end in verses 7–9. The most salient feature of the Pravargya is the offering of the gharma-drink, referred to specifically in verses 8–9, the heated milk-offering that boils until it overflows. The last, and most important, implicit comparison between frogs and priests turns on this ritual offering: the prodigious discharge of eggs after anuran mating, especially by many pairs simultaneously, must have reminded the poet of the frothy bubbling overflow of the boiling milk. And since the thousands of eggs released are a tangible sign of fertility and increase, the frogs are seen as assuring increase for us as well, in the final verse (10), culminating in the "Pressing of Thousands."

1. Having lain still for a year, like brahmins following their commandment,

the frogs have spoken forth a speech quickened by Parjanya [=Thunder].

2. When the heavenly waters have come to him, lying like a dried leather bag in the pond,

like the bellow of cows with their calves, the call of the frogs comes together here.

3. When it has rained on them, who are yearning and thirsting, when the rainy season has come,

saying "akhkhala" [/repeating syllables] like a son to a father at lessons, one goes up close to the other who is speaking.

4. One of the two grasps the other from behind, when they have become exhilarated in the discharge of the waters,

when the frog, rained upon, has hopped and hopped, and the speckled one mixes his speech with the green one.

5. Once one of them speaks the speech of the other, like a pupil that of his teacher,

then a whole section of them speaks as if in unison, when you of good speech speak amid the waters.

6. One of them has a cow's bellow, one a goat's bleat; one is speckled, one green.

Bearing the same name but different forms, they ornament their voice in many ways as they speak.

6. Like brahmins at an "Overnight" soma ritual, speaking around a soma vessel full like a pond,

you cycle around to that day of the year, which, o frogs, is the one marking the rainy season.

8. The brahmins, having soma, have made speech, creating their yearly sacred formulation.

The Adhvaryu-priests, having the hot ritual milk-drink at the Pravargya ritual, sweating, become visible; none are hidden.

9. They guarded the godly establishment of the twelve-month; these men do not confound the season.

In a year, when the rainy season has come, the heated ritual milk-drinks obtain their own release.

10. The one with a cow's bellow has given, the one with a goat's bleat has given, the speckled one has given, the green one has given us goods.

The frogs, giving hundred of cows, lengthened their/our life at a "Pressing of Thousands."

I.179 Agastya and Lopāmudrā (Anukramaṇī: Rati "Delight")

Lopamūdrā 1–2, Agastya 3–4, student 5–6
triṣṭubh meter, except bṛhatī 5

This memorable hymn compresses much matter in a few verses. The first four verses consist of a dialogue between the seer Agastya, the poet of the hymn cycle in which this hymn is embedded (I.165–191), and his wife Lopāmudrā. It concerns, and contains in embryo, a persistent theme in Indian religious literature and thought, the competing and incompatible goals of male religious figures: ascetic practice and the production of sons, and it also presents the figure who mediates these goals: the sexually eager woman who seduces the ascetic, who can thus attain the second goal without actively abandoning the first (see, e.g., Jamison, 1996: 15–17).

Lopāmudrā speaks the first two verses, urging her husband to allow them both to cease their ritual labors and have sex. She mentions the deleterious effects of old age (vs. 1c) and cites as a precedent for her proposed course of action the pious ancients who nevertheless also stopped working from time to time (vs. 2). In our view (and that of the Anukramaṇī and Sāyaṇa, inter alia, contra a number of modern scholars, who assign vs. 4 to Lopāmudrā), Agastya speaks the next two verses (3–4). In verse 3 he counters her proposal with a vigorous call to renewed religious endeavor, which he casts as a battle against a tricky and numerous enemy that they, as a married couple (*mithunaú*), can defeat together. The word *mithunaú* is a charged one, because it can refer specifically to a *sexual* pairing. And this is what appears to be rather graphically illustrated in verse 4, where Agastya succumbs to his lust, as Lopāmudrā engages him in intercourse. The "steadfast" (*dhī́ra*) man is undone by the "flighty" (*ádhīra*) woman.

The next two verses (5–6) are assigned by the Anukramaṇī to a student, and at least verse 5 may contain the expiatory statement of someone, quite possibly a brahmacārin or Vedic student, who has broken a vow, quite possibly the vow of chastity, and has undertaken ritual purification. The myth embodied in the previous dialogue acts as a Legendenzauber, a magic spell that provides a mythological precedent for the misdeed and its expiation. (See Thieme 1964: 76.) The final verse (6) summarizes the happy results for Agastya, despite— indeed because of—his lapse: he attained offspring as well as power, and a place among the gods.

Although verse 5 provides support for the expiatory theory, we are inclined to think there is something more going on, and that the conflict between Agastya and Lopāmudrā reflects a theological struggle dimly perceptible beneath the surface of the late Ṛgveda—the struggle between the innovative theologians who favor introducing the new ritual model involving the Sacrificer's Wife as partner on the ritual stage, and the conservatives who consider it a dangerous model with potentially disastrous side effects (see pp. 49–50). Agastya in verse 3 appears to be a spokesman for the innovators, urging an energetic ritual partnership between husband and wife—a partnership that deteriorates in the next verse into a mere sexual encounter. In this reading Agastya must undertake the penance in verse 5, and although everything comes out right for him, the hymn cannot be seen as a ringing endorsement of the introduction of the Sacrificer's Wife.

1. [Lopāmudrā:] "For many autumns have I been laboring, evening and morning, through the aging dawns.
Old age diminishes the beauty of bodies. Bullish (men) should now come to their wives."
2. [Lopāmudrā:] "For even those ancients, who served truth and at one with the gods spoke truths,
even they got out of harness, for they did not reach the end. Wives should now unite with their bullish husbands."
3. [Agastya:] "Not in vain is the labor that the gods help.
Let us two take on all contenders; let us two win here the contest of a hundred strategems, when as a united couple we will drive on."
4. [Agastya:] "The lust of a mounting bull [/waxing reed = penis] has come to me, lust arisen from here, from there, from everywhere.
Lopāmudrā makes the bullish one flow out; the steadfast man does the flighty woman suck while he is snorting."
5. [Student or Agastya:] "This soma within my heart, just drunk, do I adjure:
Whatever offense we have commited, let him forgive that, for of many desires is mortal man."
6. Agastya, digging with spades, seeking offspring, descendants, power—
with regard to both "colors" [=offspring and ascetic power] the mighty seer throve. He arrived at his hopes which came true among the gods.

X.159 Against Co-wives

Śacī Paulomī
anuṣṭubh

As noted above (p. 162), the R̥gveda contains two charms against co-wives, X.145 and X.159, both found, like most personal charms, in the late Xth Maṇḍala. Like X.145, this hymn is in the voice of a woman, speaking in the first person, against her co-wives. But, whereas in X.145 she is in the act of performing the spell with which she hopes to vanquish her co-wife, in this hymn her triumph is complete. She recites a victory paean, in the appropriate high rhetorical style—albeit with some dips into the vernacular, such as the diminutivized derivative of the personal pronoun in verse 1, *māmaká* "li'l ole me." The tone is not only triumphant but also violent and aggressive. It is worth noting that in verse 3 she extends her victory to her sons and her daughter; as the early parts of the Rāmāyaṇa teach us, one of the most important reasons that co-wives plot against each other is to secure preferment for their children.

1. Up has gone yonder sun; up this good fortune of li'l ole me.
I, a cunning woman, now have gained victory over my husband, so that I am victorious.
2. I am the beacon; I am the head; I am the powerful debater.
Only my will should my husband follow, when I am victorious.
3. My sons are rival-smiters, and my daughter is a wide ruler.
And I am a complete conqueror. To my husband my signal-call is the highest.
4. The oblation through which Indra, when he performed it, became the highest brilliant one,
that oblation I have now performed, o gods: I have therefore become without co-wives.
5. Without co-wives, smiting co-wives, conquering, overcoming—
I have ripped off the luster of the other women, like the gifts of the feckless.
6. I have completely conquered them, overcoming the co-wives,
so that I will rule widely over this hero and over his people.

X.90 Puruṣa

Nārāyaṇa

anuṣṭubh meter, except triṣṭubh 16

This is one of the best-known and most influential hymns of the Ṛgveda (see pp. 216–17). Its central symbol is the *púruṣa*, the "man," "person," or "human being." On the surface, this hymn tells of the sacrifice of a cosmic Man, from whose parts the world was created. This theme of creation through sacrifice is widespread in various cultures, but this hymn is not simply the retelling of an ancient tradition. The púruṣa here serves as a symbol of the sacrifice itself, which in the later Vedic tradition is a locus of creative power. The púruṣa is thus similar to the later Prajāpati, who in the brāhmaṇas personifies the sacrifice and who creates by dispersing himself into his creation. This late hymn represents a verse commentary on the sacrifice that prefigures the prose commentaries of the brāhmaṇas. It is also notable because it is the only Ṛgvedic mention of the four varṇas, the hierarchical division of the social order that forms the theoretical basis for the caste system (see pp. 33–34).

The identity of the Man and the sacrifice is established in the opening verse, for his thousand heads, eyes, and feet recall Agni, the sacrificial fire, and his macrocosmic equivalent, the Sun (cf. Brown 1931: 109–110). The Man comprehends the earth and extends beyond it. As Mus (1968: 549) has pointed out, the "ten-fingers' breadth" by which he exceeds the world measures from the Man's hair line to the mouth. The Man's mouth represents speech, which marks the boundary between the imperceptible world of thought and the perceptible world, which is created by speech. His mouth is also associated with eating, and in verse 2 the Man rises beyond the world "through food," that is, by making the world his food. In later texts the "eater" is the master and the "eaten" is one who benefits the master (cf. Rau 1957: 34–35). The image may therefore reflect the Man's dominance over the world.

This theme of dominance or rule continues also in verse 5 in the mutual generation of the Man and the Virāj. The word *virā́j* can mean either "brilliant" or "ruling, rule." The latter is the more likely sense here, and this connects the hymn to Vedic ideals of the king, who in his consecration encompasses the world in a similar way that the Man does here (Proferes 2007, especially chapter 3). Since the term *virā́j* is grammatically feminine, it complements púruṣa, which is masculine in grammar and connotation.

The Man is the "offering" (vs. 6), the sacrificial victim (15), but he is also the sacrifice itself that the gods, the Sādhyas, and seers performed (7). Through this sacrifice the elements of subsequent sacrifices emerged: the "clotted-mixture" (8), the verses, chants, meters, and sacrificial formulae (9), and the sacrificial animals (10). The parts of the sacrifice also became the three upper varṇas (11–12): his mouth the brahmins, masters of knowledge and speech; his arms, the rulers, the possessors of power; and his thighs, the freemen or clansmen, who are the productive support of society. These three classes form parts of the sacrifice because they can participate in the sacrifice. The śūdras or "servants" are not part of the sacrifice but rather emerge from the feet of the Man, a symbol of their low social status and their exclusion from the sacrifice. Finally, the elements of the cosmos and gods themselves come forth from the sacrifice (13–14). This primeval sacrifice thus establishes the "first foundations" for the performance of the sacrifice and for the ritual, social, divine, and visible worlds (16).

The identity of the Sādhyas (in vss. 7 and 16) is not clear. They appear to be ancient sacrificers who have attained god-like status or even the status of gods through their ritual performance.

1. The Man has a thousand heads, a thousand eyes, and a thousand feet.
   Having covered the earth on all sides, he extended ten fingers' breadth beyond.

2. The Man alone is this whole world: what has come into being and what is to be.
   Moreover, he is master of immortality when he climbs beyond this world through food.

3. So much is his greatness, but the Man is more than this:
a quarter of him is all living beings; three quarters are the immortal in heaven.
4. With his three quarters the Man went upwards, but a quarter of him came to be here again.
From there he strode out in different directions towards what eats and what does not eat.
5. From him the Virāj was born; from the Virāj the Man.
Upon his birth, he reached beyond the earth from behind and also from in front.
6. When, with the Man as the offering, the gods extended the sacrifice,
spring was its melted butter, summer its fire-wood, autumn its offering.
7. On the ritual grass they consecrated that sacrifice, the Man, born at the beginning.
With him the gods sacrificed, also the Sādhyas and those who were seers.
8. From that sacrifice, when it was offered in full, the clotted-butter mixture was collected.
It [=the sacrifice] was made into the animals: those of the air, and both those belonging to the wilderness and those belonging to the village.
9. From this sacrifice, when it was offered in full, the verses and chants were born.
Meters were born from it. The sacrificial formula—from it that was born.
10. From it horses were born and whatever animals have teeth on both jaws.
Cows were born from it. From it were born goats and sheep.
11. When they apportioned the Man, into how many parts did they arrange him?
What was his mouth? What his two arms? What are said to be his two thighs, his two feet?
12. The brahmin was his mouth. The ruler was made his two arms.
As to his thighs—that is what the freeman was. From his two feet the servant was born.
13. The moon was born from his mind. From his eye the sun was born.
From his mouth Indra and Agni, from his breath Vāyu was born.
14. From his navel was the midspace. From his head the heaven developed.
From his two feet the earth, and the directions from his ear. Thus they arranged the worlds.

15. Its enclosing sticks were seven; the kindling sticks were made three times seven,

when the gods, extending the sacrifice, bound the Man as the sacrificial animal.

16. With the sacrifice the gods performed the sacrifice for themselves: these were the first foundations.

These, its greatness, accompanied it to heaven's vault, where the ancient Sādhyas and the gods are.

X.129 Creation

Prajāpati Parameṣṭhin

triṣṭubh meter

This is not only one of the most famous hymns of the R̥gveda, but also one of the most significant for its influence on later Indian cosmogonies. Because it is elusive and suggestive, rather than directly narrative, it has given rise to a wide variety of interpretations. The interpretation we offer here follows the more extensive discussion in Brereton 1999, which also refers to earlier literature and alternative interpretations.

If this is a cosmogonic hymn, it is certainly a strange one, because the last verse does not arrive at an answer but ends with a question. This incompleteness is formally marked by both metrical and syntactic irregularities. The meter of the second pāda of verse 7, 7b, is two syllables short, leaving the audience to anticipate two beats that are not there, and the syntax of the last pāda, 7d, is incomplete since the poem ends with a relative clause without a main clause. A close look at the rest of the hymn explains the reason for these poetic strategies.

In verse 1 there is a progression from negations—what existed was neither existing nor non-existing and neither space nor heaven existed—to questions (1c) and to possibilities (1d). Verse 2 also begins with negation, here the negation of death, of deathlessness, and of the signs of night and day. The only narrative progress in these two verses is the greater specificity in verse 2 about what is negated: there are no mortals nor immortals, there is no moon nor sun. And whereas the second half of verse 1 continued with questions and possibilities, the second half of verse 2 provides an answer to the question of what existed: there existed "that One," which "breathed without wind." In pāda 1c the poet asked what "stirred," or more literally what "moved back and forth," and in 2c the implicit answer is that the "breathing" of the One moves back and forth. If 2c answers the question of 1c and indeed if verse 2 brings into greater definition what verse 1 suggests, then "that One" in verse 2 is the previously undefined thing that was neither existent nor non-existent in verse 1.

Verse 3 sharpens the sense that nothing has yet happened, nothing material at least. It apparently starts over once again: 3a ends "in the beginning" just as 1a ends "at that time" and 2a "then." But where verses 1 and 2 asked questions or hinted at answers, verse 3 asserts that there was something, namely "darkness" covered by darkness, and describes a "thing coming into being" covered by "emptiness." In verse 3, therefore, "that One" still does not have substance, but it is beginning to have shape, since something is "covered" by something else. As Thieme (1964: 66–67) has observed, that shape is the shape of an egg, and it is this egg-like shape that at the end of verse 3 "was born" or hatched through heat.

Thus far there has been little development of substance, although there has been an evolution of concept. An unidentified subject that neither exists nor does not exist is introduced in verse 1. It has taken conceptual form as the "One" in verse 2, and finally assumed an egg-like shape in verse 3. In verse 4 there is a shift that apparently breaks the continuity of the hymn: thought gives rise to desire, which is concretized as the "primal semen," the origin of beings. However, there is one thing that connects verses 3 and 4 and maintains the hymn's continuity: "desire" in the first line of verse 4 corresponds to "heat" in the last line of verse 3. If so, then "thought" in verse 4 should also correspond to the "One" in verse 3. And so it does, for "thought" is the hidden metaphor in verses 1–3. In verse 1 it is thought that neither exists nor does not exist because thought is something real but at the same time something not real, since it is not externally perceptible. Or, to put it another way, thought has shape but no substance, as verse 3 says. This hymn, therefore, shows an omphalos structure, in which the middle verse, verse 4, contains the key to the hymn. Here that key is the revelation that thought is the One, which is the ultimate source of creation. It is not surprising, therefore, that the "connection" between "existing" and "not-existing," the connection that is thought, was discovered by poets "though inspired thinking" (4). In verse 5 this "connection" also becomes a dividing "cord," since thinking makes distinctions, and through it there emerges the division between males (the "placers of semen" and the "offering") and females ("greatnesses," i.e., pregnancies, and "independent will").

But even if thought is the ultimate and primal creative act, the origin of the world is still unknown, even by the gods (vs. 6). If there is an overseer of the world, he might know, or he might not (7). The lack of an answer means that "thinking" will not come to an end. The poem ends with metrical and syntactic irresolution and with a question in order that its hearers are left thinking and thereby left repeating the fundamental act of creation—the act of thinking.

1. The non-existent did not exist, nor did the existent exist at that time. There existed neither the airy space nor heaven beyond.

What moved back and forth? From where and in whose protection? Did water exist, a deep depth?

2. Death did not exist nor deathlessness then. There existed no sign of night nor of day.

That One breathed without wind by its independent will. There existed nothing else beyond that.

3. Darkness existed, hidden by darkness, in the beginning. All this was a signless ocean.

What existed as a thing coming into being, concealed by emptiness—that One was born by the power of heat.

4. Then, in the beginning, from thought there evolved desire, which existed as the primal semen.

Searching in their hearts through inspired thought, poets found the connection of the existent in the non-existent.

5. Their cord was stretched across: Did something exist below it? Did something exist above?

There existed placers of semen and there existed greatnesses. There was independent will below, offering above.

6. Who really knows? Who shall here proclaim it?—from where was it born, from where this creation?

The gods are on this side of the creation of this world. So then who does know from where it came to be?

7. This creation—from where it came to be, if it was produced or if not—

he who is the overseer of this world in the furthest heaven, he surely knows. Or if he does not know . . . ?

Bibliography

Alsdorf, Ludwig. 1962. "Indian Studies in Germany." *The Indo-Asian Culture* 10: 296–314, 456–61.

Bergaigne, Abel. 1889. "Recherches sur l'histoire de la liturgie védique." *Journal Asiatique*: 5–32, 121–97.

Bhat, M. S. 1987. *Vedic Tantrism: A Study of the R̥gvidhāna of Śaunaka with Text and Translation*. Delhi: Motilal Banarsidass.

Bloomfield, Maurice. 1916. *Rig-veda Repetitions: The Repeated Verses and Distichs and Stanzas of the Rig-veda in Systematic Presentation and with Critical Discussion*. Harvard Oriental Series, vols. 20, 24. Cambridge, MA: Harvard University Press. Rpt. New Delhi: Meharchand Lachhmandas, 1981.

Brereton, Joel P. 1981. *The R̥gvedic Ādityas*. American Oriental Series, vol. 63. New Haven: American Oriental Society.

Brereton, Joel P. 1999. "Edifying Puzzlement: R̥gveda 10.129 and the Uses of Enigma." *Journal of the American Oriental Society* 119: 248–60.

Brereton, Joel P. 2012. "Gods' Work: The R̥bhus in the *R̥gveda*." In *Indologica: T. Ya. Elizarenkova Memorial Volume*, part 2, ed. L. Kulikov and M. Rusanov, 111–34. Moscow: Russian State University for the Humanities.

Brereton, Joel P. 2016. "Reconstructing R̥gvedic Religion: *Deva*s, *Asura*s, and Rites of Kingship." In *Vedic Investigations: Papers of the 12th World Sanskrit Conference*, vol. 1, ed. Asko Parpola and Petteri Koskikallio, 35–58. Delhi: Motilal Banarsidass.

Bronkhorst, Johannes. 1982. "The R̥gveda-Prātiśākhya and Its Śākhā." *Studien zur Indologie und Iranistik* 8/9: 77–95.

Bronkhorst, Johannes, and Madhav Deshpande, eds. 1999. *Aryan and Non-Aryan in South Asia*. Harvard Oriental Series, Opera Minora, vol. 3. Cambridge, MA: Department of Sanskrit and Indian Studies, Harvard University.

Bronner, Yigal. 2010. *Extreme Poetry: The South Asian Movement of Simultaneous Narration*. New York: Columbia University Press.

Brown, W. Norman. 1931. "Sources and Nature of *pū́ruṣa* in the Puruṣasūkta (Rigveda 10.91 [*sic*])." *Journal of the American Oriental Society* 51: 108–18.

Caland, Willem. 1953. *Śāṅkhāyana-Śrautasūtra*. Nagpur: The International Academy of Indian Culture.

Caland, Willem, and V. Henry. 1906–1907. *L'Agniṣṭoma: Description complète de la forme normale de sacrifice de soma dans le culte védique*. 2 vols. Paris: Ernest Leroux.

Chaubey, B. B. 1983. "Nature and Methods of Brāhmaṇic Interpretation." *Annals of the Bhandarkar Oriental Research Institute* 64: 77–88.

Chaubey, B. B. 2009. *Āśvalāyana-Saṃhitā of the Ṛgveda (with Padapāṭha, Detailed Introduction and Two Indices)*. 2 vols. New Delhi: Indira Gandhi National Centre for the Arts.

Clark, Matthew. 2017. *The Tawny One: Soma, Haoma, and Ayahuasca*. London: Muswell Hill Press.

Doniger [O'Flaherty], Wendy. 1981. *The Rig Veda: An Anthology*. Harmondsworth, UK: Penguin Books. Rpt. 2005.

Falk, Harry. 1986. *Bruderschaft und Würfelspiel:. Untersuchungen zur Entwicklungsgeschichte des vedischen Opfers*. Freiberg: Hedwig Falk.

Falk, Harry. 1988. "Savitṛ und die Savitrī." *Wiener Zeitschrift für die Kunde Südasiens* 32: 5–33.

Falk, Harry. 1989. "Soma I and II." *Bulletin of the School of Oriental and African Studies* 52: 77–90.

Falk, Harry. 2002–2003. "Decent Drugs for Decent People: Further Thoughts on the Nature of Soma." *Orientalia Suecana* 51/52: 141–55.

Elizarenkova, T. Ya. 1989–1999. *Rigveda*. 3 vols. Moskva: Nauka.

Flattery, David, and Martin Schwartz. 1989. *Haoma and Harmaline*. Berkeley and Los Angeles: University of California Press.

Gautama, A. S. 2012–2013. *Śāṅkhāyanaśākhīya Ṛgvedasaṃhitā*. Ujjain: Maharṣi Sāndīpani Rāṣṭriya Veda Vidyā Pratiṣṭhānam.

Geldner, Karl Friedrich. 1951. *Der Rig-Veda aus dem Sanskrit ins Deutsche übersetzt und mit einem laufenden Kommentar versehen*. 3 vols. Cambridge, MA: Harvard University Press.

Gotō, Toshifumi. 2009. "*Aśvín-* and *Nā́satya-* in the Ṛgveda and Their Prehistoric Background." In *Linguistics, Archaeology and Human Past in South Asia*, ed. Toshiki Osada, 199–226. Delhi: Manohar.

Grassmann, Hermann. 1872–1875. *Wörterbuch zum Rig-Veda*. Leipzig. 6th ed., ed. Maria Kozianka. Wiesbaden: Harrassowitz, 1996.

Hale, Wash Edward. 1986. Ásura- *in Early Vedic Religion*. Delhi: Motilal Banarsidass.

Griffiths, Arlo, and Jan E. M. Houben, eds. 2004. *The Vedas: Texts, Language and Ritual: Proceedings of the Third International Vedic Workshop, Leiden 2002*. Groningen: Egbert Forsten.

Heesterman, Jan. 1993. *The Broken World of Sacrifice: An Essay in Ancient Indian Ritual*. Chicago & London: University of Chicago Press

Hillebrandt, Alfred. 1902. *Vedische Mythologie. Dritter Band*. Breslau: M. & H. Marcus.

Hock, Hans Henrik. 1999a. "Out of India? The Linguistic Evidence." In Bronkhorst and Deshpande 1999, 1–18.

Hock, Hans Henrik. 1999b. "Through a Glass Darkly: Modern 'Racial' Interpretations vs. Textual and General Prehistoric Evidence on *ārya* and *dāsa / dasyu* in Vedic Society." In Bronkhorst and Deshpande 1999, 145–74.

Ikari, Yasuke. 1989. "Some Aspects of the Idea of Rebirth in Vedic Literature." *Indo shisōshi kenkyū* 6: 155–64.

Jamison, Stephanie W. 1982. "Case Disharmony in RVic Similes." *Indo-Iranian Journal* 24: 251–71.

Jamison, Stephanie W. 1991. *The Ravenous Hyenas and the Wounded Sun: Myth and Ritual in Ancient India*. Ithaca: Cornell University Press.

Jamison, Stephanie W. 1991–1992. "Natural History Notes on the Rigvedic 'Frog' Hymn." *Annals of the Bhandarkar Oriental Research Institute* 72–73: 137–44.

Jamison, Stephanie W. 1996. *Sacrificed Wife / Sacrificer's Wife: Women, Ritual, and Hospitality in Ancient India*. New York: Oxford University Press.

Jamison, Stephanie W. 2001. "The Rigvedic Svayaṃvara? Formulaic Evidence." In *Vidyārṇavavandanam: Essays in Honour of Asko Parpola, Studia Orientalia,* vol. 94, ed. K. Karttunen and P. Koskikallio, 303–15. Helsinki: Finnish Oriental Society.

Jamison, Stephanie W. 2003. "Vedic *vrā́*: Evidence for the Svayaṃvara in the Rig Veda?" In *Paitimāna: Essays in Iranian, Indo-European, and Indian Studies in Honor of Hanns-Peter Schmidt,* ed. Siamak Adhami, 39–56. Costa Mesa, CA: Mazda Publishers.

Jamison, Stephanie W. 2004. "Poetry and Purpose of the Rigveda: Structuring Enigmas." In Griffiths and Houben 2004, 237–49.

Jamison, Stephanie W. 2006. "Poetic 'Repair' in the Rig Veda." In *La Langue poétique indo-européenne: Actes du Colloque de travail de la Société des Études Indo-Européennes (Indogermanische Gesellschaft / Society for Indo-European Studies) Paris, 22–24 octobre 2003*, ed. Georges-Jean Pinault and Daniel Petit, 133–40. Leuven/Paris: Peeters.

Jamison, Stephanie W. 2007. *The Rig Veda between Two Worlds / Le R̥gveda entre deux mondes*. Publications de l'Institut de Civilisation Indienne 74. Paris: De Boccard.

Jamison, Stephanie W. 2008. "Women's Language in the Rig Veda?" In *Indologic:. T. Ya. Elizarenkova Memorial Volume*, part 1, ed. L. Kulikov and M. Rusano, 153–65. Moscow: Russian State University for Humanities.

Jamison, Stephanie W. 2009a. "The Function of Animals in the Rig Veda, RV X.28, and the Origins of Story Literature in India." In *Penser, dire et représenter l'animal dans le monde indien* (Proceedings of the conference of same name, Paris, March 2002), ed. Nalini Balbir and Georges-Jean Pinault, 197–218. Paris: Champion.

Jamison, Stephanie W. 2009b. "Sociolinguistic Remarks on the Indo-Iranian *-ka-Suffix: A Marker of Colloquial Register." *Indo-Iranian Journal* 52: 311–29.

Jamison, Stephanie W. 2011. "The Secret Lives of Texts" (Presidential Address, American Oriental Society 2010). *Journal of the American Oriental Society* 131: 1–7.

Jamison, Stephanie W. 2015. "Śleṣa in the R̥gveda? Poetic Effects in R̥V X.29.1." *International Journal of Hindu Studies* 19: 157–70 (Festschrift Edwin Gerow).

Jamison, Stephanie W. 2016a. "The Divine Revolution of R̥gveda X.124: A New Interpretation. Beyond Asuras and Devas." In *On Meaning and Mantras: Essays in Honor of Frits Staal*, ed. George Thompson and Richard Payne, 289–306. Moraga, CA: Institute of Buddhist Studies and BDK America.

Jamison, Stephanie W. 2016b. "R̥gveda X.109: The 'Brahman's Wife' and the Ritual Patnī." In *The Vedas in Indian Culture and History: Proceedings of the Fourth International Vedic Conference (Austin, Texas 2007)*, ed. Joel P. Brereton, 207–20. Florence: Società Editrice Fiorentina.

Jamison, Stephanie W. 2018. "'Sacrificer's Wife' in the Rig Veda: Ritual Innovation?" In *Creating the Veda, Living the Veda: Selected Papers from the 13th World Sanskrit Conference*, ed. Joel P. Brereton and Theodore N. Proferes, 19–30. Helsinki: Finnish Academy of Science and Letters.

Jamison, Stephanie W. 2019. "Vedic Ritual: The Sacralization of the Mundane and the Domestication of the Sacred." In *Self, Sacrifice, and Cosmos: Late Vedic Thought, Ritual, and Philosophy. Papers in Honor of Dr. Ganesh Umakant Thite's Contributions to Vedic Studies*, ed. Lauren Bausch, 64–80. Delhi: Primus Books.

Jamison, Stephanie W., and Joel P. Brereton. 2014. *The Rigveda: The Earliest Religious Poetry of India*. 3 vols. Oxford University Press: New York.

Knipe, David M. 1997. "Becoming a Veda in the Godavari Delta." In *India and Beyond:. Aspects of Literature, Meaning, Ritual and Thought. Essays in Honour of Frits Staal*, ed. Dick van der Meij, 306–32. Leiden: International Institute for Asian Studies.

Knipe, David M. 2015. *Vedic Voices: Intimate Narratives of a Living Andhra Tradition*. New York: Oxford University Press.

Maurer, Walter H. 1986. *Pinnacles of India's Past: Selections from the R̥gveda*. University of Pennsylvania Studies on South Asia, vol. 2. Amsterdam: John Benjamins.

Minkowski, Christopher. 2002. "Nīlakaṇṭha Caturdhara's Mantrakāśīkhaṇḍa." *Journal of the American Oriental Society* 122: 329–44.

Minkowski, Christopher. n.d. "Nīlakaṇṭha Caturdhara and the Genre of Mantrarahasyaprakāśikā." http://www.columbia.edu/itc/mealac/pollock/sks/papers/minkowski_nilakantha.pdf. Accessed June 2018.

Mus, Paul. 1968. "Où Finit Puruṣa?" In *Mélanges d'indianisme à la mémoire de Louis Renou*, 539–63. Paris: de Boccard.

Nooten, Barend A. van, and Gary B. Holland. 1994. *Rig Veda: A Metrically Restored Text with an Introduction and Notes*. Harvard Oriental Series, vol. 50. Cambridge, MA: Dept. of Sanskrit and Indian Studies, Harvard University.

Oberlies, Thomas. 1993. "Die Aśvin: Götter der Zwischenbereiche." *Studien zur Indologie und Iranistik* 18: 169–89.

Oberlies, Thomas. 1998. *Die Religion des R̥gveda. Erster Teil: Das Religiose System des R̥gveda*. Vienna: Publications of the de Nobili Research Library, XXVI.

Oberlies, Thomas. 1999. *Die Religion des R̥gveda. Zwieter Teil: Kompositionsanalyse der Soma-Hymnen des R̥gveda*. Vienna: Publications of the de Nobili Research Library, XXVII.

Oberlies, Thomas. 2012. *Der Rigveda und seine Religion*. Berlin: Verlag der Weltreligionen.

Oldenberg, Hermann. 1894. *Die Religion des Veda*. Berlin: Wilhelm Hertz.

Olivelle, Patrick. 1998. *The Early Upaniṣads: Annotated Text and Translation*. New York: Oxford University Press.

Olivelle, Patrick. 2005. *Manu's Code of Law: A Critical Edition and Translation of the* Mānanva-Dharmaśāstra. New York: Oxford University Press.

Parameswara Aithal, K. 1993. *Veda-lakṣaṇa, Vedic Ancillary Literature: A Descriptive Bibliography*. Delhi: Motilal Barnarsidass.

Parpola, Asko. 2015. *The Roots of Hinduism: The Early Aryans and the Indus Civilization*. New York: Oxford University Press.

Proferes, Theodore. 2003. "Remarks on the Transition from R̥gvedic Composition to Śrauta Compilation." *Indo-Iranian Journal* 46, no. 1: 1–12.

Proferes, Theodore. 2007. *Vedic Ideals of Sovereignty and the Poetics of Power*. New Haven: American Oriental Society.

Raghavan, V. 1962. *The Present Position of Vedic Recitation and Vedic Sakhas*. The Veda Kumbhakonam: Dharma Paripalana Sabha.

Rau, Wilhelm. 1957. *Staat und Gesellschaft im Alten Indien*. Wiesbaden: Harrassowitz.

Reddy, P. Bhaskar. 1991. *The Inscriptions of Simhachalam: A Cultural Study*. Diss. Sri Venkateswara University. Tirupati: Oriental Research Institute, Sri Venkatewsara University.

Renou, Louis. 1947. *Les écoles védiques et la formations du Veda*. Paris: Imprimerie Nationale.

Renou, Louis. 1955–1969. *Études védiques et pāṇinéennes*. 17 vols. Paris: de Boccard.

Sastri, P. S. 1947. "Figures of Speech in R̥gveda." *Annals of the Bhandarkar Oriental Research Institute* 28, nos. 1/2: 34–64.

Scharfe, Hartmut. 2002. *Education in Ancient India*. Handbook of Oriental Studies, India, vol. 16. Leiden: Brill.

Scheftelowitz, Isidor. 1906. *Die Apokryphen des R̥gveda*. Rpt. Hildesheim: Georg Olms Verlagsbuchhandlung, 1966.

Schlerath, Bernfried. 1980. "Indo-Iranisch **var* 'wählen.'" *Studien zur Indologie und Iranistik* 6/6: 199–208.

Schmidt, Hanns-Peter. 1968. *Br̥haspati und Indra:. Untersuchungen zur vedischen Mythologie und Kulturgeschichte*. Wiesbaden: Harrassowitz.

Schmidt, Hanns-Peter. 1987. *Some Women's Rites and Rights in the Veda*. Poona: Bhandarkar Oriental Research Institute.

Siegling, Wilhelm. 1906. *Die Rezensionen des Caraṇavyūha*. Diss. Friedrich-Wilhelms-Universität zu Berlin.

Simon, Richard. 1889. *Beiträge zur Kenntnis der Vedischen Schulen*. Kiel: Haeseler.

Sontakke, N. S., et al., eds. 1933–1951. *R̥gveda -Saṃhitā with the Commentary of Sāyaṇācārya*. Rpt. Pune: Vaidika Saṃśodhana Maṇḍala: Pune, 1972.

Staal, J. Frits. 1961. *Nambudiri Veda Recitation*. The Hague: Mouton.

Staal, J. Frits. 1983. *Agni: The Vedic Ritual of the Fire Altar*. 2 vols. Berkeley: Asian Humanities Press.

Stuhrman, Rainer. 2006. "R̥gvedische Lichtaufnahmen: Soma botanisch, pharmakolisch, in den Augen der Kavis." *Electronic Journal of Vedic Studies* 13, no. 1: 1–93.

Thieme, Paul. 1938. *Der Fremdling im Rigveda: Eine Studie über die Bedeutung der Worte* ari, arya, aryaman *und* ārya. Leipzig: Deutsche Morgenländische Gesellschaft. Rpt. Nendeln, Liechtenstein: Kraus, 1966.

Thieme, Paul. 1954. "akhkhalīkr̥tyā." *Zeitschrift für vergleichende Sprachforschung* 71: 109. Rpt. in 1971: 138.

Thieme, Paul. 1957. *Mitra and Aryaman*. Transactions of the Connecticut Academy of Arts and Sciences, vol. 41. New Haven: Yale University Press. Rpt. in *Paul Thieme: Opera Maiora* I, ed. N. Kobayashi and W. Knobl. Kyoto: Hōzōkan, 1995.

Thieme, Paul. 1964. *Gedichte aus dem Rig-Veda*. Stuttgart: Reclam.

Thieme, Paul. 1965. "Drei rigvedische Tierbezeichnungen (*nodhā́s, śundhyū́-, admasád-*)." *Zeitschrift für vergleichende Sprachforschung* 79: 211–23. Rpt. in 1971: 214–26.

Thieme, Paul. 1971. *Kleine Schriften*. Glasenapp-Stiftung, vol. 5. Wiesbaden: Steiner. Rpt. 1984.

Thompson, George. 2003. "Soma and Ecstasy in the R̥gveda." *Electronic Journal of Vedic Studies* 9.

Velankar, H. D. 1948. "Hymns to Indra in Maṇḍala VIII." *Journal of the University of Bombay* 15, no. 2: 1–28.

Velankar, H. D. 1948–1951. "Hymns to Indra in Maṇḍala I." *Journal of the University of Bombay* 17, no. 2 (1948): 1–22; 18, no. 2 (1949): 6–25; 2, no. 2 (1951): 17–34.

Velankar, H. D. 1952–1954. "Hymns to Indra in Maṇḍala X." *Journal of the University of Bombay* 21, no. 2 (1952): 1–20; 22, no. 2 (1953): 6–26; 23, no. 2 (1954): 1–18.

Velankar, H. D. 1955. "Hymns to Agni in Maṇḍala VI." *Journal of the University of Bombay* 24, no. 2: 36–64.

Velankar, H. D. 1956. "Hymns to Agni in Maṇḍala VII." *Journal of the University of Bombay* 25, no. 2: 9–31.

Velankar, H. D. 1957. "Agni Hymns in Maṇḍala VIII." *Journal of the University of Bombay* 26, no. 2: 1–24.

Velankar, H. D. 1958–1959. "Hymns to Agni in Maṇḍala X." *Journal of the University of Bombay* 27, no. 2 (1958): 1–28; 28, no. 2 (1959): 1–19.

Velankar, H. D. 1960–1963. "Hymns to Agni in Maṇḍala I." *Journal of the University of Bombay* 29, no.2 (1960): 1–18; 31, no. 2 (1962): 1–24; 32, no. 2 (1963): 1–36.

Velankar, H. D. 1963. *R̥gveda Maṇḍala VII*. Bombay: Bharatiya Vidya Bhavan.

Velankar, H. D. 1966. *R̥gveda Maṇḍala II*. Bombay: University of Bombay.

Velankar, H. D. 1968. *R̥gveda Maṇḍala III*. Bombay: University of Bombay.

Velankar, H. D. 2003. *The Fifth Maṇḍala of the R̥g-Veda*, ed. S. G. Moghe. Delhi: Koshal Book Depot.

Wasson, R. Gordon. 1968. *Soma: Divine Mushroom of Immortality*. New York: Harcourt, Brace and World.

Watkins, Calvert. 1987. "Two Anatolian Forms: Palaic *aškumāuwa-*, Cuneiform Luvian *wa-a-ar-ša*." In *Festschrift for Henry Hoenigswald on the Occasion of His 70th Birthday*, ed. George Cardona and Norman Zide, 399–404. Tübingen: Gunther Narr. Rpt. in *Selected Writings*, 1:310–14.

Watkins, Calvert. 1995. *How to Kill a Dragon: Aspects of Indo-European Poetics*. New York: Oxford University Press.

Watkins, Calvert. 2009. "The Milk of the Dawn Cows Revisited." In *East and West: Papers in Indo-European Studies*, ed. Kazuhiko Yoshida and Brent Vine, 225–39. Bremen: Hempen.

Witzel, Michael. 1983. "The R̥gveda-Saṃhitā as Known to AV-Par. 46 (Materials on Vedic Śākhās, 4)." *Indo-Iranian Journal* 25: 238–40.

Witzel, Michael. 1995a. "R̥gvedic History: Poets, Chieftains and Polities." In *The Indo-Aryans of Ancient South Asia*, ed. George Erdosy, 307–52. Berlin: de Gruyter.

Witzel, Michael. 1995b. "Early Sanskritization. Origins and Development of the Kuru State." *Electronic Journal of Vedic Studies* 1–4: 1–26.

Witzel, Michael. 2003. "Linguistic Evidence for Cultural Exchange in Prehistoric Western Central Asia." *Sino-Platonic Papers* 129.

Witzel, Michael. 2005. "Indocentrism: Autochthonous Visions of Ancient India." In *The Indo-Aryan Controversy: Evidence and Inference in Indian History*, ed. E. F. Bryant and L. L. Patton, 341–404. Abington: Routledge.

Witzel, Michael, and Toshifumi Gotō. 2007. *Rig-Veda: Das heilige Wisssen. Erster und zweiter Liederkreis aus dem vedischen Sanskrit übersetzt und herausgegeben von Michael Witzel und Toshifumi Gotō, unter Mitarbeit von Eijirō Dōyama und Mislav Ježić*. Frankfurt am Main: Verlag der Weltreligionen.

Witzel, Michael, Toshifumi Gotō, and Salvatore Scarlata. 2013. *Rig-Veda: Das heilige Wisssen. Dritter bis Fünfter Liederkreis aus dem vedischen Sanskrit übersetzt und herausgegaben von Michael Witzel (Buch III), Toshifumi Gotō (Buch IV), und Salvatore Scarlata (Buch V)*. Frankfurt am Main: Verlag der Weltreligionen.

Wojtilla, Gyula. 2003. "What Can the Ṛgveda Tell Us on Agriculture." *Acta Orientalia Academiae Scientiarum Hungaricae* 56, no. 1: 35–48.

Zeller, Gabriele. 1990. *Die vedische Zwillingsgötter: Untersuchungen zur Genese ihres Kultes*. Wiesbaden: Harrassowitz.

Passage Index

For the benefit of digital users, indexed terms that span two pages (e.g., 52–53) may, on occasion, appear on only one of those pages.

All passages from the Ṛgveda unless otherwise indicated
The appendix is indicated by *a* following the page number

Subject Index

For the benefit of digital users, indexed terms that span two pages (e.g., 52–53) may, on occasion, appear on only one of those pages.

Figures and Appendix are indicated by *f* and *a* following the page number

Printed and bound by CPI Group (UK) Ltd, Croydon, CR0 4YY